FROGMEN

FROGMEN

THE TRUE STORY OF MY JOURNEYS WITH CAPTAIN JACQUES-YVES COUSTEAU AND THE CREW OF *CALYPSO*

RICHARD E. HYMAN

Published in the United States by Iron Press,
a Venture Development, LLC company.

ISBN: 1456462172
ISBN-13: 9781456462178

First Edition
Questions regarding this book should be addressed to richard@iron-press.info

On the cover: The photograph by Richard Hyman is looking down from *Calypso*'s bow. The ship pierces the remarkably calm sea, creates a bit of white foam, and pushes the riding dolphins. Note the reflection of *Calypso* and the overhanging crew.

IRON PRESS

DEDICATION

Dedicated to:
Madame Simone Cousteau for her sweetness
Bernard Delemotte for his kindness
Joe Thompson for his friendship
Frederick Hyman, my father, for opening the door
Janett Hyman, my mother, and Florence Horne, my grandmother, who both knew that men
"go down to the sea in ships"[a]
Margaret Hyman, my loving wife, for encouraging me to write
Brent and Sarah, my children, whom I love and wish to have their own memorable journeys

---

a "They that go down to the sea in ships, that do business in great waters; These see the works of the LORD, and his wonders in the deep. For he commandeth, and raiseth the stormy wind, which lifteth up the waves thereof. They mount up to the heaven, they go down again to the depths: their soul is melted because of trouble. They reel to and fro, and stagger like a drunken man, and are at their wits' end. Then they cry unto the LORD in their trouble, and he bringeth them out of their distresses. He maketh the storm a calm, so that the waves thereof are still. Then are they glad because they be quiet; so he bringeth them unto their desired haven."
Psalms 107:23-30

"Fond memory brings the light of the days around me."

Thomas Moore

Thanks for the fond memories JYC.
Dick

PREFACE

An old *Washington Post* article mentioned that Captain Jacques-Yves Cousteau was furious about some of the books and articles written about him. I've read most of them and don't blame him, as they're full of errors.

This book is my truthful personal account, derived from my journals, photographs, tape recordings, assorted memorabilia, and memories.

It was at a time before the existence of the Internet, personal computers, smart phones, consumer GPS devices, and other helpful and entertaining technologies.

It is what I actually experienced; things that I heard, saw, felt, and thought at the time. Encouraged by others, I've reluctantly included aspects that expose my personal feelings and youthful naiveté.

I greatly admired Captain Cousteau. I've never met a harder working person. He was genuine, sincere, and passionate about what he termed our "water planet."

My journeys made an indelible impression on me. They seeded an enduring, nagging desire to return for more and to fulfill a greater purpose with my life.

I hope my story will encourage you to pursue your individual dreams and to take your own journeys, whatever they may be.

INTRODUCTION

I tell my story in first person, present tense. It's written in chronological narrative over a six-year period, beginning in chapter three, just after I turned eighteen years old, ending in chapter seven when I was twenty-four years old.

Named after my grandfather, I am referred to as Dick, a nickname for Richard.

It starts in July 1973 when I joined my father on his business trip to Los Angeles, California. I didn't know that by tagging along I'd end up spending the rest of the summer on a rare land-based Cousteau expedition into the Canadian wilderness, which would essentially change my life.

The next year, my sophomore year of college, over Thanksgiving break I flew from school in Greenville, South Carolina, to Panama City, Florida, to dive in warm springs and study stone crabs in the Gulf of Mexico.

Just a month later, in late December 1974, I rendezvoused with the Cousteau team and *Calypso* off Mexico's Yucatan Peninsula, where we studied the migration of spiny lobsters.

From there we sailed south to Belize to study grouper and coral reefs, highlighted by a visit from John Denver and the filming of his television special, which included a concert aboard *Calypso.*

Five years passed before again, in 1979, I joined the team in Norfolk, Virginia. After a few interruptions along the way, we arrived in Martinique and then went on to Venezuela. This would be my final expedition.

It was Philippe Cousteau's final journey as well. Within a month out of Norfolk he'd be dead, crashing the organization's plane in Portugal.

Calypso was a dynamic floating microcosm. She slept twenty-seven but often housed more. There were multiple nationalities, languages, and religions with associated habits and diets. Although the science was interesting and the adventure exciting, the social experience was by far the most fascinating.

Given that Captain Cousteau was the chairman of Aqua Lung International, also known as U.S. Divers Corporation, we could have used any of the most state-of-the-art dive gear, but instead we always opted for just the bare minimum.

By her own design, Madame Simone Cousteau was the only woman allowed aboard. Her official title was nurse. Her nickname was *La Bergère,* meaning "the shepherdess." Madame treated me like a son and I loved her for that.

To finance the costly expeditions, there had to be a business. With no sponsors or grants, Cousteau needed help to manage the operation. In 1971, he sought out Frederick L. Hyman, my father, who became president, chief executive officer, and Cousteau's partner.

At the time, Cousteau was about to embark on an expedition to Antarctica[b] to make a speculative feature length film. *Calypso* was in Monaco loaded with 35mm film. The bank account was virtually empty. Dad convinced Cousteau to instead shoot four one-hour television programs, requiring the exchange of 35mm[c] film for 16mm.[d] The ship left on schedule for Antarctica to shoot those one-hour programs.

---

b Antarctica is the earth's southernmost continent and the fifth-largest in area. It's surrounded by the Southern Ocean. About ninety-eight percent of it is covered by ice averaging about one mile in thickness.

c 35 mm film was the film format most commonly used for still photography and motion pictures. Invented by Thomas Edison, the film was cut into strips thirty-five millimeters wide, with six perforations per inch along both edges.

d The compact size and lower cost of 16mm made it popular for use in professional news reporting, corporate and educational films, and television production.

Dad assumed responsibility for selling the four programs and actually sold five—to Metromedia Producers Corp (MPC)—obtaining production advances to finance the expedition.

Two years later, Cousteau still wanted the feature-length film. Dad obtained releases from Metromedia and ABC, which allowed Cousteau to use footage from the television shows, enlarge the film from 16mm to 35mm, and make *Voyage to the Edge of the World,* about the Antarctic voyage. The feature film was not a commercial success. Documentaries were television favorites but not theatrical favorites. However, Dad had sold the film to an investment group that provided a profit to the newly formed Cousteau Group.

There was also a two million-dollar loan in France that had to be dealt with. Dad renegotiated it to an acceptable level of $300,000 plus an interest in Cousteau's autobiography, if ever written. These actions, along with consolidating Cousteau's five companies into one named The Cousteau Group, saved the business.

The Cousteau Group Inc., or The Group as we called it, was a for-profit company that produced thirty-six one-hour television programs known as *The Undersea World of Jacques Cousteau,* the aforementioned feature film *Voyage to the Edge of the World,* some thirty books including a twenty-volume encyclopedia entitled *The Ocean World of Jacques Cousteau,* and an eight-book series of adventure stories published by Doubleday.

In 1973, The Group contributed the seed capital to create The Cousteau Society Inc. or The Society as we called it. The Society was co-founded by Captain Cousteau, Dad, and Jacques' two sons, Jean-Michel and Philippe. Dad was the president. The Society was a non-profit member-based organization "dedicated to the protection and improvement of life." The Society believed "that only an informed and alerted public can best make the choices to provide a healthier and more productive way of life for itself and for future generations." With that objective, The Society produced television films, filmstrips and books for schools, and books for the public, all focused on important marine and environmental issues. It also organized lectures throughout the country and published articles and columns in various periodicals for distribution throughout the world.

The Society also sponsored research in fields that had little chance of being funded by government or industry and pioneered the global surveying of the "vitality" of the oceans.

With the creation of The Society, The Group ceased production of television programs, turning production over to The Society, which enjoyed the goodwill and revenues associated with future Cousteau work. This "gift" by Jacques Cousteau and Fred Hyman was the basis for the creation of The Society.

The Society also organized "Involvement Days." Between 1976 and 1977, six of these environmental festivals took place in the United States. Attended by more than fifty thousand in California, Florida, Massachusetts, Texas, Washington, and Wisconsin, people gathered to hear speeches and participate in discussions with renowned experts and to meet representatives of other non-profit environmental organizations who were also invited to participate, gratis. The result was that people become actively *involved* in local as well as global environmental causes. The festivities were fun and included exhibits, films, workshops, programs for children, and musical entertainment from artists such as Harry Chapin, David Crosby, John Denver, Don McLean, Graham Nash, Pete Seeger, James Taylor, and Paul Winter, which made Involvement Days memorable celebrations.

The Society formed a board of advisors. Members included Andrew Benson, professor of biology at Scripps Institution of Oceanography[1]; Ray Bradbury, author, lecturer, and poet[2]; John Denver, composer, musician, and entertainer[3]; Dr. Harold Edgerton, inventor, professor emeritus of electronics, Massachusetts Institute of Technology[4]; Dick Gregory, author and entertainer[5]; Dr. Henry Kendall, nuclear physicist, Massachusetts Institute of Technology, and co-founder of Union of Concerned Scientists[6]; Dr. K.O. Emery of Woods Hole Oceanographic Institute[7]; and Dr. Gabrial Nahas, physiologist and toxicologist, Columbia University College of Physicians and Surgeons.[8]

While Dad was president, The Society grew to over three hundred thousand members, enabling meaningful accomplishments in research, education, and public awareness.

Dad resigned in 1975 but continued as a member of the board until Cousteau's death twenty-two years later.

"When you dive, you begin to feel that you're an angel." [9]

Jacques-Yves Cousteau

CONTENTS

FOREWORD

Sometimes things just happen. An opportunity presents itself and the timing is perfect. My involvement with Jacques-Yves Cousteau started like that and so did my son's adventures with the Cousteau team.

When I joined Cousteau, *Calypso* was departing Monaco for Antarctica. It was to be the voyage of a wooden boat into a sea of icebergs, crossing the dangerous Cape Horn to get there. She made it there and back against long odds, and Cousteau created five television shows and a feature-length film to tell the story.

After the *team*, as Cousteau liked to call his sailors, divers, and cameramen, returned from Antarctica and had their well-deserved vacations, a small team was to leave for Canada to film a TV show on beavers. I had planned a trip to our California offices and asked Dick if he'd like to go with me. It was the beginning of summer and my son had just graduated from high school. So began his great adventures. He was offered the opportunity to join Philippe Cousteau on the beaver expedition. Dick was on summer vacation and had the time and interest, so he jumped at the chance. He climbed aboard the truck for the long drive and began writing his journals.

I say "adventures," the plural, since the Canada trip was only a trek into the woods with little diving and not a lot of glamour. He worked hard and loved it, and it inspired him to pursue more trips with the Cousteau team.

This book is about the excitement of growing up. Adventure and inspiration for a life of caring for nature is the product. An opportunity not granted to everyone but acted on by Dick. His summers were always the best part of his year, with voyages on *Calypso* and working in Washington, D.C., for NASA during some of the agency's most exciting years.

Dick has written this book in the style of a young man. It exudes the charm and enlightenment that fathers and sons (and daughters too) can relate to. It is not necessary to offer a young individual, boy or girl, the chance to sail the seas to gain a great understanding of what life has to offer. Most of us believe we endure mundane lives, but in reality what we do is exciting and adventurous to those just beginning. If you can, let youth share their joy and problems during their time of "growing up." The lessons and inspirations last a lifetime.

To me, that is the message of my son's book. I hope you like it.

– Fred Hyman

I
THE CAPTAIN

I knew him as Captain Cousteau but he was also addressed as Jacques, Commandant, and JYC (pronounced Jheek).

Jacques-Yves Cousteau was born June 11, 1910 in Saint-André-de-Cubzac, a small town near Bordeaux, France, which was also the birthplace of his parents.

He was raised in Paris but in 1920 spent the school year in New York and summer camp in Vermont. He often traveled with his father.

A sickly boy, he suffered from chronic enteritis, an inflammation of the small intestine, and anemia. He disregarded his doctor's advice to avoid strenuous activity and frequently enjoyed the water.

He was fascinated by machines and film but bored by school. As a teenager he found his share of trouble, eventually being expelled from high school and sent away to a strict boarding school, where he excelled and saved his money to buy his first movie camera.

At the age of twenty, he joined the French Naval Academy in Brest, France and at age twenty-six graduated second in his class. He was a midshipman aboard *Jeanne D'Arc* and *Primauguet* prior to training to be a naval aviator in Hourtin; that is, until a fateful day en route to a friend's wedding, when he crashed his father's Salmson sports car and nearly died. His left arm was shattered to the point that the doctors wanted to amputate, but he refused. His right arm was paralyzed. The injuries ended his dream of ever becoming a pilot.

While recuperating, he regained use of his arms and was reassigned to the Navy gunnery in Toulon, France. There, a fellow lieutenant, Philippe Tailliez, encouraged him to strengthen his injured arms by swimming. They swam together each day and soon met another swimmer, Frederic Dumas, who became a close friend.

Although Cousteau had enjoyed peering below the water's surface since the age of ten or younger, he wrote about a 1936 free dive, at the age of twenty-six, "Sometimes we are lucky enough to know that our lives have been changed, to discard the old, embrace the new and run headlong down an immutable course. It happened to me on that summer's day, when my eyes were opened by the sea."

In 1937, Cousteau married Simone Melchoir, and within the year their first son, Jean-Michel, was born. A second son, Philippe, followed a year later in 1938.

Simone's father was a director of Air Liquide S.A., a French company that created and supplied industrial gases, and helped Cousteau realize his dream to "swim with the fish." Air Liquide had an engineer, Emile Gagnan, who was designing a valve to automatically feed cooking gas into converted automobile engines. Cousteau was working on a similar valve, innovating a way to allow a human to stay underwater by breathing compressed air. In 1943, under the difficult and restrictive working conditions of German-occupied France, Cousteau and Gagnan teamed up and designed an improved demand regulator. Coupled with pressurized compressed air tanks, it was the first prototype two-stage diving regulator. Following testing[10] and redesign, a patent was filed for the first fully automatic demand valve linked to a high-pressure cylinder. They named it the Scaphandre Autonome, or the Aqualung.[11]

The advent of the Aqualung set divers free from their traditional dependence on breathing air through tethers, allowing them to swim more freely underwater for extended periods of time.

After the war, French divers used this self contained underwater breathing apparatus, also known by the acronym SCUBA to locate and remove enemy mines, which is ironic as the ship that Cousteau would make famous, *Calypso*, was formerly a U.S. minesweeper.[e]

In 1948, the French Navy promoted Cousteau to captain and gave him the latitude to begin exploring and filming.

In 1950, Cousteau made an arrangement with Loel Guinness, of the famous Irish brewing company, to lease his ship, *Calypso.* Cousteau used *Calypso* for decades as a platform from which to explore the world.

By 1951, the Aqualung was being sold in England and Canada. In 1953, Rene Bussoz sold his U.S. distribution rights and holdings in Rene Sporting Goods, a California company, to U.S. Divers.[f] Air Liquide, a French company, which owned the Aqualung patent until it expired in the early 1960s, licensed it to U.S. Divers, the manufacturer and supplier of Aqua Lung products.[g] Another company, La Spirotechnique, was an affiliate of U.S. Divers. Air Liquide, bought U.S. Divers in 1958 and changed the name to Aqua Lung America, which became part of Aqua Lung International, established by Air Liquide in 1988 and is now the world's largest diving equipment company. JYC served as chairman of the board until his death.

JYC and his partners were also credited with many other inventions, including underwater scooters and a jet-propelled submarine.

---

e The word scuba is now widely considered a word in its own right.

f JYC told Dad that when he first visited Bussoz, Bussoz ordered ten Aqua Lungs. He sold them all that year, and when JYC returned the following season to sell him more, Bussoz said, "No, the market is saturated."

g The invention itself was trademarked under one word "Aqualung". The brand is "Aqua Lung" of Aqua Lung International.

Cousteau's 1956 documentary film, *The Silent World,* virtually invented the underwater documentary. It won the Cannes Film Festival as well as an Academy Award. The book of the same title has sold more than five million copies to date.

In 1957, Cousteau retired from the French Navy to become director of the Oceanographic Museum of Monaco and to continue his expeditions.

In 1959, he produced *The Golden Fish,* a nineteen-minute French-language film, which won the Academy of Motion Picture Arts and Sciences' 1960 award for Best Short Subject, Live Action Subjects, a category that the academy subsequently renamed Live Action Short Film.

In the 1960s, as America's space program was progressing, Cousteau wanted to demonstrate that, just as in space, humans could also live below the surface of the ocean. He designed three expeditions, named Conshelf I, II, and III—as in "Continental Shelf Station," the shelf being the submerged perimeter of each continent. The first manned underwater sea habitat was in 1962, when two men, Albert Falco and Claude Wesly, termed *oceanauts,* lived ten meters deep for a week near Marseilles, France. Conshelf II followed in 1963, with five men at ten meters for a month in the Red Sea off Sudan. Finally, in 1965, the third project, Conshelf III, housed six divers for twenty-two days at a deeper 102.4 meters (336 feet) off Cap-Ferrat in the Mediterranean.

To prevent nitrogen narcosis, a dangerous result of breathing gases under elevated pressure, the oceanauts breathed a mixture of oxygen and helium, resulting in entertaining, high-pitched, Donald Duck-like voices.

Cousteau documented the oceanauts' lives underwater in a ninety-three-minute film about Conshelf II, entitled *World Without Sun,* for which he won yet another Academy Award in 1964.

Subsequently the footage shot during Conshelf III became a 1966 *National Geographic* television special produced by David Wolper and narrated by Orson Welles.[12]

Wolper was an extraordinary documentary filmmaker, receiving nine Oscar nominations and one win, four Emmys including Television Program of the Year, two Peabodys, and more than one-hundred other awards.

After Wolper introduced Cousteau to television in 1967 with the Jacques Cousteau television specials, Cousteau wrote to him saying, "I will never forget what you did to start my career."[13]

The success of these specials paved the way for a major television deal with the American Broadcasting Corporation (ABC). Cousteau agreed to deliver four one-hour-long television programs per year for the next three years. First broadcast in 1966 and running for more than eight years, Cousteau's thirty-six television episodes, named the *Undersea World of Jacques Cousteau,* made him an international household name.

After this, Cousteau continued to make documentaries, first for the Public Broadcasting System (PBS), including the *Cousteau Odyssey* series, and then, starting in 1981, *Cousteau Amazon* for Ted Turner's cable television network, Turner Broadcasting System (TBS). In total there were more than seventy-five films plus forty Emmy nominations.

Cousteau also wrote many books, including the *Living Sea* (1963), *World Without Sun* (1965), a twenty-volume encyclopedia (1980s), the *Ocean World of Jacques Cousteau,* and the *Cousteau Almanac.*

Cousteau was a member of the National Academy of Sciences and Academie Francaise. In addition to his Cannes win, two Academy Awards and his Emmys, he was honored with the Gold Palm Award (1959), Potts Medal of the Franklin Institute (1970), Presidential Medal of Freedom (1985), Television Hall of Fame (1987), National Geographic Society's Centennial Award (1988), and for his wartime exploits in the Résistance de la Legion d'Honneur (Legion of Honor).

The scientific community often unfairly criticized Cousteau, saying he was a showman, not a scientist. He never claimed to be a scientist. He viewed his role as that of a steward. He always made an effort to include one of the world's best specialists on each expedition, endeavoring to make films that were not only entertaining but also scientifically accurate.

By presenting ordinary people with amazing images and informative stories, Cousteau made an impact on a generation's awareness of the importance of the oceans.

In his final days, Cousteau continued to strongly advocate environmental protection, conservation, and the use of alternate energy sources such as wind, by advocating wind-powered double sails, even for large ocean-going commercial vessels.

When he died, the team was engaged in a five-year global expedition, named *Rediscovery of the World,* which was planned to yield twenty-five new films.

I knew Captain Cousteau as a thinker who could be approached on any topic and relied on for a well-formulated and passionately-supported opinion. If you disagreed, he would gladly debate.

He regretted that the Aqua Lung had led to spear fishing and the associated devastation of the world's coral reefs. He was an ardent opponent of spear fishing, and spear guns were strictly banned aboard *Calypso.*

He often spoke of returning on expedition to the Red Sea to study the environmental impact of oil in the Persian Gulf. I'd been scheduled to join such an expedition, but the concerns about security, war, and terrorism prevented us from going.

Cousteau feared, perhaps prophetically, that man would refuse to respect morality by developing more and better techniques to fight and exploit each other and nature. He promoted peaceful teamwork as a solution to protect one another and our natural world, something that today seems to be universally ignored and forgotten.

Jacques-Yves Cousteau died June 25, 1997, at the age of eighty-seven. His memorial service was held in Paris at Notre Dame Cathedral. The team carried his casket. He is buried in his town of birth at the Saint-André-de-Cubzac Cemetery.

"When we are at sea, we are free."

Jacques-Yves Cousteau

II
THE SHIP

The research vessel *Calypso* became perhaps the world's most famous exploration ship. Amazingly it also had an earlier life, actually two earlier lives.

Calypso is a BYMS Mark 1 Class motor minesweeper, with the yard designation BYMS-26. Constructed in 1942 by the Ballard Marine Railway Company at the foot of Twenty-fourth Avenue Northwest along the Seattle, Washington, ship canal, she and four sister ships were soon commissioned by the British into the Royal Navy as HMS J-826 and sailed from Seattle to Gibraltar. There the flotilla was dispatched to Malta, the allied naval headquarters for Mediterranean operations in World War II, and later moved to Italy. When the war ended, the group was disbanded and J-826 was returned to the U.S. Navy.

In 1949, she was sold for private use as a ferry across the five-kilometer stretch of the Mediterranean Sea between Malta and Gozo Island, the second largest island of the Maltese Archipelago.

.e new owner named her *Calypso,* derived from Gozo's nick-.ıame, the Isle of Calypso, and Homer's Greek mythological poem, the *Odyssey.* In the poem a sea nymph, Calypso, controls Gozo, imprisoning Odysseus on the island for love.

In 1950, Loel Guinness of the famous Irish brewing family bought the ship and leased it to Cousteau for one franc a year, with Cousteau assuming responsibility for her maintenance and operating expenses.

Calypso's wooden hull and shallow, ten-foot average load draft (the number of feet from the waterline to the lowest point of the ship's keel), were designed for minesweeping purposes. She was not all that big, just 139 feet long with a 25-foot beam, the width at her widest point.

Propelled by twin General Motors 8-268A straight 8 cylinder 580-horsepower diesel engines, her top speed was a painfully slow 10 knots with two motors running at 900 rpm, the equivalent of 11.5 miles per hour. (A knot is a unit of speed equal to one nautical mile, e.g. 6,076 feet per hour.)

To operate the ship, a crew of at least fourteen was required.

Cousteau converted *Calypso* from a minesweeper and ferry to a marine research and expedition platform by adding many features, including an underwater observation chamber, observation tower, navigational and communication tools (automatic pilot, gyroscopic compass, Decca radar, depth sounder, VHF radio, and satellite communications system), refrigerated darkroom (for storing film and cameras), walk-in freezer and cooler (for meat, dairy, fruit, and vegetables), four-ton capacity hydraulic crane and winch, repair workshop, industrial compressor and air tank rack, recompression chamber, a two-man diving saucer (submarine with 350-meter diving capacity), underwater scooters, inflatable boats, and a helicopter pad.

Otherwise *Calypso* had the standard characteristics of a ship, including a bridge (the location from where a ship is steered and its speed monitored and controlled), a galley (kitchen) and adjoining wardroom (eating and gathering area), and an engine room (below the galley extending aft, toward the rear or stern of the ship).

Tragically, on January 8, 1996, in Singapore harbor, a barge accidentally rammed and sunk *Calypso.* She was raised and moved to La Rochelle, France, where she sat for years, seemingly destined to rot. Wonderfully, in 2008, she was relocated to Piriou Shipyard in Concarneau, northwestern France, where an ambitious restoration project began. Unfortunately it has since stalled and her true fate remains unknown.[14]

III
LALA TO LARONGE

August 4–August 27, 1973

Dad and I left New York's John F. Kennedy International Airport (JFK) early this morning en route to Los Angeles International Airport (LAX).

Upon arrival at LAX we're greeted by Jacques Cousteau, his two sons, Jean-Michel and Philippe, and soon-to-be friends, Ivan Giacoletto and Louis Prezelin, both Cousteau divers.

It's early afternoon here in L.A. and hot as we ride with the car windows open to Cousteau's offices at 8430 Santa Monica Boulevard.

As we arrive at the modest offices, I notice the walls decorated with inspiring photographs of past expeditions. It makes me wonder what it's like.

As the men meet, I wait in the office next door, leafing through a vast library of prints and slides atop a light table.

After the meeting breaks, Philippe drives us to his home on the 8900 block of Shoreham Drive in Beverly Hills. He and his wife, Jan, have invited Dad and me to be their houseguests.

It's an open, free-feeling house in the Hollywood Hills, one block above Sunset Boulevard. From the backyard pool and patio there's a southerly view of the 9000 Sunset Building and greater Los Angeles.

Cameraman François Dorado and his wife, Anne-Lise, are also guests. They are already enjoying the pool. We join them. For the first time I put on scuba gear and Philippe gives me a lesson.

As the sun descends, we dress for dinner and then meet Captain Cousteau, Ivan, Louis, and others at an Italian restaurant just off the Sunset Strip, the name given to the mile and a half of Sunset Boulevard that passes through West Hollywood.

The dinner discussion includes mention of the need for a second driver to accompany Ivan. He will be transporting diving gear, camera equipment, and other supplies for a new expedition to film beavers in the wild. When the talk turns to me, without hesitation I volunteer, and suddenly, instead of returning home to Connecticut, I'll soon be bound for Lake La Ronge, Saskatchewan, Canada, wherever that is.

The next day Dad and I manage a quick day trip to San Diego. We visit the famous zoo and then meet Louis and his wife, Barbara, to go surfing in La Jolla. A fun evening follows as we go to their nearby home and Barbara cooks while Louis plays his guitar and sings.

Louis was born and raised in Cholet, in the region of Vendee, south of Brittany. He did his military service in Corsica as a rescue diver with the French Air Force. He joined Cousteau in 1969, and today he is a diver and photographer. His expeditions include the Blue Hole, Diving Machine, Manatee, New Caledonia, Squids, Walrus, and the Antarctic. Louis told me that among his favorite memories are diving with killer whales, who were "rough but gentle," and the also gentle giant manta rays.

After a fine dinner, Dad and I drive back to L.A.

It's just after midnight, August 7, when we drive down Shoreham and discover in Philippe's driveway a van, bursting at the gills.

In the morning Dad orders a larger vehicle, a step van. This truck is much better suited to handle the load. Its Grumman walk-in aluminum body offers plenty of room, even allowing a passenger to stand inside the cab area next to the driver. We build a bunk bed behind the driver, in front of the separated cargo area, and then transfer the supplies from the strained van. Now that it's done, we're prepared for the long road ahead.

We clean up for an enjoyable farewell dinner at Philippe's. Tomorrow Ivan and I depart on the 2,080-mile drive; a rare land-based Cousteau expedition.

Ivan doesn't speak English and my French is pretty weak, so that alone promises to be an adventure.

We depart on August 8 at 3:00 p.m. to avoid the desert's peak heat. First it's Route 10 to San Bernardino, continuing on Route 15 through Death Valley, the lowest, driest, and hottest location in the U.S.

In Barstow, we stop for gas and dinner. Ivan is intrigued by the packets of sugar on the table, each with a picture of an American scene. He gathers some extras to take along.

The next stop is Las Vegas, at midnight. It's strange emerging out of the quiet, dark desert into the loud, bright, neon city, only to fuel up and then head right back out.

We parallel the faintly outlined mountains and fields of the northwest corner of Arizona and then Saint George, Utah.

At 2:30 a.m. we gas up in Cedar City, Utah. It's my turn to drive, and even before I finish filling the tank, Ivan is fast asleep in the bunk.

I pull onto the road and head down the highway. Hundreds of shooting stars entertain me. They're so visible against the black heavens.

At 5:00 a.m. I pull into a town that's coincidentally named Beaver. It's the birthplace of Butch Cassidy, the notorious western outlaw. It's silent but for the distant crowing of a rooster. Ivan awakes and takes the wheel. I stay up, and as the sky lightens we stop to catch the sunrise with our cameras. I again take the wheel in Nephi, named after people in the Book of Mormon, and drive us to Salt Lake.

We've gone 702 miles and although we've napped, we're dazed and feel a strange numbness. We also need showers and to brush our teeth, particularly Ivan, so we pull into a motel around 10:00 a.m. and sleep until the confused maids knock on the door at 4:00 p.m. After a shower we leave for Pocatello, Idaho, where we'll spend the night.

The van's sliding door is open and there's a wonderful smell of fresh cut hay. It's a beautiful stretch of Route 15. The Bear Mountains are to the east and the Great Salt Lake is to the west.

Soon we succumb to Ogden's immaculate farms and stop for fresh, juicy fruit: peaches, green apples, grapes, and cherries. To our west are one million acres of the Caribou National Forest. Oddly, no caribou ever lived here. The name originated from a prospector named Caribou Jack.

Moving onward, the Snake River Valley introduces us to Pocatello's vast fields, farmhouses, and miles of countryside. There's a violent storm in the distance. Lightning bolts skewer the earth.

We find our motel and begin what will become the nightly ritual of calling Jan in Los Angeles. She's helping us coordinate the planned rendezvous with François and Anne-Lise, who are to haul the Cousteau helicopter north on a trailer. The plan is to meet as soon as possible. But Jan informs us that there's an unexpected helicopter repair required, and because the mechanic is ill, François and Anne-Lise's departure from L.A. has been delayed. In fact, they haven't left yet, so why did we?

Their delay is our gain. It's August 10, so now, ahead of schedule, we head north to Yellowstone National Park, passing through Blackfoot, Montana, named after the Blackfeet Indians, and the northern corner of Idaho Falls, where we exit toward one of only three Montana entrances to Yellowstone. We enter the park via the town of West Yellowstone and pick up a hitchhiker named Dave. He's an enjoyable character and fun to have along.

Established in 1872, Yellowstone is actually the first national park in the world. It measures sixty-three miles north to south and fifty-four miles east to west. Of its 2.3 million acres, ninety-six percent are in Wyoming, three percent in Montana, and one percent in Idaho.

Twelve miles in we stop at an area known for its hundreds of hot springs, mudpots, and what are called fumaroles, which are openings in the earth's crust where groundwater mixes with hot gases to emit a steam composed of carbon dioxide, sulfur dioxide, hydrochloric acid, and hydrogen sulfide. More than ten thousand of these geothermal features exist throughout the park. I'm surprised to learn that Yellowstone has one of the world's largest active volcanoes and a nearly hundred-square-mile crater as a result of another partially collapsed volcano.

We move onward toward the Old Faithful area, also known as the Upper Geyser Basin. Our timing is perfect. We arrive just as the famous 185-foot cone geyser, Old Faithful, erupts into the air. Albeit a more predictable attraction, erupting about every sixty-five minutes, Old Faithful is not the tallest geyser in Yellowstone. That distinction belongs to Steamboat Geyser, in the Norris Geyser Basin, which shoots more than three hundred feet into the air. It can, however, be days and even decades between Steamboat's eruptions.

Yellowstone actually has nine geyser basins and as many as five hundred geysers, half of all the geysers in the world.

We drive fifty miles deeper into the park to Inspiration Point, where we view the Yellowstone River rushing over an enormous waterfall yielding a rainbow-enhanced cloud of mist. During the last volcanic eruption, a lava flow stopped just west of this canyon, the Grand Canyon of Yellowstone, and created an underground thermal basin that still produces steam, contributing to the size of the cloud of mist.

At dusk, as we depart the park, I'm excited to see a pair of moose and then a dozen grazing elk.

Dave joins us for chow in West Yellowstone. Ivan collects some more sugar. Then we call Jan, who informs us that François is still delayed, this time due to a broken shock on the trailer. We leave Dave and head north.

The next morning, the eleventh, we encounter another hitchhiker, Josh. He's got a broken bicycle, which he lugs through our open sliding door and up the three steps. Later we drop him in Butte.

Continuing toward Missoula, we stop for gas and notice pick-up trucks with horses and trailers. We ask if there's a rodeo nearby and are told there's going to be a small rodeo this evening in Deer Lodge, only sixteen miles from here. Ivan is fascinated by the idea of a rodeo and I'm pretty excited myself, so with time to spare we decide to head to Deer Lodge.

Deer Lodge is nestled in a valley between the Continental Divide and the Flint Creek Mountain Range. Its name derived from a forty-foot cone, formed by thermal spring deposits that still emit visible vapor resembling smoke rising from an Indian lodge.

The Continental Divide, also called the Great Divide, is a major line dividing the North American continent's watersheds and resulting flow of water, either westward toward the Pacific Ocean or eastward toward the Atlantic or Arctic Oceans. It runs from the Seward Peninsula in Alaska through Western Canada, along the crest of the Rocky Mountains to New Mexico, and continues along the top of Mexico's Sierra Madres all of the way to the tip of South America.

It's a small local rodeo, more of a social town gathering. Everyone's drinking beer and cheering for their children, grandchildren, brothers, and sisters. They're all in jeans and chaps and wearing cowboy hats, so we stick out like sore thumbs, but the people are friendly and we have a great time. We leave ten minutes early to beat the crowd.

A confrontation with a rain shower slows our progress, but otherwise we enjoy a pleasant and scenic trip to Missoula. Once there, we phone Jan, who gives us more bad news: François has been further delayed by yet another problem with the twenty-eight-foot helicopter trailer.

I call home to tell Dad my idea of postponing the upcoming freshman year of college and staying the winter for the entire expedition. He disagrees, and I'm disappointed, fearing I'm going to miss a once-in-a lifetime opportunity.

On the twelfth, we finally enter the 1.5 million-acre Blackfeet Indian Reservation.[15] The reservation, the largest remaining community of Blackfeet Indians, is set in the foothills of the Rocky Mountains, which the Blackfeet aptly call the "Backbone of the World." They were once one of the most powerful tribes in the northwest. Great warriors, who at their peak controlled a massive territory outlined by the North Saskatchewan River in Alberta and the Missouri and Yellowstone Rivers in Montana.

There are at least two theories as to the origin of the Blackfeet name. One is from a reference to the color of their black moccasins, which were said to be either painted or more likely darkened by the char from crossing the burnt prairies. The other is a story from the Legend of the Sun, in which it is said that an old man was told during a vision to paint the feet of the eldest with black medicine. Doing so gave the old man's sons the power to catch the buffalo. The old man then decreed that his descendents should be called Blackfeet.

The name of their language is *Siksiksa,* which translates to Blackfoot; however, the constitution under which their tribal council was formed translates to Blackfeet.

We spend the night at a motel inside the reservation in Browning, Montana, the seat of the tribal government.

François is finally underway, so we'll rendezvous the day after tomorrow. Then, together, we'll cross the nearby Canadian border. Since we're waiting for François, tomorrow is another free day. We plan to visit Glacier National Park (Glacier), which is only thirteen miles to our west.

In 1910, President Taft signed a bill establishing Glacier and preserving over one million acres of forests, alpine meadows, and lakes. At first, in fact for decades, access to the park's interior was limited to horseback. With the advent of the automobile came demand for a road, leading to an eleven-year project constructing the Going-to-the-Sun Road. Eventually completed in 1932, the road is today considered to be an engineering feat and one of the most scenic roads in North America.

We actually take Going-to-the-Sun Road, in our truck, no less. Our first stop is Sun Point. Looking down, we see Saint Mary's Lake. Above there's a glacier, nestled within the majestic snow-topped Rocky Mountains, standing high upon their throne.

Continuing, we see Going-to-the-Sun Mountain and more snow-capped mountains and glaciers. The timberline, where the lush clusters of pine trees suddenly stop, is clearly evident. Eventually we hit "The Loop" and make a sudden turn to the south proceeding along Packers Roost. We stop for a break. A melting roadside glacier gifts us with sparkling fresh water.

These roads are extraordinary, commanding much respect as they wind and twist about. One false move does mean disaster. Below are pines, cedars, rocks, waterfalls, and the Flathead River. Above there's a clear blue sky and an occasional cotton candy cloud. It's a clear view of heaven.

We descend until we reach the southern side of Lake McDonald and follow the lake to the town of West Glacier. Heading onward, back toward Browning, we're actually now on the same road that we arrived on yesterday. It's been one spectacular circle. We pass

Browning and head farther north to the town of Babb. Once there we find a motel and call Jan, who informs us that François is already in Helena and that he'll meet us here tomorrow morning. *Bonne nuit* (good night).

On the fourteenth, François, Anne-Lise, and Bob McKeegan, the helicopter pilot, arrive at the motel early in the afternoon. We enjoy lunch and then leave for the Canadian border.

The crossing goes smoothly—too smoothly, really. Our presentation of Cousteau letterhead seemed to help.

We proceed into southern Alberta,[16] the province named after Princess Louise Caroline Alberta, the fourth daughter of Queen Victoria. We're in the southern prairie region, known for desert-like summer heat, to which we can attest. We bake as we drive with the sliding door wide open. The northern part of the province has forest and alpine regions, but here in the prairie, there are endless miles of dry grasses, hardy buffalo bean, and sage. Bordering the highway is mile after mile of brilliant purple clover.

Tonight's stopping point is Calgary, which was Blackfoot territory for eleven thousand years, until European settlers began arriving in 1860 to hunt buffalo and sell bootleg whiskey.

On the morning of the fifteenth, we make the mistake of leaving during rush hour and are immediately separated. Ivan and I have lost our directions, but we eventually find our way onto the correct road and head out of town. We don't know where François, Anne-Lise, and Bob are.

Hundreds of miles pass. We drive along vast fields of wheat, oats, barley, rye, flaxseed, and canola. Eventually leaving the province of Alberta, we enter the province of Saskatchewan, its name derived from the Cree Indian word *kisiskatchewan*, meaning the river that flows swiftly, a reference to the area's major river.

Now we're lost again. This time in Saskatchewan's largest city, Saskatoon, named by the Cree after a local indigenous berry. I drive onto and over too many curbs before finally getting on the correct road to Prince Albert, the oldest city in Saskatchewan.

Prince Albert is situated in the middle of the province on the banks of the North Saskatchewan River. It bridges two lands, the open, rich agricultural southern prairie and the northern forest and abundant lakes. The Saskatchewan provincial flag mirrors this with its upper green half and lower gold half.

Reverend James Nisbet settled Prince Albert in 1866 and named it in honor of the son of the Prince of Wales. Some notable figures who lived in Prince Albert were Lucy Maud Montgomery, the author of *Anne of Green Gables*, and actor Boris Karloff of *Dracula* fame.

Since we're still separated from François, we look around town and then the airport for the not so inconspicuous bright yellow helicopter. There's no sign, so we find a motel and check in with Jan.

We're surprised on the sixteenth to have breakfast with François, Anne-Lise, and Bob. They arrived in Prince Albert early this morning and Jan directed them to our motel.

After breakfast Bob and I are deposited at the airport along with the helicopter, which is affectionately nicknamed *Felix*.

Ivan, François, and Anne-Lise are driving north to *Lac* La Ronge (Lake La Ronge). I'm not sure why we're not continuing to trailer *Felix,* but instead Bob and I are to fly.

Felix is a Hughes 300C model. It's rated to seat three people, including the pilot. To do so the middle control stick is removed and replaced with a seat cushion for a second passenger. The Cousteau team keeps it configured for two people because there's usually a need to carry extra cargo or for the one passenger, a photographer, to maneuver while filming.

Bob and I unwrap, clean, and fasten the two twenty-five-foot rotor blades, which had been secured to the trailer bed during the drive. Then we climb aboard, start the engine, and as quick as that we're en route to La Ronge, at least so we think. Soon, 150 kilometers into the trip, at an altitude of one thousand feet and a sixty-five-knot speed (seventy-five mph), the engine begins to overheat. Bob attempts several in-flight cooling maneuvers, but they're unsuccessful, so he reverses course and desperately retreats to Prince Albert. We must avoid ditching in the heavily wooded wilderness below.

We barely make it back to the airport. After a breath of relief, we maneuver *Felix* into a small, primitive hangar. Bob goes straight to work, completely disassembling the engine. He tells me that as a pilot in Vietnam, he was trained for situations like this, in case he was ever downed in the jungle. I can't help him much other than by keeping the coffee coming. We work through the afternoon and all through the night.

Bob explains that in Vietnam he flew the larger UH-1A helicopter on "dust-off" missions, slang for emergency medical evacuation (MEDEVAC) of injured soldiers from combat zones.[17]

Regarding the UH, in 1960, the U.S. Army awarded Hughes the first order for the HU-1A aircraft, designated *Iroquois* after the Native Americans. The HU designation stood for "helicopter utility," which led to the nickname Huey. For some reason in 1962, the Department of Defense reversed the initials, making it UH.

The Army used thousands of Hueys in Vietnam. They generally carried a crew of four (two pilots and two door gunners) plus an infantry section of eight to ten soldiers. UH-1 aircraft were configured for many purposes, with nicknames and capacity depending upon the function. For example, if serving as a gunship, outfitted with rocket and grenade launchers and machine guns, it was referred to as a Frog or a Hog. If it only had guns without launchers it was known as a Cobra or Guns. When stripped down and used to transport troops, or for medical transport, it was termed a Slick because other than the two door gunners it had no weapons.

The medevacs were defenseless, unarmored aircraft configured to accommodate six stretchers. The Army displayed a large red cross on the side, protecting those aboard under the laws and treaties of the Geneva Convention.

By the afternoon of the seventeenth, Bob has Humpty put back together again. He says dirty points and a loose piece of metal rattling around inside the engine caused the problem.

We leave for La Ronge again, but as Bob wants to make up for lost time, it's an even more exhilarating trip, flying lower and faster over forest, streams, rivers, and lakes. *Felix* touches down at La Ronge's Athabaska Airways terminal at 5:00 p.m., where Philippe meets us and drives us into town.

My first impression of La Ronge on this Friday evening is that it appears sad. Many of the people, mostly Cree Indians, seem to be drunk and unhappy.

We arrive at the rented house where we're all staying together. Jan, Philippe, Ivan, Louis, François, and Anne-Lise are already here. I meet Guy Jouas, a soundman, and François Charlet who is affectionately known as Tonton. François Dorado, Tonton, Louis, Ivan, and Philippe are all cameramen.

Unlike the unhappy souls in town, we have a fun dinner and then listen to Louis playing his acoustic guitar while Anne-Lise sings and François plays the drums.

La Ronge is situated in the wilderness of Saskatchewan's Northern Management Zone, about six hundred miles north of the U.S. border. The next nearest point of civilization is Pinehouse, an aboriginal settlement of nine hundred people, one hundred miles to the south.

It's believed that the French fur traders named this place because *ronge* is derived from the French ronger, meaning to gnaw, in reference to the beavers that inhabit the forests and shores.

The original inhabitants were Native Americans who canoed and dog-sledded here via the many connected rivers and lakes. The French named them Cree, originating from the tribe's name *Kristineaux*, or *Kri* for short.[18]

Being that the Cree were accomplished hunters, when the European trappers arrived, they traded for fur. The lake's shore has several overgrown trading posts.

Today there are about twelve thousand Cree living in nine distinct settlements across 375,000 square kilometers of land. They're all members of the same tribe but are described as being in different bands. The La Ronge Cree are known as the James Bay Cree because they live east-southeast of James Bay.

Although we've made it to La Ronge, we're still not to our final destination. We need to get to Foster Lake (Foster), where we'll establish a camp and build a cabin for the team to live in this winter while they film the documentary *Beavers of the North Country*. Foster isn't accessible by road, so we'll fly one hundred miles north via seaplane and helicopter.

It's the morning of the eighteenth and I'm helping Bob put the pontoons on the helicopter. They're needed because at Foster, until we clear a landing pad in the woods, we'll anchor *Felix* on the water. We slide the two landing crossbars into a sort of tunnel on each of the two long yellow inflatable floats. All along the bottom of each float we insert sturdy bolts that pass through a grommet on one side of the durable fabric, then the landing tube, and then another grommet on the other side of the pontoon. Each bolt is fastened with a nut, and then we inflate the floats, lifting *Felix* about eighteen inches. Bob and Philippe take a test flight. I return to the house and join Jan and Louis for a canoe ride on the lake.

When Bob returns, I suggest that he and Ivan join me for another canoe trip. Well, look out, these two clowns give me a bath. We cross a small bay and explore an island. During the return trip I'm removed as captain and sent to be the kneeler in the middle of the canoe. Between Ivan's splashing and a dozen near capsizes I'm now a wet rag. But it's really a fun excursion and we have already agreed to do it again tomorrow. Next time I'll wear shorts and I'm going to paddle.

Early on the morning of the nineteenth, we board the chartered Athabaska Airways de Havilland Otter for our first trip to

Foster Lake. It's a fixed-wing floatplane with metal pontoons designed to land on water.

I sit behind the pilot, atop a pile of lumber, nails and insulation and look out the window at a breathtaking sunrise reflecting off the intertwined lakes and rivers. Splash down is near Foster's southern shore. The pilot revs the propellers and coaxes the plane to the beach. Our camp will be here, a perfect spot, on the edge of a sheltered bay nestled within the rugged woods. We're at latitude 56 degrees, 30.595 minutes, and longitude 105 degrees, 24.084 minutes.

We unload supplies, stack lumber, and then explore the area. Afterward we start clearing the campsite. There's a lot of work to be done. The next plane arrives with our lunch. First we unload more lumber and supplies, and then we eat.

The first task is clearing an area to pitch our tents. We also need to clear an area for the helicopter to land and eventually an area for the cabin. Unbelievably we only have one small chain saw, a handsaw, and a pair of pruning shears. That's it!

In the late afternoon, a third and final plane arrives with more supplies and Tonton. We unload, continue clearing, and then leave for La Ronge, where we'll spend our last night in a house and a real bed. It's a quiet flight back. We're tired and mesmerized by the now late afternoon sun reflecting on the network of water below.

Dinner is again the highlight of the day as everyone is so happy and friendly.

I'm up early on the twentieth. Surprisingly two planes have already made deliveries to camp.

Now it's our turn to fly. Ivan, Tonton, Guy, and I climb aboard a completely full plane and again sit on the lumber. We land, cruise to the beach, unload, and while waiting for the next plane, we fish for two hours. The water is crystal clear. I can see the large northern pike take my lure.

Finally we hear the Otter in the distance and watch as it comes in low on the horizon, just over the treetops. It makes a smooth landing and motors to shore.

We unload, arrange trunks, pitch tents, and build beds. I enlarge the helicopter pad and rake up any sharp sticks that could puncture *Felix*'s floats. Eventually we break for another wonderful dinner, this time at our new camp.

Figure 1 - Felix landing at Foster Lake

Jan and Anne-Lise prepare dinner. Afterward we all walk the short thirty meters or so to the lake's shore. The sky is glowing. It's the Northern Lights, also known as the Aurora Borealis. The colorful light show is caused by the sun's charged particles colliding with gases in the earth's atmosphere.

It's the next morning now and I'm upset that last night Louis was stuck sleeping in the open with nothing but a parka and a space blanket. He didn't have a tent or even a sleeping bag. I feel that I'm the extra one along and I should take the discomfort. Louis is such a great guy and he's always going out of his way for me.

In La Ronge we hired two Cree carpenters to help us build the cabin. They have just arrived and will stay with us until the cabin is completed.

Bob, Ivan, and I clear more trees, first for the house and then for the helicopter pad. I use the chain saw until the chain flies off. Work gloves would be nice, but without them I take a deep cut in my index finger. The wound throbs and could probably use stitches, but we don't have a doctor, so I bandage it and go back to work. Once we clear enough, the carpenters begin laying out the cabin's foundation.

After lunch I continue work on the helicopter pad and chop wood for the oven before capping off the day with a cold swim.

The next day, I work all day with the Indians, which is great. We lay the heavy floor beams on top of the concrete blocks and then nail the plywood sub-floor to the beams, creating a level raised floor.

I also start insulating the floor. It's an unpleasant job, but I like that I can call it my own. I crawl underneath the house with my back in the earth, roots, and freshly cut stumps. Just inches above my face I staple the pink fiberglass insulation in between the floor beams. I don't have a mask or goggles, so I wrap a handkerchief around my nose and mouth, leaving my now itchy eyes exposed. I complete two-thirds of the floor before it's time to quit for dinner. After dinner Ivan and I fish, but strangely we have no luck.

Figure 2 - That's me nailing a wall brace.

We're up early again for yet another great day, with plenty of fresh air and hard work. First I finish the floor insulation and then help Ivan build his "special house," the outhouse. Later Bob and I roll one of the fifty-gallon fuel drums up from the beach and about seventy-five meters over to the helicopter pad, where we set up the fuel pump. Then I help the carpenters with the house, first nailing the sub-floor, then framing walls and starting the siding.

It's already August 24, and I'm running out of time.

Figure 3 - The seaplane near the cabin

After breakfast we correct a construction mistake from yesterday, then raise the back wall and start framing the fourth and final wall. We've decided to modify the design of the house and enclose what was to be the outdoor porch area. That means it needs insulation. So after lunch I crawl back underneath and insulate the now interior porch area. When I crawl out I see that the fourth wall has been raised. The house is really taking shape.

Before dinner we take a refreshing swim in the cold lake. Then it starts to rain and continues through the night. The only shelters we have are our small tents and a clear plastic tarp above the dining table.

In the morning the Indians teach me a better way to split wood. Then they go fishing in the rain. It's very raw and cold. While they're fishing, I chop away. We need wood for the stove, for cooking, making tea, and to huddle around for warmth.

They return with eight large northern pike, gray-green colored elongated fish with sharply pointed heads sporting sharp teeth. We stop work for a fresh fish lunch, eating outside in the rain. Cold water occasionally dribbles off an edge of the tarp and down my neck or onto my plate. It's quite an experience. Actually I never thought the tarp would work as well as it does.

Figure 4 - Dining in the rain

After lunch it's back to work chopping even more wood. Until we all take a break for tea and cognac. It tastes especially good in this August chill. Then it is a cognac-induced nap for all.

When we awake the rain has slowed to just a light mist. I help with the house as we try to get more work done before the rain returns. The whole soggy group is up here raising the roof and hammering away. It's quite a sight and fun.

Night now and it's pouring again. Anne-Lise and I leave tomorrow. Jan has prepared a delicious farewell dinner of roast beef, noodles, and muffins.

It was a great final day with everyone staying close to camp, giving us the opportunity to see each other and talk. I don't want to leave. I've grown close to these people and enjoy the hard work, the nature, and the sense of adventure.

In the morning, Jan makes a great breakfast. I chop wood, pack, and work on the house. Then the plane arrives. Fortunately Bill Jackson, the pilot, hasn't eaten lunch yet, so we have a little more time as Jan prepares something for him.

After Bill finishes, Tonton films some staged floatplane take offs and landings. Then we all gather for François to take a few quick photographs of the team.

Figure 5 - Front left to right: Tonton, Louis, Guy, Kelly (the dog), and Jan
Back left to right: Bob, me, Philippe, Ivan, and Anne-Lise

Afterward Anne-Lise and I board the plane bound for La Ronge.

In La Ronge Anne-Lise and I find a couple of rooms at Reeds Camp. I do a ton of laundry for the campers, which Bill will take back on his next visit. She and I have a quiet dinner and call it a night.

I've made new friends on this expedition and learned new things about people, nature, and myself. I hope that the group I've left behind has a successful expedition and that the photos I've taken capture the beauty of the U.S. and Canada. The Cousteau organization and these individuals are concerned with protecting, enjoying, and loving nature, as all people should.

On August 27, Anne-Lise and I awake early and leave La Ronge aboard an American Airlines DC-3 bound for Prince Albert, the leg I'd previously flown with Bob aboard *Felix*. Upon arrival we run to catch the Norcanair double prop plane bound for Saskatoon, on which we are the only passengers. In Saskatoon we have a cup of coffee together and then say good-bye, each leaving on different Air Canada flights.

Anne-Lise is bound for Paris via connection in Montreal. Montreal seems like a logical connection for me too, but for some reason my itinerary has me flying to Winnipeg. From Winnipeg, all the New York flights are full, so I fly to Toronto, where I connect with my sixth and final leg to New York. I'm aboard now, enjoying some dry roasted peanuts and a beer. Mom and Dad will meet me at LaGuardia Airport.

I'm returning to a good home and a great family. I'm grateful to God, my father, my family, and the Cousteau organization for making this trip possible.

"If you lose your head, you're finished."

Jacques-Yves Cousteau

"I think some people should be boiled in oil!"

Fran Gaar

IV

AQUA LUNG SCHOOL OF NEW YORK

July 1974

To climb the organizational ladder and fully experience Cousteau's undersea world, I must get advanced certification before my next expedition. I select Fran Gaar, PADI, W-M #1, to be my instructor. Fran is not your ordinary dive instructor and that's why I want her. She is the dean of scuba instructors in New York City and the director and founder of the Aqua Lung School of New York, located in, of all places, Manhattan. At age nine, Fran became the youngest swimming champion in Maryland state history. She went on to an illustrious water-based career and is distinguished as the first woman in the world to have been certified as a master instructor by the Professional Association of Diving Instructors (PADI), as signified by the aforementioned #1.

Fran was the first instructor to train New York City Fire Department rescue teams. She also taught legendary wreck diver Evelyn Dudas, the first woman to dive on the *Andrea Doria* and one of the first women to use mixed gases.[h]

Fran was the aquatic supervisor for the television program *Sea Hunt* and the famous live *Sea Hunt* show at the 1964 New York World's Fair, where she also soloed as Miss Aquafair. Fair visitors called this the best buy; for fifty cents they saw an eighteen-minute live underwater show narrated by Lloyd Bridges. The show would begin with Lloyd explaining the purpose of the various components of scuba gear while Fran climbed into the forty-thousand-gallon tank designed by Buster Crabbe. Fran would then do an underwater ballet, followed by the *Sea Hunt* show, featuring two champion swimmers doing an underwater drama called *Mike Nelson Meets the Sea Monster from Outer Space.* No kidding.

Fran was also featured as Miss Pickerel on the NBC-TV show of the same name and served as stunt coach, water choreographer, and understudy for Esther Williams in the Esther Williams television specials.

Although less than convenient, selecting Fran is a good choice. Twice a week I catch the 6:08 p.m. New Haven Railroad from Westport, Connecticut's Saugatuck station for the hour train ride to Grand Central Terminal in mid-town Manhattan, New York.

From Grand Central I walk to class, held in the basement of a rundown hotel pool. Last week I was sitting on the pool deck with my back against the wall while taking a written exam, and when I leaned forward, two tiles came off the wall, stuck to my back.

---

h The most common diving gas is compressed air, comprised of a mixture of 21% oxygen, 78% nitrogen, and ~1% other trace gases. The nitrogen component causes side effects, particularly at greater depths, e.g. deeper than ~40 meters (~131 feet). The maximum depth on compressed air is said to be 66.2 metres (~217 feet). There are multiple types of mixed gases but a more common mixture is nitrox, which contains a greater percentage of oxygen. With less nitrogen, diver decompress time is reduced, allowing for a longer dive. The mixture does not, however, allow the diver to go any deeper. In fact the opposite is true; it necessitates a shallower maximum operating depth.

I agree with Fran's quote, "I think some people should be boiled in oil." She said this when discussing sharks and the frenzy and fear that writers and movie producers sensationalize. She also said, "To frighten a whole generation of youngsters and their parents with distortions such as *Jaws* is ignorant and selfish. Considering that sharks don't get diseases maybe we should concentrate on trying to learn something from them instead of continuing this dreadful exploitation."

I like Fran a lot. She's teaching me that emotional stability, physical conditioning, and good swimming are the necessary requirements to becoming an expert diver.

After class, Juan, a classmate, gives me a ride back to Grand Central in his old Toyota Corolla. He's a nice guy and the rides are always appreciated. It's usually a quiet ride as we're both tired from class and the late hour. He drops me off around midnight and I catch the 12:22 a.m. train home. If I miss it then I have to take the 1:30 milk train, a local, which drops mail at every depot and arrives in Westport at 2:51 a.m.

V
THANKSGIVING

November 1974

It's Thanksgiving break my sophomore year of college, and I'm flying from school in Greenville, South Carolina, to Panama City, Florida.

Upon arrival I grab a taxi to the dock. For the first time I see Cousteau's ship, the research vessel *Calypso.*

I'm offered a choice: sail aboard *Calypso* to work on an oceanography project taking water samples in the Gulf of Mexico or join a dive team bound for a day in warm, clear, inland springs. Despite the ship's attraction, the decision is easy; I opt to dive.

Led by Bernard Delemotte, a Cousteau veteran, a half dozen of us spend the next day diving and filming several nearby springs. Then we return to port for a raucous dinner.

The following morning we climb aboard two stone crab fishing boats. We're to spend three days filming. I learn that these Florida stone crabs inhabit shallow water within bays, grass flats, and rock jetties, where they can feed on clams, scallops, and conchs, and burrow to find refuge from their only significant predator, other than man, the octopus.

An adult's hard protective shell, called a carapace or exoskeleton, is about three and a half inches long and four inches wide. Given the chance, the crabs will live seven to eight years, becoming sexually mature at two to three years of age. Before mating, the male must wait for the female to molt her shell. She'll spawn four to six times each season, depending on her size, producing two hundred thousand to one million eggs each time.

The law restricts crabbers to the taking of just one claw, from grown males only. This is because claws will actually regenerate (grow back), but not quickly enough if they are both taken.

We're soon shocked as, even while we catch them on film, the fishermen repeatedly break the law, selfishly harvesting both claws from all sizes of both male and female crabs. Then they release helpless, defenseless, live torsos, now unable to feed or burrow. These fishermen are ignorantly destroying a species as well as their legacy.

"What is a scientist after all? It is a curious man looking through a keyhole, the keyhole of nature, trying to know what's going on."

Jacques-Yves Cousteau

VI
MIAMI TO MUJERES

THE CREW OF *CALYPSO*

COMMANDANT
Jacques-Yves Cousteau

NURSE
Simone Cousteau

CAPTAIN
Camille Alibert

CHIEF DIVERS
Philippe Cousteau
Bernard Delemotte
Michel Deloire
Albert Falco

DIVERS
Raymond Bravo
Jean Jerome Carcopino
Patrick Delemotte
Ivan Giacoletto
Lev Poliakov
Louis Prezelin
Joe Thompson

SPECIAL GUESTS
John Denver
Dr. William Herrnkind
Dr. George Low
Kris O'Connor

FIRST MATE & SECOND CAPTAIN
Paul Zuena

DECKHANDS
Richard Hyman
Jeff Tworzydlo

STEWARD
Raymond Amaddio

SOUNDMAN
Daniel Belanger

ELECTRICIAN
Jean Desoeuvres

MECHANICS
Armand Davso
Michel Fourcade
Jean-Marie France, Chief

RADIO
Rick Martin
Ron Ristad
Michel Treboz

PILOT
Jerry Baxter Sr.

DOCTOR
Michel Gau

CHEF
Philippe Leconte

COOK
Manuel

STUDENTS
Hussein Abd El-Reheim
Parviz Babaee
Jack Hill

GUIDE
Valvula

December 26, 1974–February 10, 1975

It is early Thursday morning when I leave New York bound for Cozumel, Mexico, stopping in Miami, where I rendezvous with Dr. George Low, the deputy administrator of the National Aeronautics and Space Administration (NASA). We leave Miami for Cozumel, where we're supposed to meet Dr. William Herrnkind,[19] a Florida State University professor and marine biologist who specializes in the behavior of the Caribbean spiny lobster. He's nowhere to be found so we catch our charter flight to Isla Mujeres, Mexico, in the Gulf of Mexico.[20] Upon arrival we meet Jack Hill, a Texas A&M University student, and Jerry Baxter the new American helicopter pilot.

Jerry leaves with George on the thirty-minute flight to *Calypso.* The ship is anchored off Isla Contoy, twenty miles north of Mujeres and forty miles east of the Yucatan Peninsula.[21] After depositing George on *Calypso,* Jerry returns to fetch me.

This is a new chopper, a Hughes 300C, the same model as *Felix,* who met a dim fate last month, on November 17. Former pilot Jay Prather and cameraman Joe Thompson were preparing for a morning takeoff to film oceanographic experiments conducted by teams aboard Zodiacs off the southwest passage of the Mississippi River when a rogue wave in otherwise calm seas rocked the untethered *Felix* off the port side of *Calypso* into the sea. Jay and Joe were unharmed, but the helicopter was a total loss. This new bird's name is *Phoenix.* I don't think I'll ever get used to any other name than my old friend *Felix.*

As we fly I can now see Contoy and *Calypso* in the distance.

Figure 6 - Isla Contoy

Jerry closes in and brings *Phoenix* in for landing. We climb out of the helicopter to find the Cousteau team buzzing with excitement, speculating that the migration of the lobsters has begun. Contoy is known for tremendous lobster catches, so we're here to make a film, *The Incredible March of the Spiny Lobster.*

It's good to see my old friends from previous expeditions: Ivan, Bernard, Louis, and Philippe.

I'm so anxious to explore the not so distant island of Contoy.

During my seven-week stay, I'll serve as a deckhand. It's an entry-level job at the bottom of the ladder. I'll carry out any order from the captain or the first mate, including standing watch, steering, navigation, and maintenance. I'll also work on an independent research project for university credit. It was difficult getting approval from Furman University, where I'm a sophomore, because only juniors and seniors are allowed to do independent study. Also, although I have completed the prerequisite courses, I've not yet taken the required advanced science classes or declared a major. Dr. Van Price approved what is supposed to be a geology project. I'm not sure what geology there will be, but I appreciate him having vision and being flexible.

After completing the lobster film we plan to sail south to Belize. At least that's what JYC says today. I now know the team well enough to realize that decisions are made spontaneously; by the seat of the Speedo.

JYC telexes Fred Hyman at The Society office in Westport, Connecticut.

> "THE WIND YESTERDAY VEERED TO THE SOUTHEAST, BRINGING TURBID WATER AND INTERRUPTING THE ARRIVAL OF LOBSTERS. THEN YESTERDAY EVENING A DEPRESSION WELL ANNOUNCED ON THE SATELLLITE PHOTOS BROUGHT HEAVIER RAINS AND WINDS DURING THE NIGHT. TODAY WE ENTER A SAD AND WET DAY, WHICH WILL BE RESENTED IN THE CAMP. IT SEEMS TO BE A LIKELY SIGN OF A STRONG NORTH WIND TO BE FOLLOWED BY THE MYSTERIOUS AND MASSIVE ARRIVAL OF THE LOBSTERS. AT LEAST THIS IS THE GENERAL BELIEF AND FORECAST OF THE LOCAL FISHERMEN WHO ARE EVERY YEAR GETTING A MIRACULOUS BONANZA IN THREE DAYS. THEY SHOULD KNOW."

He asks Fred to work out the formalities with the Belize government. JYC seeks Belize's approval for us to dive on Glover Reef for about three weeks in mid to late January. This is a new and sudden plan. JYC wants a Cousteau executive to fly to Belize to make arrangements. Upon our arrival in Belize, JYC plans to present the government with his film *Blue Hole*, previously filmed on Belize's Lighthouse Reef.

I've seen the telex terminal in Westport but never took great notice of it. Now I'm fascinated to see that by using the TELegraph

EXchange Service even at sea, via satellite, we can exchange text messages with other subscribers around the clock and around the globe. We can also send and receive voice telephone messages and facsimiles via satellite.

Calypso operates off a twenty-four-hour clock, also known as military time, beginning at midnight, which is 0000 as opposed to noon, which is 1200. At 8:00 p.m., or 2000, the usual time for the second sitting of dinner, I join Simone Cousteau (Madame), JYC, and George. The fare is fresh lobster.

2000 is also shower hour. With twenty-seven men aboard, I grab a very quick shower. The water is rationed. I get wet, soap up, rinse off, and that's it. It's the old-fashioned pull-chain type shower. It's a new experience and not one that I cherish.

Now I'm in my cabin, which is the diver's cabin. I have two roommates, Raymond and Ivan. The fourth bunk is currently empty.

I just spoke with Parviz Babaee, the second Texas A&M graduate student aboard. He's Iranian and on watch on the bridge. He explains that, when anchored, we have one person stand watch alone and that when the ship is not at anchor and underway, two people stand watch together, normally either JYC, the ship's captain, or the first mate, teamed with one of the divers. All of the divers double as navigators.

The captain for this expedition is Camille Alibert. He's from Brittany, France. A seaman for forty-six years; fifteen years in the French Navy, twenty-four years in the merchant marine, and the last seven with Cousteau.

Being on watch requires you to be alert, constantly checking the radar[i] and the ship's position, to ensure that the anchor is holding and that the ship is not drifting. It's also important to keep a look out for other ships that might be on a collision course. Also, every fifteen minutes or so you need to walk around the ship to ensure there is nothing unusual going on, like a fire or even invading pirates. No kidding.

i Acronym for "Radio Detecting and Ranging"

I naively volunteer to stand watch in the future, not realizing that this will become one of my primary roles.

Parviz agrees to let me observe his academic weather research. I'm thinking that this is a possible topic for my independent study.

We're still wondering what happened to Dr. Herrnkind and why he wasn't in Cozumel. I prepare a telex informing the Westport office that George and I arrived and asking them to call Lynne Herrnkind, Bill's wife, to ascertain his whereabouts.

It's late now. A couple dozen small wooden Mujeres-based fishing boats are quietly anchored nearby. These fishermen supposedly make enough money from their brief several-day lobster harvest to support their family and modest standard of living for the entire year.

The natives tell us that the migration won't begin until there's a north wind. Parviz predicts good weather, which ironically is bad news.

Despite earlier involvement with the Cousteau team, this is my first night sleeping aboard *Calypso.* The sea is calm and the ship is wonderfully peaceful.

The next morning, it's a typical French breakfast of coffee and dry toast. Today's special is an extended conversation with George and JYC.

People mill around as we discuss the upcoming space flight with the Russians, mass transit, American cars, rockets, weather, submarines, and what JYC calls the "energy problem, not a crisis."

Cousteau is interested in networking satellite-based technology and ocean-based sensors to remotely monitor the health of the oceans. He says there should be a coordinated global effort between all of the nations possessing space technology.

JYC discusses how fishing is hunting and high-tech fishing is just a more scientific way to slaughter. Instead of raping the sea, we must intelligently farm the sea, just as we do the land. Marine culture is still in the early stage because not enough is known about the ocean. Fishing is an intermediate evil that will unfortunately continue until we learn how, where, and what to farm in the sea. Using technology to improve fishing is bad, though, and in the long run a disaster. He compares it to hypothetically improved hunting with machine guns and toxic gases. JYC adds that satellite imagery can help man responsibly farm the sea in ways such as detecting the luminescence of chlorophyll and the temperature of cold upwelling water currents to indicate enriched phytoplankton and potentially optimal farming locations.

Listening to JYC and George is fascinating and stimulating. George is forty-eight years old, married to Mary, and has five children, Mark, Diane, George, John, and Nancy.[j]

Today I move off of the ship to Contoy where I'll camp with Bernard, Jerry, Parviz, Hussein Abd El-Reheim, a third Texas A&M student, cameraman Jean Jerome Carcopino (Carco), and soundman Daniel Belanger.

The island is a protected reserve about four miles long and only about two hundred meters across at its widest part. The only person who lives on Contoy is the solitary lighthouse keeper. Otherwise there are occasional campers, depending upon the time of year.

The thinking is that when the desired north wind comes, *Calypso* may need to leave for Mujeres' safe harbor and leave a land-based team at the camp to continue diving and filming. The camp won't be as well equipped as *Calypso*, but having divers with

j George earned a Bachelor and Master of Aeronautical Engineering degree from Rensselaer Polytechnic Institute. After a stint at General Dynamics he joined the National Advisory Committee for Aeronautics (NACA), a federal agency focused on aeronautical research, as an engineer at the Lewis Flight Propulsion Laboratory in Cleveland, Ohio. He became head of the Fluid Mechanics Section and then chief of the Special Projects Branch, working on various space matters, including orbit calculations, reentry paths, and rendezvous techniques. When NACA was closed and the National Aeronautics and Space Administration (NASA) was born, George moved to agency headquarters in Washington, D.C., where he served as chief of Manned Space Flight, including the Mercury, Gemini, and Apollo programs. Then he relocated to NASA's Manned Spacecraft Center in Houston, Texas, as deputy center director. In 1967, after the Apollo 1 tragedy left three crew members dead, George became manager of the Apollo Spacecraft Program Office and implemented failure modes and effects analysis, a rigorous process to identify potential failure modes and proactively redesign them out, which greatly contributed to the return of the Apollo program and achievement of the lunar landing. In 1969, George became deputy administrator of NASA, where he's championed development of the Space Shuttle, Skylab, and Apollo-Soyuz.

cameras stationed on the island may prevent us from missing a filming opportunity.

It is 0800 and raining. The wind is from the northeast. Maybe Parviz was wrong; it's not such a nice day. We anxiously hope that this is enough of a north wind to move the lobsters and thus the ship.

We miss the earlier 0640 satellite flyover and are anxious for the next one at 0910 to see the weather images.

There are two new shipboard terminals, one in the radio room and the other in JYC's cabin. They interface with an 850-pound egg-shaped Comsat antenna atop the radio room, which communicates with three 720-pound Marisat satellites that are positioned in geostationary orbit to enable global maritime communications.

Parviz explains that there are two types of satellites, geosynchronous and synchronous. Geosynchronous meaning that the satellite rotates with the earth and stays in roughly the same location above the same part of the earth, whereas the second, synchronous, rotates westward around the earth, as though the earth is still.

One of the birds we rely on is the ATS3 geosynchronous satellite. We regularly receive and transmit communications and images from it. We also use the synchronized NOAA[22] satellites. When they pass overhead and we're within their footprint, we obtain weather images. The information is crude but helpful in forecasting. We can calculate wind strength and direction, cloud cover, and temperature.

NASA first worked with Cousteau in November 1972, when Locke Stuart of NASA's Missions Utilization Office and Dave Nace of NASA's Goddard Space Flight Center sailed aboard *Calypso* down the east coast of South America. That winter of 1972 and the spring of 1973, *Calypso* traveled to the Antarctic with installed NASA equipment, a direct readout weather satellite receiving station, a satellite communications terminal, a fluorometer, and a temperature sensor.

Recently, in October 1974, they teamed again, in a joint venture with Texas A&M and the U.S. Environmental Protection Agency. *Calypso* sailed a circular route, departing Galveston Bay, Texas, for the Yucatan Peninsula of Mexico, where sleeping sharks were filmed. Then in early November, *Calypso* continued to Key West, Florida and up Florida's west coast into the Gulf of Mexico, sampling water in locations including Tampa, Panama City, Tambalier Bay, Mississippi River plume, Mobile Bay, Desoto Canyon and Pensacola. This is what the team was doing when I saw *Calypso* last November in Panama City.

The scientific purpose of the voyage was to obtain data on the waters of the Gulf of Mexico, particularly the coastal waters. More specifically, scientists aboard *Calypso* collected ocean water samples called "ground truth" in support of high altitude NASA U-2 aircraft overflights equipped with an ocean color scanner. The correlated data simulated space-based imaging, to validate potential derivation of data from future spacecraft like the planned Nimbus-G research and development satellite.

In a normal day's operation, preparation for sampling began at 0600. At 0730 a confirmation was established via satellite communications to U-2 operations. The first site of the day, e.g. site A, would begin at 0800 and be completed by 0930. This process, in coordination with U-2 overflights, would continue through the day. The evening involved pouring, labeling, filtering, collecting, and summarizing data.

The Landsat 1 earth resource satellite, equipped with a multispectral scanner, was also used to provide helpful data, while other satellites provided the project with logistical support, such as navigation, weather, and communications.

The resulting data has yielded an index to enable scientists to interpret and track satellite-based observations about the ocean. JYC's idea is that satellites, aircraft, instrumented buoys, and other manned or unmanned devices might someday replace today's inefficient gathering of ocean data, which has traditionally been limited to ships. He believes we must leverage remote sensing and tele-measurements derived from anchored interrogating sensors, both passing data through satellites, to have an ongoing real-time global survey of the health of the oceans.[23]

The gathered data is already helping scientists measure the gulf's water quality and associated pollution. Of particular interest is the impact of oil drilling, cold-water upwelling areas, red tide blooms, and the Mississippi River's silt plume.

Although the majority of the initial data has been obtained, Hussein continues his study of hydrography, taking five-liter water samples in van Dorn-type bottles placed at depths of zero, five, ten, fifteen, and twenty meters and making notes on ocean conditions.

Some water from each sample is immediately filtered, and the filter pad is frozen for subsequent determination of chlorophyll and carotenoids in accordance with procedures specified by Strickland and Parsons in *A Practical Handbook of Seawater Analysis.*

Being that we're outside of U.S. waters, the U-2 flights had to stop. I'm assisting Hussein by measuring and recording data on water clarity, the speed and direction of currents, and the height and direction of waves. We're also recording information about the ocean's depth and the sea floor, called substrate, recording the type of sand, coral, rock, grass, and vegetation.

It's afternoon now, very clear and sunny. I learn the Beaufort Wind Scale,[24] devised in 1805 by British Rear-Admiral Sir Francis Beaufort, based on observations of the effects of the wind. Our current easterly fifteen knots is known as a "moderate breeze."

The Mexicans say that if the wind dies tonight, the lobsters will march tomorrow (maybe).

Unlike breakfast, lunch is substantial. Today it's delicious soup, roast beef, potatoes, noodles, rice, French bread, wine, and cheese. The fare is nicely prepared and there's plenty of wine.

We dine shirtless and shoeless in the cozy, sometimes cramped combination wardroom and mess hall. Real naval wardrooms are only used by commissioned and warrant officers, not the captain or junior people, but on *Calypso* we're obviously all together. I assume that was also the case when *Calypso* was an active minesweeper, as there is no other second dining room.

The wardroom is only about seven feet fore to aft (front to back) by fifteen feet port to starboard (left to right). A durable plastic orange tablecloth covers the dining table, which runs the width of the room. A fixed vinyl-covered booth seat extends port to starboard along the aft end of the table and two moveable benches, which each seat three men, are on the fore side of the table. There are no assigned seats, other than JYC, who always sits at the portside head of the table.

Figure 7 - JYC holds court during dinner.

A partitioning wall partially separates the wardroom from the small galley. On the wall facing the dining table is a built-in bookcase. Each of the three shelves has a single horizontal metal rod to secure the books from spilling.

Being *Calypso*'s only indoor common space, the wardroom is also where we meet to plan dives, congregate to socialize, and occasionally celebrate or watch a film.

It's time for Bernard and me to board a Zodiac and leave for Contoy. We have three Mark 3 Grand Raid Zodiacs. They're eighteen-foot, dark gray, durable rubber rafts, each with a wooden floor and a fifty-horse power Johnson outboard motor. They are excellent diving platforms, and when Bernard is driving, they literally fly. He steers standing, one hand on the motor's throttle and the other grasping a line, as if he's riding an aquatic mechanical bull.

We arrive on the sheltered western shore of the narrow island and drag the Zodiac onto the beach. Our campsite will be here, just twenty meters from the water. A lesser distance to the east is a shallow brackish lagoon surrounded by mangrove forests. To the north and south are low-lying bushes, palms, and pine trees.

The entire island is a bird sanctuary, bustling with activity. There's a pelican rookery, cormorant nests, egrets, flamingoes, gulls, herons, petrels, spoonbills, and countless other beautiful migratory species.

The lobsters are said to parade along the white sand of this western shore, taking shelter in the nearby shallow rock and coral shoreline. This species, the South American spiny lobster migrates annually. In the Bahamas the migration is in September, in Cuba it's October, Mexico in January, and in Belize, February. The local Mexican fishermen believe that the same lobsters travel the entire route from the Bahamas to Belize, passing along the Yucatan. That is doubtful. They're likely different regional lobster populations. One thing for sure is that every year tens, if not hundreds, of thousands of lobsters do move considerable distances en masse. It's a mystery as to where they start, where they're going, and why they're migrating at all.

We immediately settle into island rituals, beginning with a siesta—at least for everyone but me. George arrives from *Calypso.* He wants to see our camp and the island. So he and I take a long hike. We see large iguanas sunning themselves, blue and white heron feeding, and dozens of yellow canaries singing in the bushes. We discover a camp of Mexico university students and another camp of *National Geographic* photographers. Then, despite the sharks, we go snorkeling and see a wonderful variety of fish, coral, and jellyfish.

The next time I go to *Calypso* I need to pick up a longer camera lens and more film.

With the addition of two Mexican fishermen, we're now up to nine campers. Brothers Manuel and Valvula are from Isla Mujeres. Valvula, the stockier of the two, will be our guide. JYC previously met him when the team filmed *Sleeping Sharks of the Yucatan* near Mujeres. Manuel, Valvula's taller, leaner brother, will be our camp cook. The brothers know all of the local fishermen and they've already helped us trade our cigarettes for freshly netted fish. Manuel is now using the fish to make soup for dinner.

Bernard says that the lobsters are going to be difficult. He thinks the Mexicans are wrong about any movement tomorrow. He's been diving and only saw one lobster with any color change. Color is an important clue because supposedly when the lobsters pass from the deeper, darker substrate to the shallower, lighter, sandy shoreline their color changes from a darker green-blue to a lighter tan-orange.

Bernard is gifted with a sixth sense for nature. Because of this I suspect he's correct, that the lobster march won't occur so soon.

The fishermen's theory is that every year the migrating lobsters detour into Contoy's shallower coastline for shelter during bad weather. When the weather clears they move back to deep water and resume their migration. We question this theory because in bad weather the shallower coastal water is not calmer and is actually more turbulent. However, maybe this protected western shore and overhanging coral do provide shelter during a storm.

This evening we learn that Dr. Herrnkind has been delayed because he has the flu.

The fish soup and campfire-grilled mutton snapper for dinner is not quite the same as the shipboard meals, but it's still good.

We test the lighting for land night filming and then take a Zodiac one hundred meters off *Calypso*'s bow to dive on a fisherman's net.

We want to see if he's caught any migrating lobsters. The fisherman's thirty-meter-long net is empty.

These fishermen use nets to catch the lobsters. In the Bahamas, Cuba, and Florida, fishermen use snares, hooks, and traps. In Florida and the Bahamas there's an ever-increasing number of fishermen, and despite strict regulations, the lobster crop is in decline. In some other international waters, there are no regulatory controls at all, which may ultimately threaten the species.

One positive step toward habitat preservation was President Franklin Roosevelt's 1935 creation of the Dry Tortugas National Park. Located seventy miles west of Key West, these seven islands and their surrounding shoals were discovered by Ponce de Leon in 1513. He named them Tortuga, meaning "turtle" in Spanish. The explorer stocked his ships with fresh sea turtle meat, but since the islands had no fresh water he termed them dry.

More than ninety percent of the spiny lobsters caught in the U.S. are caught off Florida's coast. In the last ten years the catch has increased six fold and prices have tripled. With such demand, illegal fishing is a grave concern. Studies show that in unprotected fishing areas near the Tortugas, the lobster population and the average lobster body size have decreased, the result of over fishing and illegal harvesting of younger adolescent lobsters. Inside the preserve, where lobsters are protected and allowed to reach sexual maturity and reproduce, a healthier, larger population is being sustained.

After the dive on the net, we stop at *Calypso* for ice, food, and equipment and then leave for Contoy, now two miles east off *Calypso*'s starboard bow.

Upon reaching the shore we encounter two American girls and an Italian man who are returning from getting water at the lighthouse. They join us for a drink and then unfortunately have to leave for their camp.

Later I spot a star burning red, green, and white. We play with sand crabs and go to sleep.

At least we try to sleep. It's a hell of a night. Somebody left a tent flap open so the mosquitoes, no-see-ums, and sand fleas have infested the tent. We don't have any bug spray, it's hot, and there's no breeze.

At 0200 Jerry stokes the campfire and lies in the smoke. That doesn't help, so he takes a Zodiac and anchors offshore. Bernard awakes and is worried about Jerry being missing.

In the morning they argue. Jerry says he doesn't care what Bernard says. He needed relief and if necessary he was prepared to take the helicopter to Mujeres. I think the fact that Jerry had previously disappeared to the *National Geographic* camp to allegedly help them fix their generator has fueled Bernard's aggravation.

These damn bugs; my body is covered with bites.

Bernard has calmed down. Now with good humor he declares himself to be the governor of Contoy. He reads a proclamation and honors us for surviving last night's onslaught.

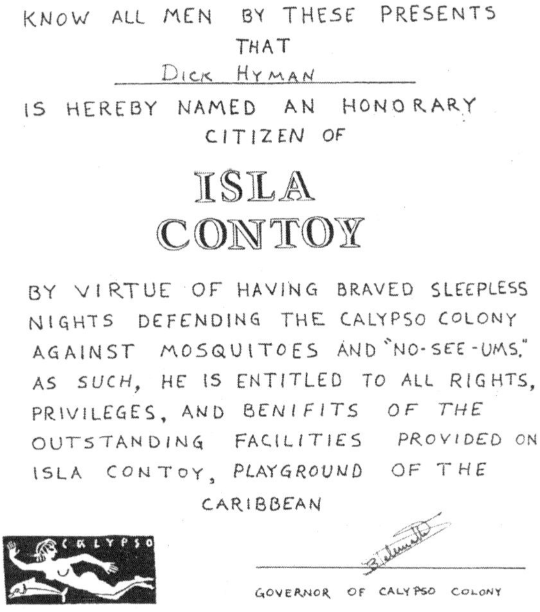

KNOW ALL MEN BY THESE PRESENTS
THAT
DICK HYMAN
IS HEREBY NAMED AN HONORARY
CITIZEN OF

ISLA
CONTOY

BY VIRTUE OF HAVING BRAVED SLEEPLESS NIGHTS DEFENDING THE CALYPSO COLONY AGAINST MOSQUITOES AND "NO-SEE-UMS." AS SUCH, HE IS ENTITLED TO ALL RIGHTS, PRIVILEGES, AND BENIFITS OF THE OUTSTANDING FACILITIES PROVIDED ON ISLA CONTOY, PLAYGROUND OF THE CARIBBEAN

CALYPSO

GOVERNOR OF CALYPSO COLONY

Figure 8 - Bernard's Proclamation

As the easterly wind continues we discuss the likelihood that the lobsters still haven't begun to march.

Bernard, George, and I make a one-hour dive. We see barracuda, red snapper, batfish, small jacks, sharks, spider crabs, horseshoe crabs, rays, urchins, starfish, horse conch, and holothurians but disappointingly no lobster.

To me, diving with George of NASA is symbolic. JYC often compares the undersea world to outer space, calling it the "liquid universe."

The fishermen are unhappy about us constantly diving on their nets so we've stopped doing so and have begun setting our own nets. The fishermen are superstitious and blame us for the delayed march. I can't say that I blame them.

After breakfast we inspect one of our nets and find two lobsters, which is no bonanza, but it's better than yesterday's tally of zero.

We learn that the *National Geographic* camp's generator is indeed broken. We take it to Jean-Marie, *Calypso*'s chief mechanic, who says it has blown a valve. He's a former submariner and a piece of work. He struts around in a tiny, grease-covered Speedo, talking in a deep baritone voice. He is always very friendly to me and most polite. Jean-Marie welds the valve shaft together, and unbelievably the generator is now working.

We take advantage of this visit to *Calypso* to refill our air tanks, send and receive telexes, and obtain new weather data. There isn't anything exciting going on aboard the ship, just Paul repairing some fishing nets. While we've been stuck at the campsite we imagine that we're missing action on *Calypso.* In reality, on Contoy we have a better opportunity to move around and explore.

We depart *Calypso* and head for camp. Once back on the island we return the now repaired generator to the *National Geographic* camp, have lunch, and a short siesta. Afterward I study and snorkel along the shore.

As evening descends, the camp is quiet. Bernard, Carco, Daniel, and Jerry are all aboard *Calypso,* but they'll be back soon for Manuel's dinner.

I've begun organizing information about the weather, lobsters, and Contoy's ecosystem in order to choose a subject to study. I'm leaning toward studying the migration of the spiny lobster.

The tension is building. Everyone is trying to be patient. We're hoping for a storm.

Merde (shit), I just realized that my camera's ASA has been set wrong. Therefore my first roll of film won't be any good. ASA refers to the film speed as determined by the American Standards Association's work with Kodak. Every time I load new film with a different ASA, I must manually adjust my Nikon camera's ASA to match the film's ASA.

Bernard's younger brother Patrick has now joined us at camp. He's a quiet guy and, like Bernard, a gifted diver.

Bernard, Patrick, and Valvula just left in the chaland. It's an eighteen-foot launch with a banged-up white metal exterior and a V-hull. It's a rugged workboat used for hauling supplies, including a generator wired to underwater lights. I don't know why we call this boat a chaland, though, because a real chaland is wide-bottomed, more stable, and raked on both ends, traditionally constructed with cypress planks or, more recently, plywood or aluminum.

The guys in the chaland return and are again quickly off in a Zodiac, joined by Michel Deloire, a chief diver from the ship. Valvula and I follow in the chaland.

We arrive at a net. They descend. Valvula and I are above in the chaland. Valvula is steering and I'm tending the cable for the first time. This involves standing and feeding electrical cable to Patrick, who is lighting the scene below. The cable is connected to a loud diesel-powered portable generator sitting on the floor of the chaland. Patrick holds the high-intensity eight-kilowatt light and tugs once for more line, twice to stop, and three times if he wants some portion of cable retrieved. I'm told that tending the cable can be tricky, particularly when in heavier seas because the waves make it difficult for the tender to feel the diver's tugs. It's easy to miss a tug or mistakenly imagine you feel one that isn't there.

Figure 9 - Diving from a Zodiac to inspect nets

Valvula steers the chaland, following the bubbles, attempting to stay close atop the divers. I feel like I'm doing a poor job, but it's my first time and I'm doing the best I can. They will dive again later tonight so if I get another chance I'll do better.

The night passes and it's now another day. Unfortunately George is leaving today. He's been very nice to me and I've enjoyed spending time with him. He's invited me to visit his home in northern Virginia, near Washington, D.C., and I intend to do so.

The wind is still from the east, but when we check the nets this morning we have six lobsters, fairly good news.

Nearby there's tremendous activity, as hundreds of seabirds dive on a large school of baitfish. Bernard, Daniel, Valvula, and I film from two Zodiacs.

Afterward we board *Calypso,* clean some fish that we'd traded for, load supplies onto a Zodiac, and then return to camp.

It's still morning and beautiful, so Patrick and I pump up a softening Zodiac and take it offshore to dive on a shallow coral reef.

We harvest a few dozen sea urchins and sit in the Zodiac eating some of them raw, cutting the bottom open and spooning out the meat with our dive knives. Satisfied, we take the remaining urchins back to camp to make urchin omelets for lunch.

Michel and Bernard are aboard *Calypso* for a chiefs meeting. They're deciding whether *Calypso* should leave for Cuba to perform scientific research. If *Calypso* sails to Cuba and completes the research, she won't return to Contoy for at least a month. For us to stay here and camp without the mother ship could be difficult.

Bernard returns to camp, informing us that the decision has been made. If the lobsters haven't arrived here by January third, which is five days from now, then we'll stay at the camp and *Calypso* will go to Cuba.

I'm scheduled to tend the cable again tonight. Hopefully I'll do a better job.

Bernard asks me if I want to stay aboard *Calypso.* I tell him I think it's better if I stay here at camp because it offers more opportunities and that I just want to do my share and cause no trouble. Jerry offers his perspective, telling me that *Calypso* is very casual. Everyone has his own assignment and nobody is concerned with anyone else's. That's the helicopter pilot's perspective anyway.

I've barely seen JYC. He's been busy with George. JYC hasn't even been to the camp yet.

Patrick and I take a Zodiac to again snorkel, collect, and eat more urchins. We plan the same for tomorrow. I'm encouraged that we've established a work schedule, including dives every morning and night.

On tonight's dive Manuel gives me a hand with the light cable and we do well. Afterward we visit a peaceful *Calypso,* where I prepare the daily telex, asking for Alinat in Monaco[k] to arrange for the previously requested spare parts and mail to be sent along with the next arriving crew members, Furlan or Davso, both engineers. They're also to bring Gitanes (a brand of French cigarettes), blue pipe tobacco, and Toscani cigars.

---

k Jean Alinat, Assistant Director, Musée Océanographique, Monaco (Museum and Aquarium).

I almost stay aboard for the night but decide to sleep back at camp. Upon return to camp, Manuel and I collect firewood for a midnight snack of grilled grouper and white wine. There's a hint of a refreshing northeast wind; lobsters tomorrow?

Bernard and Michel walk south to see if the other campers will join us for some fish. I hope so. It would be nice to have some company. The southern campers agree to pay a midnight visit. There are three girls from Wisconsin and four boys from Berkeley, California.

It's Monday morning and Manuel is preparing what he calls frittatas. They're like scrambled eggs cooked in the frying pan over the fire. The Mexicans do eat breakfast, which is a major benefit to camping. After breakfast we head out to the nets with hope of finding lobsters.

In just a few days I've noticed how everything is so relaxed here. It is a much slower way of life, without the intense pressure of the large city and university.

It turns out that it wasn't so difficult to gain approval from Belize. The trip is set. Belize is our next destination.

JYC receives a telex from Fred, which includes the following.

> "WE CONFIRM HONDURAS ARRANGEMENTS
> MADE BY BONNIE AND THEY ARE EXPECTING
> YOU. WE CONTINUE TO SEARCH FOR
> THE 3 CRATES, WHICH AS YOU KNOW,
> LISE CONFIRMS ARE IN MEXICO. WE WILL
> CONTINUE AT OUR END BUT YOU MAY WELL
> RECEIVE THEM EVEN BEFORE WE KNOW. I
> AM CONFIDENT THAT OUR GOOD FRIEND
> ENRIQUE LIMA'S GREAT INFLUENCE COULD BE
> A BIG HELP WITH AERONAVES.
>
> DR. HERRNKIND COMING TOMORROW,
> TUESDAY 12/31 BUT HIS ROUTING VERY
> DIFFICULT DUE TO NO FLIGHT AVAILABILITY
> TO COZUMEL. HIS ROUTE IS MIAMI-MERIDA-BUS

TO PUERTO JUAREZ-FERRY TO ISLA MUJERES.
HE LEAVES MIAMI 8 A.M. AND SHOULD ARRIVE
ISLA MUJERES LATE AFTERNOON.

WE ALL WISH CALYPSO AND HER CREW THE
HAPPIEST AND HEALTHIEST OF NEW YEARS."

The day passes, and now at night we move most of the camera gear on Contoy out to the ship. After completing the move, we eat a late dinner at camp before hitting the sleeping bags.

We awake the next morning to New Year's Eve day. *Calypso* has already departed for Cape Catoche, thirty miles to the north, in search of a reported lobster queue. Catoche is the first Mexican land visited by Spaniards in 1517. If the Cousteau team finds lobsters they'll stay the night. If not they'll return.

Manuel and Valvula are leaving now for Mujeres to celebrate with their families, so Patrick and I are left alone on Contoy, with an injured bird. She's a double-crested cormorant, about two feet long, with a four-foot wingspan. Her feathers are deep dark brown, almost black, contrasting her bright orange throat pouch below a hooked bill. We repair her broken wing and tether her to a post. She's resting comfortably, nestled on the ground with her black webbed feet tucked underneath.

Contoy offers a safe habitat for this cormorant colony. Hundreds of nests made of sticks and seaweed adorn the trees and shrubs, in which females lay three to five eggs. For a month both parents take turns incubating the eggs and then share in feeding and caring for the chicks, which fledge in about thirty-five days. This species doesn't have well-developed oil glands and therefore isn't very waterproofed. So after diving underwater for fish they dry their feathers by perching on tree limbs or coral outcroppings, stretching out their wings in the sun and breeze.

Patrick and I check the nets, which again yield disappointing results: only three lobsters. Then we unsuccessfully try to fix our broken Coleman stove. Without the stove we have no fire, disrupting our plan of omelets for lunch, so it'll be more raw urchins instead.

In the afternoon we take the Zodiac and dive offshore, then return to camp before hiking to the eastern surf side of the island. Here frigate birds ride updrafts above surf-covered twenty-foot-high coral outcroppings.

Their name, frigates, or man-o-war birds, is derived from their grace in the air and piratical tendencies. They harass airborne pelicans, cormorants, and gulls until they drop their catch. Aside from feeding on stolen fish, they prey on young sea birds and turtles, jellyfish, and squid. They're the most aerial of the tropical water birds, with a staggering seven-foot wingspan; the largest of any bird in proportion to its small three- to four-pound body. They soar effortlessly for hours, appearing motionless hundreds of feet in the air. While so graceful in flight, they're equally awkward on land. Like the cormorant, their feathers get waterlogged, requiring them to periodically pause to spread and dry their wings.

Scattered among the eastern shore's outcroppings are small sand beaches where there's evidence of butchered loggerhead sea turtles. Sadly, interrupted from laying eggs, their carcasses are left on the beach.

We explore a beached shipwreck and then climb atop the island. From the north we can see an approaching *Calypso.* To the west is this year's final sunset.

Calypso's quick return means they didn't find lobsters. Not the best news, but given it's New Year's Eve, it means Patrick and I won't be stuck alone on the island, so we're happy.

We hustle back to camp and jump in a Zodiac to greet *Calypso.* We rendezvous and climb aboard. There's a delicious lobster dinner and a New Year's Eve party, featuring the screening of one of Cousteau's Antarctic programs. We have lots of laughs. I stay the night.

In the morning, New Year's Day, we sail southwest, trying to locate a wreck we've heard about. The seas are a good twenty feet. Captain Cousteau takes this most inopportune time to familiarize me with the bridge and the navigational instruments. I'm pretty unresponsive, lightheaded from the sea.

It's too rough to dive so we return to the Contoy anchorage for shelter. I resist this first threat of seasickness.

Dr. Herrnkind (Dr. H) arrives mid-afternoon. He's busy with Captain Cousteau, but I look forward to spending some time with him. I join the two of them at the first sitting of dinner and we have an interesting discussion on an eclectic mix of topics including weather, boats, spear fishing, and atomic bombs.

After dinner we watch a lobster film that Dr. H brought with him. Then we head back to camp.

The next day, JYC departs *Calypso* via helicopter, bound for Cozumel airport, en route to the U.S. for a couple days. Then *Calypso* leaves for the day. We stay at the island to pull the nets. Today they are unusually badly fouled with seaweed, crabs, and fish. I spend the rest of the day cleaning the nets, a boring task that I have to do by myself.

Hopefully the lobsters will arrive soon. This waiting is non-productive and putting us behind schedule.

Depending upon the Cuba trip, it looks as though I'll be on Contoy for at least another week. I hope to get some scientific materials and information on lobsters from Dr. H so that I can begin my research.

Well, no sooner do I say that than *Calypso* returns. There's another change in plans. The Cuba trip is off. Many of us campers now go aboard *Calypso,* and tomorrow we'll depart for Mujeres to refuel.

Calypso is at anchor and I take my first watch, solo, 2300 to 0030. I suspect it will soon become boring, but for now I like it. It gives me time to read or write and a little peace.

In the morning I finally break the ice with Dr. H, who's staying aboard for the trip to Mujeres instead of camping. He introduces me to the subject of lobsters and their migration. It's more interesting than I thought and I've decided to make this the focus of my independent study. Dr. H is brilliant and funny and seems like a real good guy.

Unlike the Maine lobster, *Panularis americanus,* with claws, the Western Atlantic spiny lobster, *Panularis argus,* is a species that has two long antennae instead of claws. These antennae and the body armor are covered with small, extremely sharp, forward-pointing spines, giving it the name "spiny lobster."

These lobsters march en masse aligned head-to-tail via queues. Crustaceans like king and spider crabs also migrate, but in groups or clusters rather than in this unique single file fashion. The lobster queues are usually ten to fifteen lobsters in length but can extend to be as large as sixty-five or more.

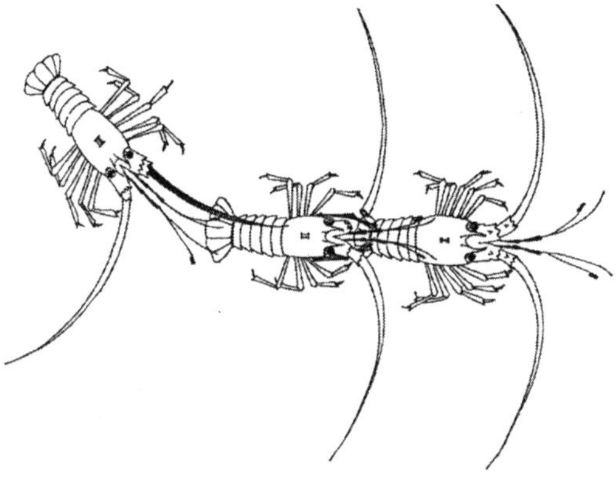

Science Magazine, William Hernnkind
Figure 10 - Spiny lobster queuing behavior

The lobsters use their spiny antennae for defense and to form and maintain queues. Accompanying pairs of flexible antennules, which are nearly two-thirds the length of the body are used to literally keep in touch with the tail of the lobster ahead and for fine-tuning alignment.

The lobsters' behavior is somewhat similar to that of migrating birds, but instead of forming a V, like birds, the lobsters form more of a straight a line or queue. Like birds, the first lobster in a line has the greatest resistance. The others follow, walking behind each other, drafting off the lobster immediately ahead of them to reduce drag. When the leader gets tired it steps aside and re-joins the rear of the queue as the lobster that was second in line assumes the lead. Once underway a queue moves smoothly, with only slight turns as necessary, covering up to seven miles in a day.

If the lobsters are marching and something frightens or obstructs a queue, or an accidental break in formation occurs, they close ranks, with the leaders slowing down and the followers moving alongside, resulting in a double or even triple file. Then they rotate into a wagon train-like circle, called a pod. They compact the circle, with their more vulnerable tails centered and curled underneath, the spiny antennae pointed outward and upward to defend the group from above and all sides. Predators such as grouper, sharks, jewfish, triggerfish, and octopuses crave the underside of the lobster's soft abdominal tail.

While en route, lobsters seem to know exactly where they're going. They're driven by an innate navigation system. During the peak of migration, the normally nocturnal spiny lobster, which prefers to feed at night and hide during the day, drives onward, non-stop, around the clock. Dr. H once put a group of lobsters in a small vinyl pool and they marched in a circle non-stop for two weeks.

The males grow faster and larger than the females. If left alone, healthy and with plenty of food, they'll live twenty-five years and grow as large as twenty-five pounds. The females are smaller, perhaps due to energy exerted when they produce eggs during reproduction. The number of eggs laid depends on the size of the lobster but estimates show that a relatively small nine-inch female can lay 500,000 eggs. A twelve-inch lobster will lay twice that. Eggs are attached to her underside, where they're fertilized and incubated. She regularly cleans and aerates the eggs by gently stroking them with her legs and flexing her abdomen. After two to three weeks she picks away the flat, leaf-shaped, planktonic organism, releasing the larvae into the sea. They will grow to a size of about two inches their first year, adding an inch per year thereafter.

Dr. H doesn't believe the locals' theory that migrations start in the Bahamas and end all the way in Belize. He says the migrations are regional, covering about fifty miles. It's impossible to be sure because the lobsters shed their shells at least twice a year. Any tracking tags would not remain attached for a long enough period of time.

Interestingly, these Mexican fishermen catch the lobsters and detach the tails from the bodies, only taking the more valuable tails to market. Fearing that dumping the torsos into the water will scare away future migrations, the fishermen pile the lobster remains above the tide line along the island's shore. Although wasteful, this greatly facilitates our research. We'll be able to measure and record data from recent as well as historical catches.

It is late when we arrive at Mujeres' solitary Puerto Juarez dock. After a quick walk around town there's a casual buffet dinner aboard *Calypso*. Later, Jeff Tworzydlo, the friendly American deckhand, and I go back into town to see the sights—or lack thereof. It's just a small, rundown tourist town. We meet some young Americans and their father and join them for a beer.

Isla Mujeres is the easternmost point of Mexico, discovered by Francisco Hernandez Cordova in 1517. In ancient Mayan times the island was the sanctuary for the Mayan goddess Ixchel, the goddess of fertility, reason, medicine, and the moon. That's how Mujeres got its name. It means "the Isle of Women." Apparently the goddess doesn't live here anymore, which is too bad for us sailors.

Upon return to the ship I prepare the daily communiqué to be telexed to the Cousteau offices in New York or Westport and sometimes Los Angeles or Paris. I'm responding to the following excerpt of today's January 3 message received from Dad, which includes information he received from Lise.

"WE JUST RECEIVED THIS MORNING THE FOLLOWING INFORMATION FROM LISE RE: THE THREE MISSING CASES. WE ASSUME 'MEXICO AIRPORT' MEANS MEXICO CITY BUT WE ARE ASKING LISE FOR CONFIRMATION.

> The 3 cases are in Mexico Airport at Customs since Dec 17…I had this news this morning from Air France Paris who called last week AF Mexico who can't help because Customs says they have no proforma invoice so they can't send the cases to Mujeres.

AS YOU ARE IN MUJERES TODAY, I SUGGEST YOU SEND SOMEONE TO MEXICO CITY VIA COZUMEL CHECKING ALL THE WAY AND ARMED WITH SOME NEW TWENTIES. WE WILL CALL ENRIQUE TO ALERT HIM AND ASK FOR HELP. WE NEVER RECEIVED PROFORMA, DID YOU?

DAVSO WILL JOIN YOU AND GO TO MUJERES VIA PARIS, MEXICO AND COZUMEL. HE WILL TAKE WITH HIM SPARE PARTS YOU REQUESTED AND CALYPSO MAIL.

CHEERS, FRED"

I'm up early to help Jeff swab the decks and embark fuel, oil, water, fresh vegetables, and fruit. We too have the three lost but now found cases of equipment mentioned in the telex above. The last time *Calypso* took on these essential supplies was in New Orleans, so we're in desperate need to replenish everything. Fortunately our existing meat supply is good, so we don't have to rely on Mujeres meat.

Otherwise it's a rather slow day. I read scientific papers about lobsters, take a siesta, and then a solitary walk on Mujeres' surf side. It's depressing. There's no beach, just rough coral and a garbage dump next to a poor community.

I head back to *Calypso* where I translate and type the following outgoing telex for Albert Falco, also known as Beber. He's a good guy, a veteran diver, who's been with Cousteau since 1952. He doesn't speak much English, but we're still able to communicate.

"CALYPSO HAS EMBARKED:
a) 26 TONNES OF GAS OIL (CALYPSO)
b) 600 LITRES GASOLINE (ZODIACS)
c) 400 LITRES GASOLINE (HELICOPTER)
d) 4 DRUMS OIL – REMULAT 30
e) FRESH WATER AND FOOD

ALL PAID IN CASH

BEST REGARDS TO EVERYONE AND LOVE TO THE FAMILY.

BEBER AND DICK"

I just had a quick shower and am now in my bunk anxiously waiting for dinner. Ivan asks me to move below into Michel Fourcade's cabin because we're expecting more Texas A&M students and need to make room. Michel is an engineer. I'd like to settle in one cabin and prefer to stay here in the divers' cabin. I'm not moving until I have to. I expect to be returning to Camp Contoy tomorrow anyway, because now we have too many people on the ship.

I stay the night in the divers' cabin. At 0700, Armand Davso wakes us up. He just arrived yesterday and wants me to move out right now. Davso is an interesting fellow and often hilarious, but not right now. He's short with a buzz haircut and a funny face.

He's hyperactive and speaks a mile a minute. Davso began with Cousteau as a diver twenty years ago, and now he's an inventor and mechanic, designing new underwater camera housings and propulsion vehicles while also repairing cameras and lights.

I get up and throw my clothes in a hold below. I don't know where I'm supposed to go. We return to Contoy today so maybe I'll return to camp. Now I'd like to stay on the ship. I'm scheduled for tonight's watch 2100–2300 so I assume I'll stay aboard, but I'm not sure where I'll sleep. There are now more people aboard than there are bunks.

We depart Mujeres by 0800. I steer the calm five-hour sail, and we arrive at Contoy at 1300.

I've started doing more work for Paul Zuena, the first mate and second captain. Paul is an extremely hard worker with a good sense of humor, at least when he relaxes, which isn't too often. He's from a family of fishermen in Marseille, France. Married ten years, he has two girls. His fortieth birthday will be February 23. This is his sixteenth year with Cousteau. He told me that his best expedition was to Antarctica in 1972.

Jeff reports to Paul. The three of us go to work resetting a net. I drive the chaland for the first time. Its V-shaped hull makes it less stable than the Zodiacs and it is quite challenging.

When done and back aboard, Jeff, Parviz, Michel, Xerox, and I jump from a rope swing we've rigged off the stern crane. Xerox's real name is Rick Martin; a radioman and Xerox employee, he's here primarily to service the copy machine, no kidding, so we call him Xerox.

We're off in the chaland again. I help Paul, Jeff, and Dr. H take up a net and reset another. In the past two days we've caught seventeen lobsters. I measured and recorded the size and sex of each lobster. Recently there have been more small young lobsters. I wonder if that's a reflection of them being over fished. We usually release everything we catch and instead trade cigarettes or wine for our seafood.

I drive the chaland back to the ship and do much better. Paul has taught me a lot today.

We're possibly going to set up a large tank on *Calypso* to view and film a couple of lobsters feeding.

More lobster fishermen continue to arrive. The time must be getting near.

It's January 6 and a new week. I ate at the early sitting of dinner and now, after midnight, I compose the daily communication to Westport, including requested supplies for JYC to bring with him when he returns.

> "TO FRED HYMAN: CALYPSO ARRIVED SAFELY AT CONTOY. ALL CAMP MEMBERS WELL. LOBSTERS NOT ARRIVED BUT INDICATIONS ARE GOOD.
>
> TO CAPTAIN COUSTEAU: PLEASE BRING MOSQUITO REPELLENT (1 CASE OF CUTTERS). ALSO, DAVSO DID NOT RECEIVE THE TELEX ASKING FOR GITANES, SO PLEASE BRING SOME. ALSO MANY PEOPLE HAVE NO NEWS FROM FRANCE. CAN YOU ASK LISE WHAT IS HAPPENING?
>
> THERE IS ALSO A REQUEST FROM RICK THE RADIOMAN. IF POSSIBLE HE WOULD LIKE YOU TO PICK UP AN ANTENNA FOR THE SHIP'S AIRCRAFT RADIO. THE BEST FOR CALYPSO IS A GAIN VERTICAL GROUND PLANE TYPE. FREQUENCY WE USE IS 127.5 MHZ. WE ALSO NEED 100 FEET OF RG 58 AU COAX CABLE.
>
> CAN YOU BRING SIX TUBES OF SILICONE SEAL FOR THE AQUARIUM?"

It's an uneventful day. I cleaned another net and then a virus or something hit me. I couldn't shake it and eventually had to sleep.

After vomiting, I felt better but weak, so I stayed in my new bunk below in the bow until this morning's 0330 watch.

Last night an outboard motor was stolen from the aft work deck. It had to be the fishermen. It may have happened during my watch. There's no way to be sure. I'd like to have stopped them, but realistically if I'd encountered them they'd probably have slit my throat, unless I vomited on them first.

Paul was actually up with me for half of my watch because when the wind shifted we started to drift anchor, so I woke him. Perhaps the drifting anchor was not a coincidence but rather an intentional diversion to the crime. I'm mad about this and want to search the fishing boats, but that's unrealistic. Plus whoever took the motor is probably long gone by now.

I'm still feeling pretty sick, but at least I've been able to keep some toast and juice down.

Dr. H shows me his slides and asks me to continue doing more research after he leaves. He again says that the local speculation of lobsters coming to this area of Contoy for shelter does not make sense. He believes that during the ice age lobsters moved to deeper, warmer water to avoid the encroaching glaciers and that this instinct was forever imprinted on the species. He's open to the possibility that local environmental conditions such as the prevailing wind or currents might influence these particular lobsters, but he believes they just pass around the island and continue into deeper water. He wants to place some temporary sonic tags and transmitters on the lobsters to track their short-term path around the island.

We're not paying enough attention to Dr. H's expertise. To me it is a reflection of the French stubbornness and insistence on being better than Americans.

The fishermen no longer set nets in deeper offshore water. Now they're concentrating on the anticipated shoreline migratory

7 JAN 1975 ISLA CATOCHE. WE HAVE SPENT TWO HOURS FOLLOWING THREE LOBSTERS THAT WERE MAKING THEIR WAY NORTH. MICHEL SHOT TWO ROLLS OF FILM UNDERWATER OF THEIR BEHAVIOR. WE STAY AT ANCHORAGE AT CATOCHE FOR THE NIGHT. WE RETURN TO CONTOI JAN 8 AT 8:00 AM. JERRY WILL BE IN MUJERES ON THURS JAN 10 AT 230 PM TO PICK UP JYC AND JOE THOMPSON. IT RAINED ON THE CAMP AT CONTOI. BUT THE WEATHER REMAINS THE SAME WITH NO NORTHEAST WIND. LATE LAST NIGHT WHILE ANCHORED AT CONTOI, A 25 HP JOHNSON OUTBORD MOTOR WAS STOLEN FROM A ZODIAC SITTING ON THE REAR DECK OF CALYPSO. AUTHORITIES IN MUJERES WERE NOTIFIED AND GIVEN THE ENGINE SERIAL NUMBER. BEST REGARDS, ALBERT FALCO

TX 8 JAN 75
635 PM

Figure 11 - Translated and faxed communiqué from Falco

Dr. H comments that he's surprised we don't wear buoyancy compensators. A BC is a bladder-like safety device that is worn by a diver to help adjust buoyancy. The diver inflates it by either manually breathing into it via an attached tube or by puncturing an attached CO2 cartridge. The objective is to maintain neutral buoyancy when diving. It's also handy to fully inflate the BC after completing a dive while resting at the surface waiting to be picked up by a boat. PADI considers BCs to be a mandatory piece of equipment, but we don't have a single one on the ship.

Our equipment is rudimentary. We strap lead to our belts, an air tank or two on our backs, connect a regulator, and don fins. Only one or two of us carry a depth gauge and watch. For protection we sometimes strap knives to our calves or carry a homemade shark stick, a stick with a nail on the end, to push away sharks.

Dr. H wants to be sure to meet Jose of Mujeres' Marine Laboratory. Jose has been studying these local lobster migrations for ten years. Dr. H also wants to speak with Enrique Lima to confirm the accuracy of last year's reported 160-ton catch. That sounds way too high to me.

Following lunch I wander the island's shore, hoping to find a fresh carcass pile or two. Not the most pleasant thing to wish for, particularly on a full recovering stomach, but finding a new large pile would indicate that there were catches overnight.

I find a couple of fresh lobster piles, one of twenty-five and a larger one of forty. As the guts spill and flies swarm, I handle the carapace and again measure and record length, width, condition, color, and sex.

Walking along the beach I come across a new camp where two fishermen are butchering a couple juvenile nurse sharks. The origin of the name "nurse" is uncertain. It may be derived from *nusse*, which was originally applied to cat sharks of the same scientific family. Although they have teeth, they are harmless to humans. They prey on unsuspecting sleeping rays, octopi, squid, clams, and crustaceans, using their small mouths to suck them in. Being a nocturnal predator, they rest in the shallows or caves during day and move to deeper water and reefs at night.

I next come across a new camp, where strangely a solitary old fisherman has a fire inside his tent. He's cooking fresh lobster and a loggerhead turtle.

I proceed to the lighthouse and climb the narrow interior spiral stairwell to the top. From here I can clearly see the ocean floor's white sand and vegetation beneath the scattered fishing boats.

While en route back to camp, I collect crushed shells for the planned shipboard aquarium.

Upon arrival at camp I see Bernard and Falco snorkeling in the lagoon. The water is warm and very shallow, but since we're filming they're dressed in the trademark Cousteau black-hooded wet suit, with a brilliant yellow line down the side. They're crawling after horseshoe crabs, which have also been crawling the earth's coastal waters since before the dinosaurs.

Like the spiny lobster, the horseshoe crab is of the Arthropod phylum. It's an invertebrate, meaning without a backbone. Even though its hard shell and claws make it resemble a crab, the horseshoe crab is really more closely related to scorpions and spiders, as is the lobster.

A very forward tourist group happens upon our camp. It's the first time we've seen anything like this on Contoy. We get rid of them, and I take a Zodiac to *Calypso* to give the new data to Dr. H.

We have a long discussion and are in the middle of a great review of my research project outline when Paul interrupts, wanting me to help Jeff swab the deck. I'm irritated, but I do what he says. Then I get ready for dinner, eat, and hit the sack early.

I'm up for 0200 watch. During watch I type some materials for Captain Alibert. At 0330 I wake Hussein for his turn.

Later, back in the bunk, Paul wakes me at 0600 for a pressing matter: to paint the anchor chain.

JYC's still away but expected back this afternoon, along with Joe Thompson.

In the afternoon we set up the aquarium and then take some time for fun and swim off *Calypso*'s stern.

The weather's nice, too nice. It's sunny with an unusual southerly breeze. The water is warm, 24°C (75°F), with great visibility.

Later now and JYC is landing. Joe won't arrive until tomorrow. He's coming on a chartered boat with a load of equipment.

I feel that I am a part of the team. I have research underway as well, so things are good.

I miss my brother Mark and think of him often.

The day passes and it's evening, so I head to camp. Someone just has to be there to keep an eye on things and it's my turn. I don't mind. It's not really watch, so at least this way I'll miss watch on the ship and can get an uninterrupted night's sleep. We probably should be standing watch at camp too, but we don't. We just sleep. Anything could happen.

The wind picks up in the middle of the night. By dawn there's a stiff southerly near gale and rough seas. We fortify the camp and then a new group of campers arrive from the ship. They'll stay behind on the stormy island. I again head for Mujeres aboard *Calypso.*

Since Raymond, the ship's steward, has now replaced Valvula on the island as the cook, I've taken over as steward. While en route to Mujeres I make it halfway through serving the first sitting of dinner and then I become seasick.

We always try to have a buddy when getting sick because *Calypso*'s railings are so low that it's way too easy to fall overboard. Xerox joins me in the darkness of the aft deck. Twenty-foot seas overflow the stern. We're wet, cold, and ill. Eventually we stumble into the adjacent dive shed, lie down on the hard plank floor, cover ourselves with yellow slickers, and fall asleep. The water flows in and out of the shed, sloshing onto our sleeping bodies.

By morning we're at Mujeres. It's a cool, damp morning. I steward and clean up breakfast before accompanying Madame on a short walk to town to buy provisions. She buys me a glass of milk, which tastes great, although I'm quite certain it's not from a cow.

Upon our return there's a pleasant aroma emanating from *Calypso*'s tiny kitchen. In this tropical climate, the oven's added warmth is not normally welcomed, but on colder rainy days like today it brings wonderful comfort.

I clean up lunch and then take a walk by myself to clear my head. I didn't realize how much I cherish being able to sit and relax at meals. I don't like working the meals. I guess I'll only have to do it for a couple of days, so it won't be too bad.

My friend Joe Thompson finally arrives, as happy as ever. Joe is the first American trained by JYC. He's worked with JYC for eleven years as a cinematographer and submarine pilot. Back home in San Diego, California, he has his own motion picture production company, Seavision Productions, at 8835 Balboa Avenue.

I write a quick letter to Mom, Dad, and Mark and head back into town with Madame to buy bread.

The wind has died and there's a light rain. The high-pressure system to the north has passed, but the satellites indicate that another storm system is building.

We had planned to leave Mujeres at 1200, but with a second front moving our way we decide to stay put for the day. There's a twenty-knot southerly fresh breeze. We hope this will shift and come from the north. If it doesn't we'll leave for Contoy late tonight or early in the morning.

The day passes. In the evening we have a buffet dinner. A buffet is rare but welcomed by me as it makes my job easier. Unless Raymond stays at the camp, I think this is my last meal as the steward.

Well, it's finally happened! There's a forty-knot northerly gale. We embark for Contoy but then turn around and return to port because we learn there's a second weather system following right behind. This is what we've been waiting for to trigger the migration.

Earlier today before the wind picked up, JYC flew in the chopper to Contoy and spotted a boat with many netted lobsters. A fishing boat is now arriving here in Mujeres with a reported four hundred lobsters. We check it out. It's more like two hundred lobsters, but it's still quite impressive.

We curiously and anxiously watch the fishermen unload and hound them with our film crew. The fishermen had tried to outrun the storm and therefore didn't have time to remove the lobster tails at Contoy. Now, even though they're in the Bay of Mujeres and close to market, they still don't try to sell the full lobster. Instead they remove the tails and here do throw the rest of the body overboard.

Dr. H and I walk the Mujeres shore, unsuccessfully searching for lobster carcasses, and figure that any other boats that made it to Mujeres with whole lobsters threw the heads overboard instead of taking them to shore. We speculate that this is because there aren't known migrations inside the bay, so the fishermen aren't concerned about migrating lobsters being frightened away by seeing underwater carcasses. We hope that when we return to Contoy we'll find many new piles to study. We are, however, afraid that most of the fishing boats rushed to Mujeres for shelter before removing the tails, so there won't be too many new piles at Contoy.

I ask JYC if he has any more reading material on the lobsters. He doesn't have any, but does offer a paper on the Belize reef.

JYC presents an interesting theory about the migration. He says that yesterday's catch were actually the lobsters that marched ahead of the arrival of the northern gale. He says maybe they have an inner sense that tells them that "the north" (wind) is coming. The theory is a bit off, though, as the storm was actually preceded by a south wind.

Or was the march just set up by the restless, unsettled sea? He suggests that these lobsters started marching before the storm and continued to march during the storm. Perhaps this protects the species because they pass through catch zones while the fishermen have retreated to safe harbor. As a fewer number of fishermen would return to the catch area after the storm, only smaller, slower trailing queues would be jeopardized.

MONDAY JANUARY 13 - 1975. FOR COUSTEAU SOCIETY WESTPORT AND LOS ANGELES.
LEV, JOE AND JYC ARRIVED IN TIME IN MIAMI BUT HAD SOME DIFFICULTY IN GETTING THE FREIGHT TRANSFERRED TO MEXICANA. WE HAD TO CALL ALBURY FOR HELP. ALBURY GAVE US JEFF'S PASSPORT AND THE ZODIAC MARK ONE. I MET THE CORAL SPECIALIST THAT WAS CONTACTED TO EVENTUALLY JOIN US IN BELIZE AS WELL AS V.BROOKS WHO GAVE US DOCUMENTATION ABOUT HONDURAS. WE FLEW I IN TIME TO COZUMEL WHERE WE HAD NO TROUBLE WITH THE CUSTOM. THE VERY SMALL BONANZA PLANE WAS OBLIGED TO MAKE THREE TRIPS? TWO THURSDAY NIGHT AND ONE FRIDAY MORNING. AS THE SUN WAS ALREADY LOW, THE HELICOPTER COULD ONLY BRING ME AND SOME EQUIPMENT TO CALYPSO THURSDAY EVENING. BY THEN I HAD A FLUE AND ASKED THE TEAM TO ACT AS IF I WAS NOT THERE. FRIDAY MORNING CALYPSO SAILED FOR THE USUAL LOBSTER ROCKS AT CABO CATOCHE BUT THE WATER WAS TOO TURBID TO MAKE ANYTHING AND WE RETURNED TO CONTOI IN THE AFTERNOON. BY THEN THE HELICOPTER HAD BROUGHT LEV TO THE CAMP BUT INFORMED US THAT THE CUSTOMS IN MUJERES HAD HELD ALL OUR EQUIPMENT AND ENRIQUE LIMA WAS NOT IN TOWN...JOE THOMSON STAYED IN MUJERES. BY THEN ALSO WE RECEIVED A METEOROLOGICAL BULLETIN ANNOUNCING NORTHERN WINDS... SO WE LANDED THE COMPLETE TEAM IN THE CAMP AND WE SAILED FOR SHELTER IN MUJERES WHERE WE ARRIVED FRIDAY NIGHT. SATURDAY ALL DAY WE TRIED TO CLEAR THE CUSTOMS BUT IN VAIN. THEY SUGGESTED THAT WE SEND ALL THE EQUIPMENT BACK TO COZUMEL !!! THANK GOD ENRIQUE LIMA ARRIVED IN THE EVENING AND SUNDAY THE EQUIPMENT WAS ALL CLEARED. DURING THAT TIME THE WIND BECAME VERY STRONG BUT FROM THE WRONG DIRECTION AND SUNDAY NIGHT THE COLD FRONT AT LAST PROGRESSED TO THE SOUTH MAKING NORTH WINDS PROBABLE WITHIN 48 HOURS. I FLEW SUNDAY AFTERNOON TO CONTOI AND MADE PLANS FOR THIS MONDAY EXPEDITION TO CABO CATOCHE IF THE GALE IS NOT TOO STRONG. THEN WE SAILED AT 2 AM THIS DAY FOR CONTOI. THE SATELLITE PICTURES CONFIRM THE GOOD NEWS OF PROBABLE BAD WEATHER....

IT IS STILL TOO EARLY TO MAKE LONG RANGE PLANS FOR OUR CRUISE. BUT WHEN WE FINISH THE LOBSTERS (DOCTOR HERRNKIND ALSO STAYS ON BOARD UNTIL THEY COME) WE WILL SPEND TWO DAYS FOR ADDITIONAL SHOTS FOR THE LAST TV3 FILM NEAR MUJERES THEN ONE OR TWO DAYS FOR THE SAME PURPOSE NEAR COZUMEL THEN WE WILL VISIT ONE DAY CHINCHORRO REEF AND CALL IN BELIZE. AFTER BELIZE WE WILL LAND A CAMP ON GLOVER REEF WHILE CALYPSO WILL EXPLORE BAATAN ISLAND AND SWAN ISLAND. THE ENTIRE BELIZE STORY SHOULD LAST ABOUT THREE WEEKS. OUR TWO WEEKS DELAY DUE TO EXCEPTIONNALLY MILD WEATHER CONDITIONS FAILING TO TRIGGER THE LOBSTER MIGRATION IS SOME SORT OF FORCE MAJEURE AND I AM NOT HERE IN A POSITION TO EVALUATE HOW IT AFFECTS THE TEXAS A AND M COOPERATION. IN A FEW DAYS I WILL EXPAND ON THIS SUBJECT.

THE JOHN DENVER EPISODE COULD BE PROGRAMMED EITHER HERE IF IT COULD BE DONE RAPIDLY OR FROM BELIZE IN EIGHT OR TEN DAYS OR FROM PUERTO CORTES LATER OR WITH THE PARTICIPATION OF THE PBY ANYWHERE IF THEY CAN PAY FOR IT. PPC MUST NOW KNOW BETTER.

HAS MY BRIEFCASE BEEN RETURNED TO THALASSA ? IF SO PLEASE INFORM ME AND I WILL GIVE INSTRUCTIONS ON HOW TO SEND IT WITHOUT LOSING IT.

TOBACCO AND MATERIAL ORDERED FROM LISE COENCA AS WELL AS MAIL SHOULD BE ADRESSED TO OUR AGENT IN BELIZE BUT THE SAME SHOULD BE WELL CONTACTED TO UNDERSTAND THAT HE MUST KEEP ALL CAREFULLY UNTIL WE ARRIVE.

PHILIPPE IT IS ABSOLUTELY NECESSARY FOR ME TO PRESENT A COPY OF THE BLUE HOLE FILM TO THE AUTHORITIES IN BELIZE UPON ARRIVAL. PLEASE SEND THIS COPY TO OUR AGENT IN BELIZE WITH INSTRUCTIONS TO HOLD UNTIL OUR ARRIVAL. COPY IS THE WRONG WORD I MEAN A 16 MM SOUND PRINT. I WOULD ALSO LIKE TO FIND IN BELIZE ANOTHER COPY OF EILEEN'S REPORTS AS I HAD PUT MY COPY IN MY LOST BRIEFCASE...
I AM SLOWLY RECOVERING FROM MY FLUE BUT IT HAS HANDICAPPED ME FOR THE PAST THREE DAYS AND I AM NOT SURE THAT I WILL BE ABLE TO DIVE BEFORE A WEEK. OTHERWISE EVERYONE ON BOARD IS WELL. BE PREPARED TO RECEIVE LONG MESSAGES TOMORROW. BEST TO ALL

LAST MINUTE = NORTHWEST 35 KNOTS INCREASING. WE RETURN TO MUJERES VERY HAPPY = LOBSTERS GUARANTEED IN TWO DAYS JYC

Figure 12 - Telex from JYC sent to The Society (Westport and L.A.)

Lobster for dinner and then we watch Dr. H's slides and a film about bully netters in the Bahamas. This is another lobster fishing technique. The way it works is that two fishermen work from a skiff in shallow water. One man steers. The other man leans over the side and peers through a glass-bottomed plastic bucket. Using what looks like a butterfly net, he scoops up lobsters with the bully net.

It's now the morning of January 14, and I'm approaching my third week at Contoy.

After breakfast I clean the galley, shower, and take a walk. Showers are easier in port because there are no restrictions on water.

Dr. H gives me an interesting hour-long lesson on lobster anatomy.

We're supposed to have left for Contoy by now, but I just heard about a change in plans. I hope we go soon. I want to see the migration. We continue to shuttle Captain Cousteau and Joe back and forth to Contoy via helicopter.

The weather is clearing but JYC's told us we're not yet returning to Contoy. He says the sea is still too rough. He reports that the camp is barely standing and most of the fishing boats have left. Four large shrimp boats arrived seeking shelter from the storm and are anchored off the westerly side of the island. He also says that twenty miles to the north there is a lobster queue heading toward Contoy. I wonder how he figured that out.

Joe is back and decides that since we're stuck in port we might as well dive here. Falco joins us. We decide to first inspect the submerged carcasses that have just been dumped close to the dock. The water is filthy with oil and sewage. Although there's no visibility, I still manage to measure a quantity of lobsters and record the data. They're dominantly males and quite large at 130–140mm.

We pull ourselves out of the repulsive water up into the Zodiac and drive a mile to a sheltered area on the bay side of the lighthouse. Despite the increasing north wind, the water here is calm and clear, with a refreshing twenty-meter visibility and an abundance of coral. Our reward is an amazing view. We hover alongside a massive school of thousands of grunts. It's a gently moving silver *wall of fish,* emitting a grunting noise caused by the grinding of their teeth amplified by their swim bladder. The wall continues to flow in a never-ending circular column as we gently stroke the fearless fish.

When we're back in the Zodiac, Falco tells us about when he and JYC filmed the sleeping sharks. I ask him if he can take us to see the sharks, but unfortunately he says the site is too far offshore for us to make an unplanned Zodiac trip, unstable weather or not. Instead Falco offers to take us to the nearby underwater shrine, the submerged statue of the Madonna.

After spending much of the day exploring, we return to *Calypso* just in time for dinner. Later I have a couple apples and then joke around with Jeff, Joe, Madame, and Philippe. Joe talks about the practical jokes they pulled in the Army, and Madame describes the tricks pulled on *Calypso.*

I hollow out some lobster legs that I'd previously removed from carcasses, hoping to make something clever out of them. I have another snack and now I'm in the bunk listening to Led Zeppelin on the Marantz C-180 cassette tape player I'd picked up at Klein's in Westport before the trip.

The morning's sail to Contoy takes six hours, which is longer than usual. We finally arrive, and the team from camp excitedly comes aboard. I'm excited to dive and observe the migration and also get to the beach to analyze some piles.

We have a rather cold fifteen-knot northerly moderate breeze with bothersome ten-foot swells. The water is turbid and dirty, and the sky is overcast. It's time for me to find a space to be alone for a while. Everybody is getting to be too familiar, including Madame.

The afternoon is quiet. We're puzzled, trying to figure out if the lobsters are migrating. The water is too murky to see much of anything. A huge loggerhead sea turtle surfaces off the bow.

With the campers away, there's plenty of room at the dinner table. I just ate at the first sitting, and now sit and write during the second sitting. We're taking shifts as steward, and Parviz is on duty for dinner. I did breakfast and lunch.

Afterward we watch another one-hour Cousteau Antarctic program, *Blizzard at Hope Bay.* It's excellent and inspirational. I'm amazed that this outfit can produce something this good.

We also watch Dr. H's slides again, and I help him send a message to Lynne, saying he needs to stay several more days. We'll send another message to her in a day or two indicating his new return date. He asks her to have P. Hamilton cover tomorrow's lecture and to cancel class the day after next.

In the morning we notice that the higher barometric pressure has made the water temperature cooler. Dr. H. mentions that his Bahamas research revealed the same phenomenon at the time of migration, causing higher-density cold water to flow across the Bahamas Bank. He suspects the same may happen here, with a deep layer of cold water flowing into the Caribbean, driving the lobsters from the deep cold to shallower, warmer water.

I hustle off the ship to search for more lobsters. It appears that most fishermen did depart with the whole lobsters. There are very few new piles on shore. We're told that some of the fishermen dropped carcasses in Contoy's lagoon, something we haven't seen yet, so I take a Zodiac to check it out.

By the time I return to camp it is dusk. A staged scene is being shot: several takes of JYC and Dr. H. arriving via Zodiac, approaching the campfire, then sitting and talking. Multiple takes are necessary because in the background a couple of frigate birds are harassing another frigate and disrupting the scene.

We've now been here a few weeks. We are desperately trying to spot lobsters and get any film footage we can. We are diving around the clock, day and night. The weather is cloudy with a light northeast breeze and scattered showers. Water visibility is only two meters, but we're hopeful that it'll improve with the new tide.

The latest dive report brings bad news. There's still no sign of the lobsters, and visibility has decreased to only one foot. We hope the sea will calm so the water can clear. With such poor visibility we can't see any lobsters or film them.

Paul, Michel, and I take a quick trip in the chaland and check out a fishing boat pulling a net. Unfortunately they have caught no lobster.

The next day, a hell of a day, starts differently as Hussein did not wake me for my watch. Whoever is on watch before you is supposed to wake you when it's your turn. He was having too much fun catching crabs off the side of the ship and decided to take my watch as well.

After preparing for, serving, and cleaning up lunch, I escape, just before four returning divers would have had me start all over again.

Dr. H and I dive in the lagoon and recover and measure seventy-five more carcasses. Then we walk up the beach past the lighthouse to measure a pile I'd spotted yesterday.

Later, back aboard *Calypso,* I shave and then serve dinner. I snap at Jeff because as I'm busy clearing the dishes from the first sitting and getting ready to set the table for the second sitting, Jeff asks me to push him an ashtray that's just barely out of his reach. Chef Philippe Leconte is his usual ill-tempered self. I'm not about to be pushed around by him either.

I prepare the daily message to Westport, requesting three cases of quart cans of SAE 50 engine oil, preferably either Aeroshell 100 or Texaco, and a replacement gas cap for the chopper's fuel tank.

This place is growing on us, in good ways and bad. It's remote and beautiful, but there's pressure to film. We've been here a month without accomplishing anything.

After finishing tonight's work, I visit with Dr. H. to ask some final questions before he leaves. He's been helpful and kind and has renewed my interest in the field of scientific research.

There's a light easterly breeze and five-foot northeast swells, helping to now improve the surface water visibility to four meters. Unfortunately, below near the ocean floor, it's still poor visibility at just half a meter.

Another film from the Antarctic series is being shown in the wardroom. I'd love to watch it, but for some reason I volunteered to take the doctor's watch. Any media diversion is rare and welcome aboard *Calypso.* Perhaps we're being shown the films to keep our spirits up.

In the morning we break camp in preparation for tomorrow's departure. We'll head to Mujeres and then south to Belize.

I assemble the aquarium and help Paul and Jeff move a net from the stern to the roof of the wheelhouse, the structure that encloses the bridge and the radio room. I jump in for a quick swim, serve lunch, and catch a lift to Contoy.

Xerox and I take a final walk on Contoy. It's interesting how people see nature so differently, or don't see it at all. Xerox is compelled to pull a land crab out of its hole to photograph it, whereas I'd prefer not to disturb it.

We return to camp and help with final packing, shuttling equipment and remaining provisions out to *Calypso* via Zodiacs and the chaland. Upon completion, we take a last swim off the beach, bid farewell to the camp, and head to the mother ship.

Unfortunately while I was on the island, Dr. H departed. I didn't get to say good-bye. Per his request, I'll continue doing research and mail it to him. He asked me to track the environmental conditions before, during, and after any additional migratory activity, including getting copies of the daily weather bulletins and satellite photos, data on location, hydrography, lobster information (sex ratio, reproductive condition, carapace condition, color, queue size, and direction of movement), and fishing (catch size, method: net, spear, trap).

For the next two hours we stow all of the camp equipment. Then it is a delicious dinner, particularly since I'm no longer the steward.

As dawn breaks on our final morning, there's a brilliant sun and a comfortable ten-knot easterly breeze. The shallows gradually clear, and four-foot northeast swells gently rock us. We ready to lift anchor when suddenly Valvula approaches in a small skiff. He's got fifty lobsters; thirty he netted and twenty he caught free diving.

Figure 13 - Valvula delivers lobsters. Contoy's lighthouse is visible in the distance.

This may be the long-awaited migration, but as luck would have it, JYC is literally climbing into the helicopter and leaving for New York. Falco is in charge and decides *Calypso* must move south.

We barter for twenty of these extremely large lobsters. I promptly measure them and record other data. I borrow Lev's macro lens and take some extreme close-up photographs.

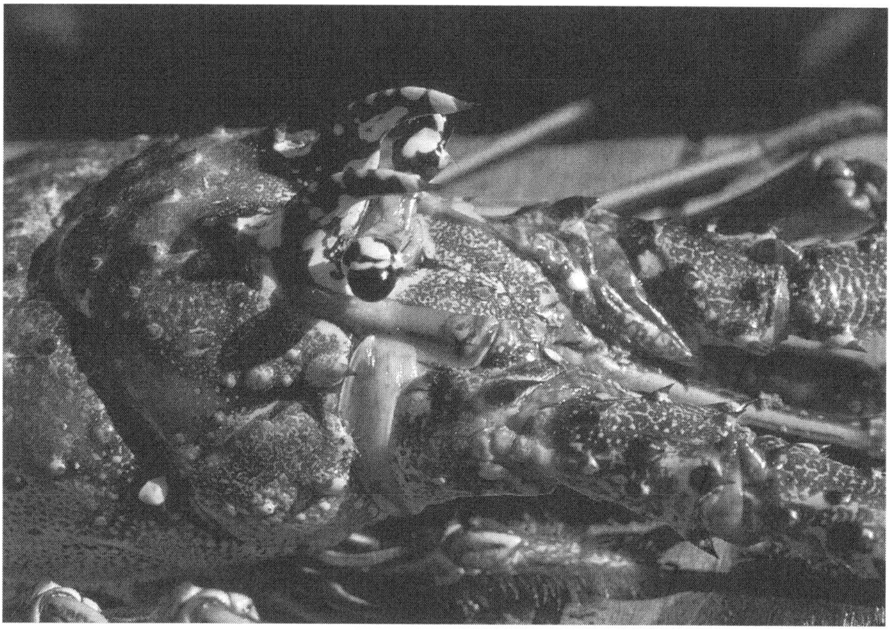

Figure 14 - Sharp horns protect the lobster's black eyeballs.

Lev is a Russian exile. He's a diver and photographer, now residing in New York City.

Once underway, Joe, Xerox, Patrick, and I visit. Then I nap outdoors in one of the onboard Zodiacs.

Lobster's the main course for lunch. Talk about fresh seafood.

When we arrive at Mujeres, we anchor out near the southern coast's ruins and again dive on the wall of fish. Carco films the scene from above in the helicopter.

Then we sail into the bay, close to the solitary dock we'd previously occupied, which is now being used by a Mexican destroyer. We'd prefer not to anchor because then we have to stand watch and shuttle back and forth to shore. So we pull alongside and tie up to the destroyer. We laugh, figuring the ship is half of the Mexican Navy. Now we can freely go ashore by hiking across the warship's deck.

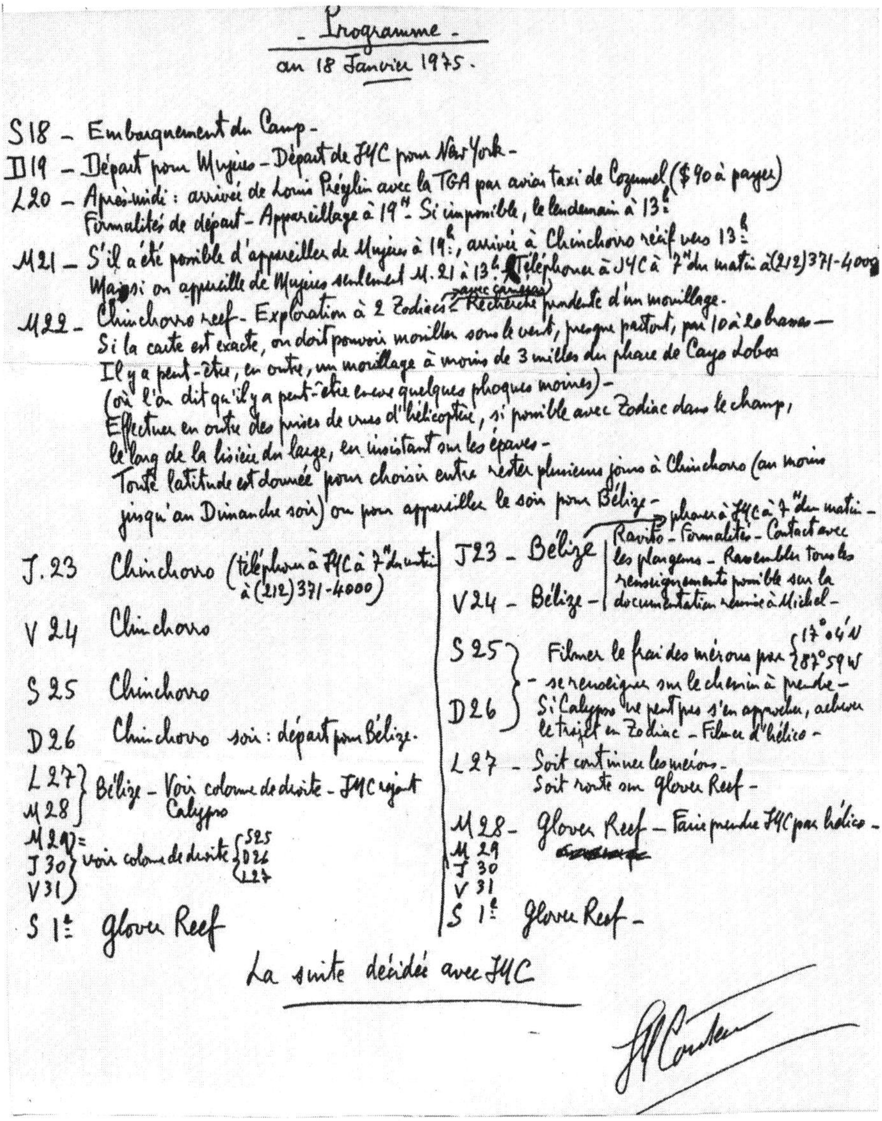

\- Programme -
au 18 Janvier 1975.

S18 – Embarquement du Camp –
D19 – Départ pour Mujeres – Départ de JYC pour New York –
L20 – Après-midi : arrivée de Louis Prezelin avec la TGA par avion taxi de Cozumel ($ 90 à payer)
Formalités de départ – Appareillage à 19 H. Si impossible, le lendemain à 13 h.
M21 – S'il a été possible d'appareiller de Mujeres à 19 h, arrivée à Chinchorro récif vers 13 h.
Mais si on appareille de Mujeres seulement M. 21 à 13 h. Téléphoner à JYC à 7 h du matin à (212) 371-4000
M22 – Chinchorro reef – Exploration à 2 Zodiacs avec caméras – Recherche pendant d'un mouillage.
Si la carte est exacte, on doit pouvoir mouiller sous le vent, presque partout, par 10 à 20 brasses –
Il y a peut-être, en outre, un mouillage à moins de 3 milles du phare de Cayo Lobos
(où l'on dit qu'il y a peut-être encore quelques phoques moines) –
Effectuer en outre des prises de vues d'hélicoptère, si possible avec Zodiac dans le champ,
le long de la lisière du large, en insistant sur les épaves –
Toute latitude est donnée pour choisir entre rester plusieurs jours à Chinchorro (au moins
jusqu'au Dimanche soir) ou pour appareiller le soir pour Bélize –

J.23 Chinchorro (téléphone à JYC à 7 h du matin à (212) 371-4000)
V24 Chinchorro
S25 Chinchorro
D26 Chinchorro soir : départ pour Bélize.
L27 } Bélize – Voir colonne de droite – JYC rejoint
M28 } Calypso
M29 =
J30 } voir colonne de droite { S25 D26 L27
V31
S 1er Glover Reef

J23 – Bélize – téléphone à JYC à 7 h du matin – Ravito – Formalités – Contact avec les plongeurs – Rassembler tous les renseignements possibles sur la documentation remise à Michel –
V24 – Bélize –
S25 } Filmer le frai des mérous par { 17°04'N 87°59'W
D26 } – se renseigner sur le chemin à prendre – Si Calypso ne peut pas s'en approcher, achever le trajet en Zodiac – Filmer d'hélico –
L27 – Soit continuer les mérous – Soit route sur Glover Reef –
M28 – Glover Reef – Faire prendre JYC par hélico –
M29
J30
V31
S 1er Glover Reef –

La suite décidée avec JYC

JY Cousteau

Figure 15 - "Programme" (schedule) Jan. 18–Feb 1, posted in the wardroom

Madame and Raymond visit the market. Soon thereafter the grateful vendors deliver the purchases, pile them high on the dock, and we march them across the destroyer onto *Calypso.*

Joe and I have a good conversation with Madame while she cuts my hair. Then I shower and we have a light buffet dinner. Jeff's depressed, so after dinner I drag him into town. We find a nice bar, have a cerveza, platano con leche, and a helado de coco and then play some pool.

It's 0100 and I'm on solo watch. I spot a white flare off the starboard stern. I wake Paul, who says that since the weather is nice and the flare was close to shore, that it doesn't represent a problem. I'm not so sure.

The next day is dark and rainy. There's a westerly fresh breeze. The harbor is relatively calm with just a light chop. Joe and I take Lev to town. He shares many stories about his life in Russia, including his friend Alexander Solzhenitsyn, a Russian writer who was awarded the Nobel Prize for Literature in 1970.

Joe and Lev need to buy some odds and ends, and I want to pick up a sweater for Mom. Our shopping is unsuccessful, though, as a torrent of rain soaks us. We're out of time and need to return to the ship for lunch.

A small fleet of fishing boats arrives. Once they get close to the factory, they anchor and load their live lobsters into dinghies. From there they detach the tails and dispose of the torsos and other remains overboard.

I want to dive in and study the carcasses and visit the factory, but first I have other work to do.

We're sending Ivan, Carco, Valvula, and another diver, Ramon Bravo, back to Contoy to live in the lighthouse after we leave for Belize. They need equipment and supplies, so I refill twelve gas cans and all of the air tanks.

As I'm doing this, a film crew leaves for the factory. Then there's chaos. The logistics of returning the campers and equipment to Contoy hasn't been thought out, the helicopter won't start, and the destroyer starts drifting, taking *Calypso* with it. So we hurriedly untie *Calypso* and move her out into the harbor. Eventually the destroyer is secured, things quiet, and we pull back alongside the destroyer. I help re-tie all of the lines, *Calypso*'s, the Zodiacs, the chaland, and the helicopter.

Based upon seeing Valvula's catch yesterday morning, it seems obvious that the migration is in full force. I'd been thinking we needed even more patience, to give Contoy just a little more time.

Now January 21, this morning's satellite images and weather transcripts indicate that a cold front is passing with a twenty-five-knot northerly wind. There's clearing to the north and west, but it's still cloudy here. The bay is calm with five meters of water visibility.

Two more fishing boats arrive. They're riding heavy in the water and loaded with lobsters. The fishermen seem unable to decide what to do. Falco doesn't know what to do either and calls JYC in New York for guidance.

There's no question that the lobster march is on. We must act and send someone to Contoy, now.

By mid-afternoon, after much wavering, we're all en route back to Contoy. The island is now in sight.

Bernard, Carco, Louis, and Ivan left earlier than us in a small boat they'd rented from the Mujeres dive shop. They're on the radio, frantically telling us that every remaining fishing boat is rapidly filling with lobsters.

As the tail of the front passes, we feel occasional sprinkles and wisps of wind. The thunderheads are now well to our south. The sea is flat and glassy.

As we approach Contoy, long, gradual, two-foot swells build from the north.

I spend the afternoon further preparing the aquarium and camp, and organizing a telex to request what seems to be a never-ending need for supplies, including the urgent need for a parts book for our generator so we can identify what's needed for the repair. It's an Onan AC 120/240 single phase, PF 1, 12.5 amps, 60 cycles, 3,600 RPM, Tecumseh motor. We're guessing we need eight valves, two interior and two exterior, including upper and lower caps and springs, a head cylinder, and a head gasket. Xerox asks me to include a request for a Raytheon depth sounder, model DE 721 A 115 volt AC.

Suddenly there's an emergency on one of the four nearby shrimp boats. Their captain stupidly used his foot to try and cushion a collision with one of the other three sister ships. He's separated his big toe, literally. It dropped into the sea. Toe overboard! We dive and search for it without success. Even if it had been found our doctor isn't equipped or skilled to reattach it. He does, however, close the wound and stops the bleeding. As a gesture of thanks, they give us a huge basket of more than one hundred pounds of fresh shrimp. So it's delicious fresh shrimp for dinner.

After the excitement, we set a net one hundred meters behind *Calypso.* Within an hour we have a lobster. It's a big one. Joe, Patrick, and Ivan dive but only find crabs. We continue to check the net every hour but there's no other lobster.

On watch now, 0330–0500. The skies are cloudy and there are no visible stars. At 0400 I wake Jean Desoeuvres, an electrician, and Joe, Patrick, and Ivan to load the Zodiacs and chaland for a planned dive. But Jean says there's a problem with the second generator needed to power the underwater lights, so I also wake Jean-Marie and Davso to work on it. Madame and Falco are now up as well, supervising. Jean-Marie and Davso get the generator up and running and at 0530, still before sunrise, Joe, Patrick, Ivan, and I dive.

I've been up since 0300 so after the dive I grab a quick nap and lunch. Then it's off to Contoy for watch. We have returned a lot of equipment to the island's new campsite at the lighthouse, and we've now instituted a watch on the island. It isn't as serious a watch as aboard *Calypso,* but we do need to have someone at the camp and awake at all times. There isn't much to do, though, so I explore a bit. My head has been hurting and my stomach upset so I don't have the energy to search for lobsters. Somehow I climb the lighthouse again, though, and eventually Xerox shows up, talking my ear off for two hours.

Later back aboard *Calypso* I'm looking at the island and noticing that near the middle, between the lighthouse and the old camp, there's an extraordinary number of pelicans diving and a mass movement of fishing boats.

The fishermen have become even more suspicious, blatantly blaming us for what's still considered a weak harvest. Not helping our cause is that once again, as soon as we return to Contoy, the lobsters vanish. The fishermen are pleased to hear that we'll be leaving for good. As a final gesture, we again barter a carton of Gitanes and a gallon of California wine for twenty lobsters. It's a bargain for us, and the fishermen are happy. Two lobsters seemingly get a reprieve, going into the aquarium instead of the pot.

As we again set sail for Mujeres, I reflect on Contoy. Special memories include the terrestrial crabs (land, ghost, hermit), frigate birds, pelicans, cormorants, lizards, iguana, scorpions, and of course Bernard's no-see-ums. Also memorable is the ocean's phosphorescence and the undersea turtles, horseshoe crabs, barracuda, red snapper, angelfish, turkeywing clams, octopi, king mackerel, huge jewfish, and the nurse and other sharks with their hitchhiking remoras.

Later, upon arrival in the Mujeres channel, we set anchor. Bernard and I disembark, taking a Zodiac and ten air tanks the three miles to the pier. We unload the tanks and settle up payments with Enrique Lima of Buzos de Caribe and pay off some other accounts too.

A Mexican television news crew interviews us. We grab a short farewell walk and then finally return to the ship. We are ready to sail south but have to wait for Jerry, who took the chopper to Cozumel two days ago to pick up a part.

The latest report from camp is one fisherman, using hooks, has caught seventy kilos (154 pounds) of lobsters. So yet again the fishermen are happy that *Calypso* is not there.

My theory is that the migration has already occurred. The largest groups passed through during the two storms, preceded and followed by smaller scattered groups. The data supports this, reflecting the migrants being considerably larger than the native lobsters.

Falco, Ivan, Lev, and I make an early morning dive along the wall of fish. The water is actually warmer than the air. There's a mild chop and good fifteen-meter visibility. A nearby rock section is chock full of a huge variety of fish and coral. We explore the area, collect some fresh sand for the aquarium, and return to the ship anchored nearby off the ruins.

Finally Jerry returns, and on January 24, we're off.

I'm left with thoughts of children and animals. It's strange that, despite Mujeres' poverty and filth, there are many tourists. The incredible diving must be the draw.

Next stop is Chinchorro Reef, where we'll begin a new film on the subject of reefs. Still in Mexican waters, Chinchorro is to the east of the main reef, the Belize Barrier Reef.

More than one thousand small islands or cays make up the 180-mile-long Belize Barrier Reef, making it the second largest reef on earth. Only Australia's Great Barrier Reef is larger. The northern end of the Belize Barrier Reef starts fifteen miles from the coast and extends eastward for sixty miles.

Progressing south, also to the east of the main reef, are three coral atolls, Turneffe, Lighthouse, and Glovers.[25] Turneffe is the largest at thirty miles long and ten miles wide. There are said to be several shipwrecks off Mauger Cay at Turneffe's northern tip and many sharks off Cay Boekl on the southern tip.[26]

Lighthouse Reef is considered to be the most beautiful, with over sixty miles of barrier reef and dramatically steep ledges.[27]

Farther south is Glovers Reef, the smallest atoll, featuring numerous shipwrecks, magnificent coral, and abundant fish.[28]

Just beyond the reefs lies the edge of the continental shelf and deep drop offs. Beyond Lighthouse the depth drops to over ten thousand feet. Perhaps that is why Columbus named the area

Honduras, meaning "unfathomable,"[1] as literally just off the shelf the sea drops to thousands of meters deep.

In 1973, the country changed its name from British Honduras to Belize. It lies on the eastern or Caribbean coast of Central America, bounded on the north and part of the west by Mexico, and on the south and the remainder of the west by Guatemala.

Sailing south, I lay face down on the hard wooden foredeck. The ship's motion hurts my hipbone but the hot sun lulls me to sleep. Later, from our small library in the wardroom, I select one of the ship's only books written in English, *Darwin and the Beagle*, written by Alan Moorehead. Charles Darwin called the Belize Barrier Reef "the most remarkable reef in the West Indies."

I touch up the yellow paint of the two-dozen air tanks. Then I help with the aquarium, which is now in nice shape. Its water is still dirty, though, so tomorrow we're going to try a charcoal filter.

Michel Deloire is anxious to film creatures in the aquarium. I don't think it will be worthwhile, but these guys seem to make magic with film.

We'll be underway all night. I have to learn more about navigation before I can take the helm at night. Despite calm seas, a rival northerly current slows lumbering *Calypso* to just seven knots. The satellite indicates our estimated time of arrival (ETA) at Chinchorro Reef to be 0600.

While sailing, there's less work. I'd prefer to be kept active, doing something constructive. But after serving so long as steward, it's nice to have a break.

We've all been in a bit of limbo since waiting for Jerry in Mujeres, so we're just happy to be underway. I look forward to studying and filming the habitat of the reef. Since we didn't obtain enough quality underwater footage to complete the lobster film, Dr. H will rendezvous with a Cousteau team in Bimini next October to film the lobster migration in the Bahamas.

---

1 Today fathom is known as a nautical unit of length equal to six feet. Originally, as defined by an act of Parliament, it was "the length of a man's arms around the object of his affections," deriving from the Old English Faethm, meaning, "embracing arms."

Sunrise reveals Chinchorro on the horizon. We approach and anchor three miles offshore. The skies are cloudy with scattered showers. Flying fish surround us and the sea is dense with floating vegetation.

The compressor is running full bore filling the air tanks. Bernard, Michel D, and Patrick are at the wardroom's table planning the day.

The two lobsters are still in the aquarium. I just fed them their favorite, fresh conch. In their natural habitat they also prey on clams, hermit crabs, sea urchins, starfish, algae, and sea cucumbers.

We've been experimenting to see if and how the lobsters respond to the taste and touch of things like vinegar, citrus, olive oil, and honey. They sense flavor by touching food with their pair of smaller, flexible, hairless antennules. When an antennule detects something good to eat, the legs gather the food and move it toward the underside of the head where smaller front legs pull the food up into the mouth, called the mandible, which looks like a beak or actually two large, dull white teeth.

After each bite the lobster cleans its antennules by drawing them under its body and whipping them forward through gathered hairy legs. When finished eating, the lobster cleans the hair on its legs like a raccoon cleans its paws. Then it lowers its tail and folds its legs underneath the torso, resting its head and entire body on the sand, like a cat settles after a meal.

Figure 16 - A lobster cleaning its antennules.

Although we normally don't fish, Paul and I take the chaland and troll around the island. We catch two three-foot barracuda. Since the chef has already cooked lunch, if he can figure out how to prepare them, we'll have them for dinner. Barracuda are normally hunted for sport and do not make good eating.

Falco, Patrick, and I go snorkeling to scout dive spots. It's fantastic, holding our breath and free diving among the giant sea fans, coral, thousands of tropical fish, conch, and best of all a two hundred-foot wreck and a dozen giant manta rays. After waiting a month for a single species, the lobster, we now have a bountiful reef to explore.

Upon return to *Calypso,* I join Captain Cousteau on the bow's deck for his daily calisthenics. Then we join the second sitting of dinner for some delicious barracuda. It's the first time in a while that my stomach feels good and I'm hungry.

Later we lose power, which causes the aquarium filter to stop. Xerox helps me fix it. Then I borrow Michel D's generator-powered lights to take still photographs of the lobsters eating their second conch of the day.

At midnight we dive and film a field of gorgons forty meters deep. They resemble a star with a centered body and five forked arms, each boasting a network of branches. This type of gorgon is commonly referred to as a brittle star. It's of the echinoderm phylum, along with sea stars, sea urchins, and sea cucumbers; echinoderms only live in salt water.

The word *echinoderm* is derived from Greek, meaning "a spiny skin." All echinoderms have small jaws that are supported by a water-vascular system, and they have tube feet, which they use to attach to objects for protection as well as to obtain food. They all can regenerate lost limbs.

The dive also reveals similarly named gorgonian fans. Members of a different phylum, these colorful coral fans traverse the prevailing current to maximize the volume of water and nutrients that flow through and are captured by them.

The word *gorgon* is derived from the Greek word *gorgós,* meaning "dreadful." In Greek mythology, gorgons such as Medusa lived near the ocean and guarded the entrance to the underworld. As monstrous feminine creatures they were covered with scales and their hair was made of living snakes.[29] They also had fangs and a beard. If you look at a gorgon she'll turn you to stone. I'm glad I didn't know about this until after the dive.

The plentiful conch, coral, and sponges prompt JYC to share with me what seems to be a recurring theme: his concern about declining populations. He cites how the number of conchs in Florida and the Caribbean has dramatically decreased, and that it is another example of how stricter regulations and farming would help sustain the species. Today's commercial fishermen harvest the young small conchs before they've reached sexual maturity. If the conch can't reproduce, the local spawning stock, and thus the sustainability of the population, is in jeopardy.

We move *Calypso* to just one hundred meters off the southern end of Chinchorro and anchor. Now I'm resting in my bunk before 2300 watch.

During watch I prepare and send a telex that includes the following information.

"LEV NEEDS TEN ROLLS OF KODAK HIGH SPEED EKTACHROME FILM.
JEAN MARIE URGENTLY NEEDS GENERAL MOTOR 6/71 (GRAY MARINE MODIFIE).

PART NO	DESCRIPTION	QTY
51 50 641	THERMOSTAT	2
D 346.550	THERMOSTAT	2
15 36 033	TACHOMETER DRIVE ASSY	2
51 84 532	FUEL PUMP ASSY	1
52 28 305	INJECTOR ASSY HV7	4
D 6.275	HEAT EXCHANGER FOR FRESH WATER	1
51 86 250	PUMP ASSY, RAW WATER (JABSCO)	1"

Breakfast is the usual unsatisfying dry toast and strong black coffee. I bum around with Lev for a while. We top off the aquarium and prepare equipment for today's planned full day of filming. Tonight we'll embark on the eight-hour sail to Belize.

I find nineteen flying fish alive on the foredeck and toss them back into the calm sea.

Patrick and I snorkel to a pod of about thirty long-beaked common dolphins playing off the starboard bow. They're curious and friendly. I swim so close I can look into their eyes and even stroke their smooth black backs. Their bellies are white and their sides an hourglass pattern of light grey.

We're just back aboard and it's already time for another team to dive. The doctor and I man the cable from the chaland. The wind and sea build, and then the clouds open up, pelting us with giant, cold raindrops.

Actually two teams are diving simultaneously. The doctor is driving and mistakenly follows the wrong team, the one with untethered strobes. The team we're supporting has lights that are connected to the generator in our boat. They're suddenly fifty meters away and yanking hard for more cable. I jockey around the generator in the center of the chaland to feed every last inch of cable that I have and am now literally at the end of my rope, leaning over the side as the divers continue to violently pull for more. Finally the doctor reverses course and gets closer to our team. We quickly straighten everything out. The dive wasn't deep, so once completed, with no required decompression, we slowly tow the irritated divers back to *Calypso.*

After lunch we repeat the process, but this time I dive and handle the underwater lights.

We roll off the Zodiac and penetrate the giant lush carpet of tan sargassum held afloat by thousands of berrylike air sacs. The current has cleared the water to twenty-five meters of crystal clear visibility. We film more conchs and retrieve one to decorate the aquarium.

Later I refill all of the gasoline tanks used for the chaland and Zodiacs. Then I exercise, read Darwin, and make yet another dive, my third of the day, just before dinner.

Now that I'm no longer camping and aboard *Calypso* full time, I learn the daily routine: that at the beginning of the first sitting of dinner Paul posts the night's watch schedule, the *programme,* on the small bulletin board just inside the portside wardroom door. Since Jeff is sick I'll man the cable on the next dive for him and then take his watch 2100–2400.

It's a new week, now January 27, and I've been at sea more than a month. I'm up at 0630 for some more dry toast. The helicopter takes off to film our early dive near the conch fishermen. Upon return, Paul and I move the nets atop the wheelhouse for storage and then swab the decks.

In the afternoon I again tend the cable. This time we try something new. We tie a Zodiac to the chaland. Each boat is equipped with a generator and cable tender. We're each responsible for a lighting man and photographer below. The two dive teams stay close together. Actually they're too close to each other and accidentally crisscross, tangling the underwater cables. We can't properly feel or interpret the tugging instructions. I feel that it is a catastrophe, but strangely, afterward, nobody is upset.

Dinner is an enjoyable change: eggs, potatoes, soup, and delicious custard.

Now we're sailing south to rougher seas. I'm hoping to keep dinner down but can't. I'm on watch and sick.

After 0500 watch all I can do is sleep, first in the Zodiac, then on the bench in the wardroom, and finally in my new bunk. I've relocated to share a crew cabin with Michel Fourcade. It's a dark, lower crew cabin in the belly of the bow, below the water line, so there's no porthole for fresh air.

I need to hit the head, the nautical term for toilet, and as I climb the ladder from the lower deck, I pass out and fall. Bernard finds me unconscious on the floor and gets the useless doctor. It's not seasickness but something else.

I sleep through the entire rainy day and awake in the evening. The weather has cleared and dinner is being served. I have scrambled eggs and chicken. The French recommend chicken for an upset stomach and are of course compelled to tell me that I'm wrong to have what I want: eggs. Is it the chicken or the egg?

Being sick makes me miss home. Yesterday I received a letter saying I'm needed home mid-February. I'd like to stay longer, but I'll have to leave then.

I'm up early the next morning for a large three-course breakfast, medicine, more medicine, and two pieces of toast.

A pilot is aboard, bringing us into the port of Belize City. He takes us to an anchorage just offshore in Belize Harbor. It's not a deepwater port, so shuttling back and forth from anchorage to the mainland is required.

The pilot brags about lobsters, saying that the Belize fishermen dive with hooks and catch eight hundred lobsters per day. This compared to only a couple dozen per day when using traps. I wonder if we should have been less focused on the nets at Contoy, whether that migration is different, or maybe we should have been at a different location to film the lobster migration.

I'll hit town as soon as I can get a ride to shore. It's sunny with a pleasant easterly breeze. The water is dirty with barely any visibility.

JYC will return today and then we're expecting a visitor, John Denver. We'll film Denver's visit, which will be aired as a segment on his television special. It should be interesting to see how a different type of show is put together and how his visit is handled.

I make it to shore and explore low-lying Belize City. It's the former capital of the country and the largest urban center, possessing a third of the country's total population. At only eighteen inches above sea level, it's built at the tip of a peninsula atop a mangrove swamp, coral, wood chips, and discarded rum bottles. After being devastated by Hattie, a wicked 1961 hurricane packing 160 mile-per-hour winds and a ten-foot tide, the city lost 260 citizens and decided to establish a new capital inland, named Belmopan.

Belize was the last British possession on the American mainland. The buildings and homes are clean and bright, designed in classic British colonial style.

I walk over the swing bridge into the bustling open-air market. The bridge connects Belize City's south and north sides. Built in 1922, it's the only manually operated swing bridge in the world, swung open each morning and evening to allow larger boats to pass up and down the last four miles of the Belize River (Haulover Creek).

The Belizeans are a mixture of Creoles from Africa, Caribs or Afro-Indians from the eastern Caribbean, Mestizos of Spanish and Indian blood, Mayans, Europeans, Lebanese, and Chinese. They derive life from both the ocean and the land. Crude rusted metal roofs shade the vendors and stacks of grouper, turtles, rays, lobsters (tails only), and shark. It's all piled atop huge, thick stone slabs. Adjacent, ancient, sturdy wooden tables overflow with tropical fruits, e.g. bananas and papayas, and vegetables.

Primitive sailboats and dugout canoes line the creek's wharf. The water often boils as scraps of freshly cleaned fish are tossed in and devoured by large catfish.

The people speak an English dialect that's difficult to understand. They're full of character and seem happy, friendly, and clean. I photograph the faces of elementary school-age children who are at recess in the school's wooden-fenced playground.

Some members of the crew have gone on a day trip to see the Mayan ruins, only seventy-five kilometers from here. I'm obliged to stay to help Daniel Belanger, the soundman, with the boom microphone when we film Denver's airport arrival.

Eventually I meet up with the film crew and we all wait for JYC at the United Brand office. He's back from New York but running late. When he arrives, we all leave for the airport. What an escapade. We arrive just in time. John's private jet is already on final approach. He lands, and we race all over the runway, taking shots as John taxis to the tiny terminal. Then the local press interviews him, he clears customs, and we leave for Belize City.

First we get John checked into the local hotel and then take him via Zodiac to *Calypso*. There's a crazy amount of filming and it's chaotic. I'm unloading supplies from a Zodiac and accidentally get my head in front of Joe's camera. This normally doesn't happen, but this scene was unrehearsed. Good old Joe is cool about it.

The chiefs disappear into Cousteau's cabin, so I shower, have dinner, and take watch. I'm missing some lingering dinner conversation below in the wardroom, but I'll take an early watch any day. John seems to be very nice.

Things are getting worse on the ship. It seems to me that the French discriminate against the Americans. The French seem to have an inferiority complex, as they're constantly intent on trying to prove that they are superior. Today Joe was excluded from work that he should have been a part of. However, I suppose, to be fair, Michel D, who's a good guy, is senior to Joe, and he manages the film crews.

Predictably, the chiefs meeting resulted in a sudden change in plans. At 0300 we'll leave for Glover Reef, a four-hour sail. That means John needs to stay aboard tonight, so someone leaves to retrieve John's belongings and check him out of the hotel.

I'm still on watch. John and JYC are talking in the adjoining radio room, two steps down aft of the bridge. JYC looks exhausted from his trip to New York and now he's trying to entertain John.

I feel like I should be more excited to meet John, but I've not really heard of him and don't know anything about him. I don't understand why people act so nutty about a celebrity. I do hope we have a chance to hear his music.

I'm up early the next morning and anxious not to miss anything. As it turns out, I'm the only one awake, except for the two on watch. The 0300 departure was delayed, so although we're underway, we're behind schedule and still three hours from Glover. I could go back to my bunk, but I'll stay on the bridge for a while. A dozen small porpoises tailgate, drafting in *Calypso*'s wake.

I decide to explore the underwater observation chamber located at the tip of the bow. I open the iron hatch, climb in, and, not wanting the waves to splash in, shut the hatch above me. It's dark and cramped and impossible to turn around, so I descend the slanted fourteen-rung iron ladder backwards, incorrectly facing forward. Being that I'm relatively tall, at the bottom I struggle to slide down and lay upon the paper-thin decade-old cushion set atop pallet-like wooden slats. Here, surrounded by eight-inch circular portholes, I see a breathtaking underwater view of the same playful porpoises, which have moved forward from the stern to the bow. They're enough to distract my stomach from the dramatic motion of *Calypso*'s bow repeatedly climbing the ten-foot waves, then free falling until crashing.

I'd incorrectly assumed that the chamber was part of the original minesweeper design, imagining it was designed so a sailor could spot submerged mines, perhaps radioing warnings up to the bridge. But I'm wrong. Way back in 1950, during *Calypso*'s conversion from a ferryboat to an oceanographic research vessel, Cousteau had the vision to add this "false nose."

The morning passes and we arrive at Glover, where we anchor five hundred meters off a small island. It's a spectacular scene; the water is calm with outstanding twenty-meter visibility, a pure white sand bottom, and a giant coral reef off the bow. I look forward to diving to study the coral and fish and exploring the island's birds, vegetation, and habitat.

John just awoke, and I'm visiting with him over more coffee and toast.

There's a brief rain shower and the sea is now a bit choppy.

I empty the aquarium, release one lobster, and am angry that the other one has died.

Paul and I fish off the stern with no luck.

JYC returns from scouting nearby Lighthouse Reef. He tells me that it's even nicer than Glover. In 1971, he was there to film the spectacular underwater circular sinkhole, the Blue Hole, that's more than 300 meters (984 feet) across and over 124 meters (407 feet) deep. JYC says that the last time they dove on it he saw fish swimming upside down, giant grouper, oarfish, and whale sharks.

JYC takes John to visit the nearby island.[m]

John and his assistant, Kris O'Connor, who is also aboard, join Bernard, Patrick, and me for a dive at dusk. Our timing is strategic, allowing us to witness the reef's magical changeover from day to night.

The brilliant theatre of this healthy living reef features an abundance of life, with different species efficiently time-sharing the same quarters. As the sun sets, the fish that have been out for the day begin to take cover. First the smaller plankton-eating fish, which generally stay closer to the reef, e.g. damselfish and

m Footage showing John and JYC walking on the island, as well as John diving, discussing the writing of the song *Calypso*, and performing at JYC's 75th birthday party. http://www.youtube.com/watch?v=RyivrvEwU6Q

wrasses, then the larger, less vulnerable herbivorous fish, which have wandered farther, come closer, congregate, and retire, e.g. surgeonfish, parrotfish, triggerfish, and filefish. Once dark, the nocturnal fish emerge from caves and coral crevices. Again the smaller fish stay close to home, while larger predators like the squirrelfish and scorpionfish boldly venture farther.

Upon return to the ship, I join JYC and John for the second sitting of dinner. JYC tells us that he has studied reefs for decades, and now with the help of experts, he wants to determine the environmental impact of oil and gas exploration, hurricanes, and other natural and man-made phenomena.

We then talk about what we saw on today's reef dive, including the school of Atlantic Spanish mackerel, hundreds of large grouper, and colorful sponges. John says that the stag horn coral are "far out." It's hard to get to know someone in just a day, but John has made a beautiful first impression. He seems to be very down to earth and honest.

After dinner, in preparation for our early morning departure to the north, I secure the lines, including tying down the helicopter.

Madame pays me a visit on watch, telling me I must be more careful about so generously offering my services, counseling that if I do, people will take advantage. For example, some people keep asking me to do their work and I continue to say yes. Madame is a beautiful lady. For her to survive twenty years on a small ship with so many men is no easy task. I'm sure that there have been many trying times for her. I try to do my best for Madame.

Given our latitude and that many satellites are positioned over the nearby equator, we play a nightly game of spotting the so-called birds. The absence of any urban afterglow enhances the contrast between the dark sky and the distant sun reflecting off the illuminated satellites. They resemble slow-moving shooting stars.

This morning's early sail is postponed because the anchor is lodged in rocks. It's hard to believe because all we see below is pure white sand. We dive and work to free the anchor, completing a new short film, *The Freeing of Calypso*. I'm just kidding, although, like most everything, we do actually film it.

Afterward Paul has me clean the bridge. I wash the windows and polish the brass. I enjoy polishing the brass instruments on the bridge because it all looks so nice when it's done. Of course, here at sea it takes just a few days for new tarnish to set in.

Daniel is being real cute, asking me to follow him around and take pictures of him. I have other things to do, and I'm remembering what Madame told me, so I ignore him.

This afternoon we begin a new film about Nassau grouper, *The Fish That Swallowed Jonah.* We're miles offshore anchored in thirty meters of water. The setting is perfect: great light, clear water, and brilliant white sand. It's a unique spot as we're bookended by both extremely deep water and treacherous shallow water. The edge of the continental shelf's two thousand-meter drop is just one hundred meters off the bow, while one hundred meters off the stern is a shallow half-meter deep reef.

Suddenly, drifting beside us in dugout canoes and other rustic vessels, are native fishermen; dark men barely dressed, in rags. They're curious, and assertively tie-up alongside *Calypso.*

Figure 17 - Native fishermen approaching Calypso

Although not yet quite invited, they climb aboard anyway. They point to the reef and their primitive one- and two-man elevated thatched huts set atop mangrove pilings and explain that they live here temporarily when fishing for grouper.

Figure 18 - Two men at their hut

It's amazing to think that none of this is planned or rehearsed. The fishermen had no knowledge that we'd be arriving and they don't even know who we are.

The fishermen keep the caught fish alive in a small pool of water in the center of their boat, and once this live well is filled, they move their now heavy boat back to a chicken wire pen adjoining their hut where they deposit their catch. The fish are kept alive until the day before the men return to the mainland market. At that time they fillet and salt the grouper and hang the fillets on the wire fence to dry in the sun. Only a few fish will be kept alive to be freshly filleted at the market.

<u>The Fisherman</u>

The Man, tired, natural, his face, dark and wrinkled,
It tells a story by itself.
His eyes, white, green, blue,
How many stories can they tell?

The Man, the weary soul of the fisherman,
He struggles for a catch while celebrating the day.
Worn and tattered clothes rest upon his bones.
Scraggly stubble grows upon his face.

The Man, like his father and his son, he is a fisherman.
His years, days, and minutes of thought,
The aged fisherman,
Imagine the experience, the tales, and wisdom of the
fisherman.

Written by Richard Hyman

I dive twice and am dead tired, but now it's time for watch 2300–0100. I write the above poem before John visits me. He asks me many questions about *Calypso,* JYC, and what it feels like to be a member of the crew. He explains that he wants to write a song about *Calypso* and that he needs to know details and my thoughts. I share my impressions and emotions with him.

I'm up again for 0300–0500 watch. The current has increased, we have a thirty-knot near gale, and the sea is rough. Regardless, the planned 0400 dive is underway.

By sunrise it's just a fifteen-knot moderate breeze with comfortable five-foot seas.

At JYC's request, I fill the aquarium and deposit two small grouper. I ask that they be cared for better than the lobsters, to which he agrees, saying we'll release them in a day.

I join the 1130 dive and work the lights. Afterward, at lunch, Kris tells some great stories and invites me to come see John's spring tour. I tell him I'll be at school in South Carolina. We review the southern swing of the schedule: 4/4 Memphis, 4/5-6 Atlanta, 4/9 Columbia, 4/10 Charlotte, 4/11 Norfolk, and agree that he'll arrange for me to see them in Atlanta.

Then we start the one-hour sail to calmer water near a chain of small islands, the Turneffe Atoll. There used to be a small town on one of the islands but it was wiped out by a hurricane. Today there's just a small fishing resort.

At Turneffe I dive with John, JYC, and Falco while manning the lights for Joe. We try to photograph John but he's so enthusiastic. He moves way too fast for us to properly film him.

I'm shocked as afterward Joe tells me that he's scared every time he dives. He's a funny guy who's like a big brother to me.

Madame christens her new six-foot Zodiac with a mini-bottle of champagne, and she and JYC leave on a joy ride.

I'm getting fed up with the French attitude. Even my friends Bernard and Patrick don't say please and thank you. I offered my services too much today and they took advantage.

Patrick and I did some spectacular snorkeling at dusk, but there were a few too many circling sharks for comfort.

It's after dark now and we're all outside on the foredeck for a party and concert. The luscious warm breeze is enhanced by plentiful special rum punch.

We start by filming the sequence intended for John's television special, "*An Evening with John Denver.*" I handle the clapboard, a device used to synchronize the picture and sound and to designate and mark particular scenes and takes.

Figure 19 - Left to right: John, Joe, me, Louis, Bernard, and Falco

Figure 20 - Left to right: JYC, John, Joe, me, Louis

Then Joe and I sing along to *Country Roads.*

<u>*Country Roads*</u>
Almost heaven, West Virginia
Blue Ridge Mountains, Shenandoah River
Life is old there, older than the trees
Younger than the mountains, blowing like a breeze

Country roads, take me home
To the place, I be-long
West Virginia, mountain momma
Take me home, country roads

All my mem'ries, gather 'round her
Miner's lady, stranger to blue water
Dark and dusty, painted on the sky
Misty taste of moonshine, teardrop in my eye

Country roads, take me home
To the place, I be-long
West Virginia, mountain momma
Take me home, country roads

I hear her voice, in the mornin' hours she calls to me
The radio reminds me of my home far away
And drivin' down the road I get a feeling'
That I should have been home yesterday, yesterday

Country roads, take me home
To the place, I be-long
West Virginia, mountain momma
Take me home, country roads"

Written by Bill Danoff, John Denver, and Taffy Nivert

Figure 21 - John

Once the filming for John's television special is done, the cameras are put away and painfully shy Madame emerges from hiding to sit next to John. He's delighted to sing Madame's many additional requests. I'm impressed by his endurance, her knowledge of his songs, and I'm happy to see Madame's pretty smile.

Figure 22 - John and Madame

The concert ends late and then I have watch. I find a quiet moment on the bridge to write John a note. I'll give it to him in the morning before he leaves. I'm also making him a key chain out of a lobster foot. How weird is that? It's all I have, and I want to give him something.

In the morning, as I'm removing links from the anchor chain, I hear that John and Kris are ready to leave. I say good-bye and then Jerry shuttles them via chopper to the mainland airport. Quickly it's back to work. I take the helm and we depart for the grouper huts. Cranky old Captain Alibert harasses me the whole way.

We near the huts and Jerry does a fly by. I turn *Calypso* into the wind. Jerry hovers the helicopter in and lands smoothly upon the aft pad. Then I swing the ship around, back onto course. Before long we're there, and once again we set anchor above the fishing ground, in between the reef and the ledge.

A nice steak for lunch, and Bernard grabs me to tend the cables. This time it's a difficult job as Falco is driving and for some reason he allows the chaland to drift forty meters away from the divers. I'm low on cable but manage to straighten Falco out in time to get back to the divers.

When the dive ends I grab a swim with a large school of dolphin. Then I start over, working the cable again, right off *Calypso*'s aft deck instead of the chaland. I've never tended the cables right off the ship, but I like it because it's less boring. While Falco, Louis, and Joe dive, I'm able to talk to the others that are hanging around.

JYC hasn't allowed me to release the grouper from the aquarium, and now he's added a third, so I'm becoming disillusioned. Why does he insist upon keeping the fish? It's obviously bad for them.

I relax in my top bunk while waiting for the second sitting of dinner. Michel's tiny turntable spins *Motherless Children, I Shot the Sheriff,* and *Let It Grow,* off Eric Clapton's *461 Ocean Boulevard* album, his actual address in Miami Beach. The rubber fan above the bunk whirls away as I think of friends, family, and girls, praying that when tonight's watch is posted, I'll have an early one.

Dinner is excellent. I dive again and work the lights. Now I'm on watch.

It's just before sunrise on February 4. Carco is already airborne, filming the fishermen as they leave their huts and paddle toward us. The following excerpt is from a telex I just sent for JYC.

> "FEBRUARY FOUR 1975. CALYPSO STILL ANCHORED OUTSIDE THE REEF NEAR GLORY CAY. ALL EXPECTATIONS NEVER MATCHED THE SPLENDOR AND VARIETY OF WHAT WE ARE

> OBSERVING AND RECORDING. HELICOPTER LAUNCHES AND OUTSIDE CAMERAS ARE WORKING IN HIGH GEAR AND DIVING GOES ON NIGHT AND DAY ALMOST WITHOUT INTERRUPTION."

The chiefs are meeting. They've decided that today we'll make as many dives as possible and try to complete the grouper film.

I'm on the first early morning dive. We film a concentrated gathering of hundreds of grouper and thousands of other tropical fish, including grunts, tangs, amberjacks, and angelfish, which are all active and hungry after their night of sleep.

For the next dive, I tend cable from the chaland. There's an accident. The metal bar that's wired to the generator and supposed to be hung over the side as an electrical ground is tossed by a wave into the boat. I'm shocked badly. It feels like the electricity is sticking the cable to my hand. After a few long seconds, Jeff, who is steering, hits the cable away and kills the generator. The lights extinguish, so the puzzled divers abort. I lie on the chaland's floor as Jeff speeds to *Calypso.*

There's nothing the doctor can do. He's again over his head. I feel like a bird, stunned after flying into a window. Eventually I shake it off, and another dive begins.

It's astonishing that we don't have more accidents. We disregard safety, both above and below the sea.

The water is wonderfully calm and clear. The sun is severe with the air temperature a hot 95°F (35°C).

Lunch is suddenly interrupted. Another dive that's underway has an emergency and is aborting. The recently repaired underwater lamp has malfunctioned and the underwater cable tender has been shocked. Also the diver handling the lights ran out of air. I wonder if the two electrical matters are somehow related. It seems obvious that they are.

The disruptions prevented us from accomplishing what we intended today, so we'll try to get more footage tonight. But of course we must first have an excellent dinner, fresh grouper, no less.

As night falls, to make up time, we organize an unusually large dive team. Since the sea is kicking up, we'll dive very close to the ship.

While climbing down the heavy stern dive ladder, a large wave lifts the ladder and crashes it into Lev. It's a hard hit, but Lev continues into the water and swims toward those of us already in the water and positioned port side of the bow.

Whether viewed from above or from within, the night dives are always a spectacular sight. Lights illuminate the water, creating radiant shades of green, bright aqua, and blue. It's lightest at the surface and darker with increased depth.

After successfully completing the dive, Jerry flies Lev to Belize for x-rays. We load the Zodiacs and chaland and I take the helm, heading *Calypso* back to Turneffe for a night in sheltered, calmer water. En route we see the lights of two oil platforms. I shudder to think what an oil spill would do to this pristine environment.

As we arrive at Turneffe, the helicopter returns, approaches, and lands. Lev is aboard. Fortunately the x-rays were negative and Lev is fine.

We have an all-hands meeting in the wardroom to discuss today's accidents. There's confusion as to what is causing the electrical problems and what needs to be done to prevent it from happening again.

A telex arrives, following up on the previous one, indicating that Mom isn't well. I'll need to leave for home at the next port.

It's after midnight and I'm trying to kill my last hour of 2300–0100 watch. I'd like to read, but I'm out of books. Xerox and I talk about college. He only had one term before being drafted. He learned about radios under fire, literally, in the jungles of Vietnam.

We're anchored on the sheltered west side of Turneffe. As morning breaks there's a calm easterly breeze. Today is a badly needed rest day. Well, sort of. We attend to the wear and tear from recent around-the-clock diving. I clean the aquarium, the dive gear, and cameras. Afterward it's playtime. We take the non-divers on a recreational dive off the side of the ship. The water is amazing with fifty meters of visibility.

Later Bernard and I jump in a Zodiac. Joe, Michel, and Falco grab one too. We're supposedly scouting for more grouper. I don't know how we are supposed to find grouper from above, particularly at full speed. We actually end up going all of the way back to the huts, about ten miles, before turning around and heading back to *Calypso*.

Madame and Captain Cousteau are off for a sunset sail in their mini-Zodiac.

I eat at the first sitting of dinner so that I can take the helm during second sitting. Tonight we'll leave Turneffe's calm water and sail back to the exposed anchorage near the grouper and the huts. More diving is planned for tomorrow.

At times I'm disillusioned about Captain Cousteau. Most of his ideas are good, but some seem kooky. I can't believe that a grouper has been left on the deck all day to dry. It was neither cleaned for eating nor released. The notion was to simulate what the fishermen do, hanging, drying, and salting the fish. If we wanted to attempt that we should have cleaned and hung the fish, not left the entire carcass boiling in the sun.

It's after midnight and I'm on watch until 0200. We're still at Turneffe. The earlier plan to return to Glory Cay and the huts was postponed. The sky is clear and seas are calm. We're at anchor, so I'm having my usual peanut butter and jelly midnight snack while reading a magazine.

As the sun rises the engines rumble to life, and it's anchors away. We head for Glory. It's a smooth sail with brilliant sun and a ten-knot easterly breeze. Upon arrival the sea calms to long, comfortable eight-foot swells. There's a three-knot southwesterly current and the water is slightly dirty with just twenty meters of visibility.

We believe that these grouper started arriving here in December and continued *grouping* throughout January. Now in

February, upon the first new moon, they'll mate and then suddenly disappear.

Grouper are of the sea bass family. There are more than four hundred species of sea bass. JYC says that as long as they have food and are not preyed upon, some grouper can grow to be thousands of pounds.

An astonishing characteristic is that all groupers are born female and later change their sex to become male.

Although most fish reproduce by having females release eggs into the sea and males fertilize the drifting eggs, grouper are different. It's believed that female groupers carry their fertilized eggs and take them farther south to deeper water, where they're then deposited.

Brothers Bernard and Patrick dive and return. Bernard claims that the females are releasing eggs and the males are fertilizing them, contradicting the above-mentioned grouper spawning behavior.

We're using a high-powered Nikon microscope to take a closer look at some collected eggs and fish scales. The scales have rings like a tree, indicating the fish's age.

With Bernard's news, we add more dives to the schedule. I join Joe and Louis on the next dive.

Fishermen continue to visit *Calypso*, trading grouper for cigarettes. They usually give us three or four ten- to twenty-pound fish for a carton of cigarettes.

It's estimated that four thousand grouper will be caught here, all with crude fishing rods or drop lines.

Some fishermen have already caught their fill and left for market. This is clear by looking at the huts and seeing the front canvas door tied shut, leaving it abandoned until they return next year. Others, with larger boats to fill, may extend their stay to fish for arriving rockfish, also known as striped bass. Other fishermen may move on to Glover Reef for larger grouper, said to weigh hundreds of pounds each. How they manage to lift the larger fish into these small boats is beyond me.

Bernard drives the Zodiac one hundred meters off the ship's bow to the ledge of the shelf. He and I then descend to a depth of 160 feet. We're off the side of the shelf in bottomless dark water that's thousands of feet deep.

We swim toward a massive rock and coral wall and ascend vertically to a plateau at one hundred feet. We continue swimming underwater back toward *Calypso* and are amazed to approach a magical stage where hundreds of dancing grouper rub one another. It's a psychedelic light show, a flash dance of fish instantly transforming from solid brown, to black with red stripes, to orange.

Amidst the splendor, exhausted females randomly drift like feathers until settling onto the white sand blanket. Weary males back their way into higher coral outcroppings. Once rested, the ladies, white as snow, arise for more, as the males swim out for another dance.

Those grouper that are not engaged are off-stage just meters away, eating voraciously, which explains the success of the fishermen. After dining, these grouper settle on the bottom, below the virtual dance floor, with their mouths wide open, inviting smaller fish and shrimp to oblige them by picking isopods and other parasites off their skin and gills. It's all a precious, delicate cycle of life.

As Bernard and I pause on the bottom, we look up at an eerie sight: dozens of dangling fishing lines and then suddenly a startling, unnaturally rapid rise of a hooked grouper being hauled to the surface.

We accidentally spook a larger grouper with a live moray eel hanging from his mouth. He spits it out and the stunned eel wriggles away. Other less fortunate grouper swim by, unable to spit out hooks and broken lines still embedded in their mouths.

Like most bony fish, grouper are equipped with a swim bladder, which helps them stabilize their body at various depths; kind of like the buoyancy compensator that I previously referred to. When a grouper is caught and hurriedly pulled to the surface, a faster ascent than nature intended, their bladder fills with air too quickly. The bloated belly resembles an inflated balloon. The fishermen mercifully puncture the bladder as they unhook the fish.

A couple dozen sharks have joined us. They aren't feeding, yet, so instead of becoming their lunch, we ascend to eat our own.

The rather intense afternoon progresses with continued hourly dives. I work the underwater lights and then join another dive using Joe's strobe to take underwater still photographs.

At times it feels that there are too many people aboard. There's certainly a division among us, with the technicians, photographers, and soundman having it pretty easy, while the crew and divers do yeoman's work.

It's fresh grouper for dinner. I attend a late second sitting.

JYC, Falco, Bernard, Patrick, Louis, and I descend the stern ladder at midnight. Using even more powerful lights, we illuminate sixty feet of spectacular clear green aqua water and capture great footage, including the team's dramatic descent. For me it's a thrilling balance of the beauty of the mysterious nocturnal world and the exhilarating fear of not knowing what's out there, just beyond the light.

Approaching the bottom, we're amazed to discover hundreds of grouper piled on top of each other, some as many as a dozen high. Bernard, JYC, and I carefully stroke a few as they sleep. Most don't move, but a few do awake, darting away with a single strong flip of the tail, which produces a loud snapping noise.

A short nap after winding down from the midnight dive and up again at 0500. Groggy, but the rising warm sun feels perfect against the cool northwest breeze.

The day brings alternating sun and overcast skies, later shifting to light air from the northeast. The four-foot swells are smooth and comfortable, while the water visibility continues to be amazing.

Grouper are still here, so we continue our hourly dives, still seeking to film them spawning. Most of the fishermen have left. Those that remain tell us that the grouper have left or will leave in order to spawn elsewhere. JYC thinks they are wrong and that the grouper will spawn here.

I believe the *wisdom of the fisherman.*

Coincidentally, as predicted by the fishermen, our dives now reveal queues of migrating lobsters. The fishermen told us that when the groupers leave, the lobsters arrive, triggered of course by a north wind and a new moon. Such natural phenomena will likely continue so long as man does not interfere or destroy.

I prepare the aquarium by cleaning the glass, installing the pump, and adding fresh sand and coral. It's ready for the planned catch of two new grouper.

Jeff and I board the chaland and follow what should be this locations' last dive. It's going to be a deep dive. We normally make the deeper dives closer to *Calypso,* just in case of an accident, but we're now two hundred meters away from the ship. Jeff steers as I tend the lights.

The dive is uneventful. When done, I retrieve the lights, coil the heavy cable on the chaland's floor, and throw weighted lines over the port side for the divers to grab. Then we slowly tow them back to the ship. They're still at depth, yet to decompress.

As we near *Calypso* the divers let go and move to the decompression line hung from *Calypso*'s stern. It's a heavy, rigid cable with a weight at the bottom. There they'll hang at designated depths for calculated periods of time. Decompression varies depending on the depth and duration of the dive. Deeper dives require more time. Since air usually runs low, we always have extra air tanks readily available to lower to the divers.

I try to sleep before my 0330 watch but am summoned to fix the damn aquarium. It's really difficult—add water and start the siphon. Anybody could have done it, but tonight is a circus and I'm a part of the first act.

Ladies and gentlemen, presenting, in ring number two, Falco, who will attempt a death-defying feat. He will put four grouper into a very small aquarium. Watch Falco as he frantically races around, standing upon a small slippery stool and falling onto the deck with two fish in his arms. Yes, he is now up and has put the grouper into the aquarium. Let's give Falco a big round of applause. What's this, the water is too high and the tank is overflowing?

The circus ends, well, at least tonight's performance.

Now the time is close enough to my watch that it's easier to not go to sleep, so I just stay up.

The sky above is clear but the horizon over Belize is thick with lightning. The shifting winds and nearby coral shelf makes for a hectic, worrisome watch, constantly checking our position, ensuring we're holding anchor. At 0500 I'm finished. With no sleep, I dive and man the lights.

We again collect eggs from a female grouper and return to the ship. Sperm is then collected from the two males in the aquarium. The eggs and the sperm are combined in a sterile basin, making for a crude fertilization attempt. Subsequently, strangely, the two seemingly confused yet aroused males playfully court one another. The more aggressive larger male has his mouth wide open as he nudges the smaller one. The larger one turns white and rolls onto his belly as his color changes to brown and then to orange.

Morning is overcast with a gentle westerly breeze and choppy northeast four-foot swells. Good fortune smiled upon us here at Glory, as in just twelve days we've shot thirty thousand feet of film. It should yield an excellent product. All that remains are a few final inserts yet to be shot in Belize City.

We've also made good progress on the reef film. More interesting reef footage is anticipated from Alcaran Reef.

Another dive is planned for this morning and then we're off.

Lev, Falco, Bernard, Ivan, and I dive, retrieving two female groupers that are now sitting in a basin on the ship's deck. I'm again disillusioned by their treatment. I've been asked to concoct an anesthetic drug to be used on them and to build a tent over the aquarium, for added shade during filming.

Suddenly there's excitement, as somehow Jeff has fallen out of a fast-moving Zodiac. He's alone and fortunately the motor was turned, so the boat is going around and around in circles instead of dashing off in a straight line. He's fine, clinging to a line and pulling himself aboard.

Parviz, JYC, and Louis are staging another phytoplankton collection.

"Phytoplankton," derived from the Greek words *phyto* (plant) and *plankton* (made to wander or drift), are single-celled plants that live in both salt and fresh water and use photosynthesis to turn sunlight into energy. This process consumes carbon dioxide and produces oxygen.

After they finish, we depart the grouper hole and the huts forever. We'll anchor at Turneffe for thc night.

It's a particularly clear evening. A soothing sun sets over the western mainland's mountains.

After a big shrimp dinner, I'm on watch 2100–2300.

I'm sad to soon be leaving *Calypso,* but it's logical to leave from Belize. I sense I'll return, so I'm not worried. Again I've learned many new things about people, the ocean, life, and myself.

I'll be leaving this unique ship and the ocean environment to re-enter the rat race. I dread the cars, classes, exams, people, television, and news. I miss many things about home, but at times life seems so worthless. Fortunately at other times life is so great.

I would like to leave school for a year and experience more adventures while I have the chance. I want my life work to be related to protecting the environment because I enjoy the simple, natural beauties of the earth.

It's just after midnight and I'm diving with Joe and Lev, lighting zooplankton off the stern's starboard side. Like phytoplankton, zooplankton are also key components of marine ecosystems. Together they are essentially the foundation of the marine food chain. Zooplankton are tiny animals, some of which remain plankton their entire lives while others are temporary larval forms of urchins, crustaceans, fish, and other creatures. It's thought that many zooplankton spend the day in deep, dark water out of sight from predators, but that they surface at night to feed on phytoplankton.

Joe films while Lev takes still shots. For some reason most everyone else is crammed inside the radio room at the microscope, shouting "microscope!" We guess that they want us to retrieve samples for them to view under the microscope. But as millions of plankton swarm to the light, somehow dozens get inside Joe's wet suit, biting him, literally eating him alive. Lev and I help Joe from the water. He's lying on the deck in great pain. The doctor attends to hundreds of bites. The French get a big kick out of this, laughing and laughing. I fail to see the humor.

The sun rises and another day passes. Despite a strong easterly breeze chopping up the sea, the currents have improved visibility to thirty meters. We leave for Glover Reef around 1500, arriving at 1800. The first anchorage isn't interesting, so we move north.

I dive at dusk and light a tremendous reef, abundant with tropical fish, gorgons, and sea fans, as Bernard rides away on a sea turtle. It was a shallow enough dive that we can still safely immediately dive again, so Ivan and I deposit the motion cameras and lights and grab still cameras. Lev and Davso join us to also shoot stills.

Untethered to the lights, we can roam farther and find even more fantastic coral and fish. There are interesting surge channels, swaths of sand running parallel to rows of coral.

We rendezvous with Lev and Davso. I know that I can't look at Davso or I'll laugh and flood my mask. He's funny enough above water, always making goofy faces. Sure enough, he taps my air tank from behind. I turn and see his funny face jammed in the mask. I laugh, flood slightly, and look away to clear my mask.

I learn that Bernard will also be leaving *Calypso* at the same time as me. He'll travel to join another smaller team on Cousteau's sailboat, the *Serenade.* She's a sixty-two-foot double-ended "N" class sloop built in 1938 by Wilmington Boatworks Company of Wilmington, California, for the famous violinist Jascha Heifetz, who kept her in Newport Beach. Russian-born Heifetz moved to Beverly Hills, California, in the 1940s and became great friends with Humphrey Bogart, who learned to sail on the *Serenade.*

We stage another dive with Bernard collecting plankton. He's treading water, unsuccessfully trying to cast a net. You really need to be standing on a platform or dry ground to be able to throw the net.

We complete the filming at Glover, and to my surprise, we're returning to the huts to release the grouper. I guess that means never say *forever,* at least not on *Calypso.*

It's just a brief stop at the huts.

We witness another spectacular sunset.

I'm sad to say that one of the captured grouper died. Before releasing the others, we tag them for the Oceanographic Museum of Monaco. But for some reason we capture two more. Now we're off to Belize. I pack, shoot some final stills, and have a wonderful dinner.

I'm still sitting at the wardroom table, writing, as we arrive at the port of Belize City. Captain Cousteau and the crew walk into the wardroom, and JYC presents me with a *Calypso* pin, a hand-carved wooden shark, and a traditional Cousteau red skullcap. I'm moved by their thoughtfulness. I've had a great time and these gifts will bring me happy memories for the rest of my life.

Figure 23 - Receiving gifts, with Madame

It's later now and still extremely hot, so I'm sleeping on deck. If there's an available flight tomorrow, I'll leave for home. Mom is in the hospital. I pray that everything goes well, and I'm glad I'll be home soon to help.

I just had a nice conversation with Madame. It was funny because we talked about girls.

The morning of February 10 arrives, and Bernard and I leave *Calypso.* He's en route to Los Angeles, where Philippe will provide further instructions on how to join *Serenade.* I'm bound for New York's JFK and then home to Connecticut.

This wonderful experience aboard *Calypso* has come to an end. I'll remember all of it.

"A dead ship is the house of tremendous life...the mixture of life and death is mysterious, even religious; a sense of peace and mood that you feel on entering a cathedral."

Jacques-Yves Cousteau

VII
THE *MONITOR* TO MARTINIQUE

<u>THE CREW OF *CALYPSO*</u>

COMMANDANT
Jacques-Yves Cousteau

NURSE
Simone Cousteau

CAPTAIN
Alain Tranouil

CHIEF MISSION
Jacques Constans

CHIEF DIVERS

Raymond Coll

Philippe Cousteau

Bernard Delemotte

Michel Deloire

Albert Falco

DIVERS

Bruno Capello

Jacques Delcoutere

Patrick Delemotte

Richard Hyman

Dominique Sumian

Joe Thompson

Marc Zonza

SPECIAL GUEST

Luis Nunez Verde

FIRST MATE & SECOND CAPTAIN

Paul Zuena

MATE

Pierre Cariou

DECKHANDS

Christian Tomasi

Nono

STEWARDS

Raymond Amaddio

Maurice Herve

Joseph Zeline

ELECTRICIANS
Jean Desoeuvres
Rémy Galliano
Michel Treboz

MECHANICS
Nöel Aubry
Jean-Marie France, Chief
Gilbert Jourdan
Jean-Paul Martin

PILOT
Ken McDaniel

DOCTORS
François Avice
Michel Gau

CHEFS
Philippe LeConte
Jean-Pierre Herve

SCIENTISTS
Ron Page Ayres
Victor Galdo

June 2–August 8, 1979 – Norfolk, Virginia

I rendezvous with some Cousteau Society staff in Fairfield, Connecticut, and we leave for New York's LaGuardia Airport to fly to Norfolk, Virginia.

We're met in Norfolk by dignitaries and taken to the Omni Hotel. They're courting us with VIP treatment, trying to attract The Society's move here from New York City.

Today we take a bus tour of the city and then the harbor with lunch served aboard the *Pride of Norfolk.* Then we visit the shipbuilding school. In the evening we attend a fun cookout in Virginia Beach.

The next day, at 0900, under the guidance of the seventy-seven-year-old river pilot R.B. Holland, *Calypso* arrives at Norfolk's National Oceanic and Atmospheric Administration (NOAA)[n] pier off Brambleton Avenue.

Calypso was recently in Monaco for extensive repairs, including replacement of her electrical system, renovation of the radio room, and installation of new telecommunications equipment. She left Monaco April 21, with stops in Gibraltar to receive the helicopter, and the Canary Islands for supplies, arriving yesterday at Fort Monroe in Hampton, Va.

We greet *Calypso,* along with Mayor Vincent Thomas, members of the city administration, naval officers, a smiling Miss Hospitality, and television reporters, as a forty-member U.S. Navy band plays John Denver's *Calypso,* now a hit.

Captain Cousteau wears his trademark double-breasted leisure suit and turtleneck while speaking to several hundred spectators and a national television crew about world oceanic and environmental policy.

Following the festivities we go to work. I help Ken McDaniel, the new helicopter pilot, unpack and install the blades.

---

n NOAA is a federal agency formed in 1970 by the consolidation of three scientific agencies, the U.S. Coast and Geodetic Survey, the Weather Bureau, and the Bureau of Commercial Fisheries.

A large spool of cable being hoisted aboard falls from the crane into the river. The accident allows the enthusiastic crowd an unusual treat—to see a Cousteau diver suit up and dive. Marc Zonza successfully descends and reattaches the spool, which is then retrieved by the crane.

When our work is done we retreat to John Sears' beach house for another fun barbecue. John is president of Home Federal Savings & Loan Association of Norfolk and very involved in numerous Norfolk civic organizations that are interested in seeing The Society relocate here.

It's the next morning now and raining. I'm a diver on this expedition so I'm back up top in the four-man divers' cabin. My cabin mate Raymond was just fired. I don't know why. There are still two other Raymonds aboard, Amaddio and Coll.

We're now completing another press conference and then driving to the 3,400-acre naval station, which berths close to one hundred ships, including aircraft carriers, cruisers, destroyers, and submarines.

Naval Station Norfolk is the world's largest naval station, supporting naval forces in the Atlantic Ocean, Mediterranean Sea, and the Indian Ocean. The facility is about eighteen nautical miles west of the entrance to the Chesapeake Bay from the Atlantic Ocean, located at the mouth of the port of Hampton Roads, a peninsula known as Sewell's Point.

The U.S. Navy hosts a luncheon aboard the nuclear-powered USS *Nimitz* aircraft carrier.[30] We tour the enormous ship that is more than three football fields in length (1,092 feet). The width is 252 feet and the height is over eighteen stories. We're told it's the most efficient carrier in the Atlantic Fleet. I ask what its top speed is, and the answer is "that's classified information." Although hard to believe, rumor has it that it's greater than fifty knots, more than fifty-seven miles per hour.

Built locally at the Newport News Shipbuilding and Dry Dock Company, the *Nimitz* was commissioned in May 1975 at Pier 12 of the naval station. First deployed in July 1976, she returned to Norfolk in February 1977, subsequently redeployed to the Mediterranean and returned here again last July.

Following lunch we head to the Norfolk-based *Monitor* Research and Recovery Foundation. We hope to sail *Calypso* from Norfolk to the wreck of the Civil War's USS *Monitor*, located off the coast of Cape Hatteras, North Carolina. It's one of only two marine sanctuaries in the United States,[31] so we first need permission from John Newton. He is the former marine superintendent of Duke University's Marine Laboratory and now leads the foundation.

In 1972 Congress passed the Marine Protection, Research and Sanctuaries Act, which established the National Marine Sanctuary Program, later renamed the National Marine Sanctuaries Act. The primary objective of the act is to protect marine resources, such as coral reefs, sunken historical vessels, and unique habitats. In 1974, North Carolina Governor James E. Holshouser Jr. nominated the *Monitor* for sanctuary status. In 1975, President Gerald Ford approved the *Monitor*'s designation as the first national marine sanctuary.

We tour the offices and review an excellent scale model of the ironclad warship. John presents us with bright yellow USS *Monitor* Rescue Team T-shirts and tells us great news: he's successfully obtained permission for us to dive on the wreck. He also plans to be aboard when we sail to search for it.

We return to *Calypso*. It is still raining. There seems to be no order on the ship; people are coming and going as they like.

It is quiet aboard, and there's no work to do, so I leave to meet my girlfriend Kathy, who's just arrived at the Omni.

In the evening we attend a dinner reception at Chrysler Hall and a speech by Captain Cousteau at the Scope Convention Center.

AN EVENING HONORING
CAPTAIN JACQUES COUSTEAU

CHRYSLER HALL — *Monday June 4, 1979*
Cocktails 6:30 p.m. — *Dinner 7:00 p.m.*
NORFOLK SCOPE — *Movie 8:30 p.m.*

The Mediterranean: Cradle or Coffin
Speech by Captain Cousteau — Ocean Policy
Cost per person for the evening $12.50

I support Norfolk's effort by submitting my application for membership in The Cousteau Society.

Name(s)

Street *City* *Telephone Number*
Please bill me $15 for annual dues.

Figure 24 - Invitation to JYC's speech. Note the affordable price. JYC wanted to reach as many people as possible. It was not about making money.

Six thousand people attend JYC's powerful speech. He proposes the Ten Commandments of the Sea, declaring that since the United Nations' recent, eighth, Law of the Sea Conference failed again to draft a comprehensive plan governing the use of natural resources taken from the sea—or any other measures to protect the sea such as a Law of the Sea resolution—we must establish international zones of responsibility to protect the oceans from man.

Ten Commandments of the Sea

1. A request that the president and the Congress of the United States update the landmark Marine Sciences Act of 1966.
2. Sensitive development of publicly owned oil and gas on the sea adjacent to the coast, and better coordination with energy policy.
3. Continued vigilance in the management and the monitoring of the coastal zone.
4. A higher national priority to improve marine traffic safety.

5. A new national policy to maintain and enhance productivity of domestic fisheries.
6. Accelerated research on maritime sources of energy and on techniques of conservation.
7. Improved administration of federally sponsored research, engineering, and education.
8. Studies of the possibly adverse long-term impacts of an international treaty dealing with use of the oceans.
9. Taking a vigorous leadership role in international forums to advocate global principles for all nations to follow in their domestic policies.
10. Developing agreements to reduce threats to world order by studying the role of the oceans in national security and reducing maritime deployment of nuclear weapons.

JYC calls upon the United States government to establish new policies to reverse the rapid deterioration of life in the ocean, stating that humanity will become more dependent on marine resources in the future as a source of food, minerals and energy, a transport mechanism for global trade, a stimulus to employment, a source of recreation, and a political and economic factor for peaceful relations. He reminds us that more than one hundred nations have coastlines that touch the sea, yet there is no U.S. or global plan or agreement.

In the morning, the Cousteau Society staff leaves to tour nearby Williamsburg. I stay aboard preparing for *Calypso*'s departure. Later in the afternoon I go shopping with Kathy. We have lunch at Alexander's and dinner by the pool. She leaves early tomorrow morning.

The next day I spend most of my time helping Ken put the pontoons on the helicopter. I remember how to do this from working with Bob on *Felix* in Canada.

All sorts of repairs are underway, and supplies constantly arrive: a dozen crates of scientific equipment, ten-dozen crates of vegetables, bread, and fruit. We form a sort of human conveyor belt, passing crates from the pier to the ship, through the doors then hatches, and down the stairs, into the bowels of *Calypso.*

The meat is hung and shelved in the walk-in refrigerated meat locker while vegetables and fruit are stacked in a walk-in cool room. Frozen goods go in the walk-in freezer. Dry goods such as potatoes, pasta, and boxed items are put in a dry hold.

I feel accepted by the crew, which helps relieve my anxiety. I was worried someone would be upset about me leaving the ship yesterday. It's too bad that I was so worried about it.

After an amusing dinner, we walk just outside the pier's security gate, where there's a relatively flat, sandy area. We play *petanque* (pronounced pay-tonk). It's like horseshoes but played with balls, similar to bocce. Originating in Provence, France, in the early 1900s, the game's objective is to toss or roll a number of steel balls as close as possible to a small wooden aim ball, called the *but* or *cochonnet* ("piglet" in French). There is no official court, so it can be played on any surface. It's a lot of fun, but Paul has a fit because I play better than he does.

I've now been in Norfolk a week. Jean-Paul, a mechanic, has moved out of my cabin to a cabin below because arriving today, to join me in this small divers' cabin, are three divers, Bruno, Patrick, and Marc. I've claimed the top right bunk, the one with a window.

The cabin's two bunks run fore to aft, with the head fore. For storage we each get a one-foot-square cubby in the wall between the bunks and a small drawer below the bottom bunks. With less than three square feet of floor space, it will be difficult for more than one of us to stand at a time.

This cabin and Captain Tranouil's cabin next door are the only cabins on the ship's second level. They're both located aft of the radio room, just a few feet ahead of the helicopter pad, smokestack, and decompression chamber. Captain Alain Tranouil replaces Captain Alibert for this expedition.

One level down, fore of the wardroom, is Captain Cousteau and Madame's cabin. On the same level but farther forward port-side are the two chief divers' cabins for Falco and Bernard. The crew shares cabins yet another level below and still farther forward. That's where I bunked last expedition.

Now I'm helping Maurice Herve, the new steward. He shows me where Madame hides the *Calypso* T-shirts. She has 250 T–shirts, but only a few members of the crew have received one. I think everybody should get a few. Maurice asks Madame to give me one and she does.

It's very hot, so I treat myself to a cold shower before the second sitting of lunch. Then Madame joins me to get our yellow fever shots.

Yellow fever is a tropical disease found in Africa and South America. It's spread to humans by the bite of an infected female mosquito, which injects the virus that causes jaundice, a yellowing of the skin and the whites of the eyes. Most infections are mild, but severe cases can lead to shock and kidney or liver failure and be life threatening.

Bernard arrives, and it's great to see him again. I'm already taking photos of him prepping the submarine, as well as Ken working on the helicopter.

Captain Tranouil bought a sailboard for windsurfing and the owner of the shop just stopped by to give the captain a bottle of wine and a T-shirt. The T-shirt is too large, so the captain gives it to me. He's nice, and we already have a good rapport. He does, however, seem to be stressed out from the recent Atlantic crossing. And we haven't even started the expedition yet.

The next afternoon is hectic, with many chores, including the loading of two hundred more cases of food and a most precious cargo, 150 cases of California red wine. Wine is served daily at lunch and dinner. At least a dozen gallon-sized bottles are consumed per day.

A few cases of Pernod are loaded as well. On Sundays, Pernod is put on the table as a treat. It's a yellowish, licorice-flavored liqueur that's usually mixed with water, which turns it milky white. It's very popular in France and on *Calypso.* Dr. Cazin's 1886 treatise on medicinal plants said of Pernod, "In moderate amounts, it excites the stomach, sharpens the appetite, facilitates digestion, and accelerates the circulatory and secretive functions."[32] To me, it sounds like some elixir you'd buy off a wagon train.

We're making good progress on all the required preparations and repairs and plan to sail tomorrow night.

As predicted, with four in the cabin it's very crowded, but bearable, I think. There certainly is no choice.

Captain Cousteau announces that he's giving a bonus to the crew that just made the Atlantic crossing. He also tells me I will be paid for this expedition. That's a nice surprise.

Even here in port I've already lost a sense for time. The days seem to run together, only separated by the different types of mostly redundant chores.

A blue van arrives from the Willoughby Bay Marina along with Johnson Outboard Motor Corporation executives who are delivering a dozen new motors. They ask me to take some publicity photographs and I gladly oblige.

We seem to have an interesting crew. I see some potential conflicts, but nothing beyond the normal human interaction in the *Calypso* microcosm. The only other American aboard this expedition will be Ken McDaniel, the helicopter pilot. Ken is enthusiastic, but he may be overboard. I now know that the glamour does wear off…real fast. He seems to be well accepted, which is important, but I'm wondering about down the road. Yesterday he left the ship without informing Paul or Falco. They were upset, but how was he supposed to know? There is little to no order on the ship.

Captain Cousteau and Dr. Harold E. "Doc" Edgerton just arrived from New York. Doc is on The Cousteau Society's council of advisors and will be joining us for the first part of the expedition, the filming of the USS *Monitor.*

Doc's association with Cousteau began in 1953. Since then Doc has been on many expeditions, experimenting with numerous devices to enhance underwater photography, including a device attached to a submerged camera that sends sound waves off the ocean floor, indicating how close the camera is to the bottom. He's also experimented with side-scan sonar, an acoustic device used to locate objects lying on the ocean floor.[o] We plan to use side-scan to locate the deep wreck of the *Monitor.*

Among Edgerton's inventions is the stroboscope, more commonly referred to as the strobe light, for use in both ultra-high-speed and still, or stop-motion, photography, thus his nickname on *Calypso* of "Papa Flash."

Some of the famous images he's captured are the splash of a milk drop into a red liquid, a shattering light bulb, the ascent of a Russian pole vaulter, the wings of a hovering hummingbird, and a bullet in flight, e.g. through an apple, a jack of diamonds playing card, and the smoke from a candle. The U.S. military even had him capture the nighttime detonation of an atomic bomb at an exposure at 1/100,000,000th of a second.[33]

He earned his master and doctorate degrees from the Massachusetts Institute of Technology (MIT), where he is professor emeritus of electronics.

Before leaving Norfolk I quickly return to the *Monitor* Research and Recovery Foundation to see the videotape of the wreck, which shows the 172-foot, 980-ton warship resting upside down 230 feet deep in what's known as the Graveyard of the Atlantic.[34]

The *Monitor,* the Union's first ironclad warship, was built by Continental Iron Works and Delamater Iron Works, in just 147 days, in a shipyard in the Greenwich Point section of Brooklyn,

o Acronym for underwater echo-ranging equipment, "Sound Navigation Ranging"

New York. This was in rapid response to the Confederacy's CSS *Merrimack,* a traditional warship that had been sunk then raised and covered with iron and renamed the USS *Virginia.*

The two ships met on March 9, 1862, in their only battle, at Hampton Roads, Virginia. Neither was sunk. They continued maneuvers in the area until May of that year, when the Union troops blocked the 275-foot *Virginia* from escaping down the river to the sea. Unable to retreat farther up the James River toward Richmond because of the ship's twenty-two-foot draft, on May 11 the Confederate crew abandoned ship and blew up the *Virginia* to prevent the enemy Union soldiers from capturing it.

The *Monitor* met its own dim fate on December 31 that same year. While the big side-wheeler USS *Rhode Island* towed the *Monitor* southward from Hampton Roads to Beaufort, North Carolina, a gale sank the *Monitor* sixteen miles off Cape Hatteras.[35] Sixteen members of the crew perished.[36]

It's evening, and now that JYC's aboard, we're ready to set sail. I'm ashore at the pay phone making a last minute call to Kathy. *Calypso* is being untied and I have to sprint to barely make it back aboard.

Within two hours we're outside the harbor's protected waters, into a stiff breeze and sixteen-foot Atlantic seas. To be out here, miles from land on the kicking sea, is the wildest feeling I've ever experienced.

As *Calypso* divers are also navigators, part of my job is to take the helm, which I do, 2000–2200. It's been a while since I steered *Calypso,* but I quickly regain technique and do well. What a thrill!

I'm on watch again, early morning at 0600, and the sea is calm, like glass. A dozen porpoises have been with us for more than twenty miles, gracefully gliding along, actually being pushed by the bow wave and only occasionally adjusting their course or balance.

Mile after mile, hundreds of flying fish pop from the sea's surface and scuttle through the air. Dozens of them pepper the bow and amidships—meaning in or toward the middle of *Calypso.*

It's a great day and so nice to see the ship and crew alive, together anticipating new adventure.

Figure 25 - JYC, representative from Monitor Research and Recovery Foundation, Philippe, Dr. Edgerton

We arrive in the vicinity of where the wreck is supposed to be. Radar and satellite positioning helped us get this close, but now it's up to the side-scan sonar to help us find the precise location.

This sanctuary is defined as a column of water above the wreck, extending one mile in diameter. By keeping it unmarked, deterioration from diving, fishing, and anchors is prevented. More importantly, if found by pirates or salvage divers, they'd loot the warship's china and silver.

Lieutenant Commander Floyd Childress, NOAA's associate director of Operations and Enforcement, is aboard to supervise, ensuring that we don't disturb the sanctuary or take anything. Because of his red hair and square personality we've sarcastically nicknamed him *Pink Floyd.* He's a straight military type who's pushy and too serious for this wacky crew. Floyd won't be diving, so his enforcement literally only scratches the surface.

It was in 1973 when, after scouring ninety-six miles of ocean floor with side-scan sonar, cameras, and other equipment, Newton, Edgerton, and others aboard Duke University's 118-foot steel oceanographic research vessel *Eastward* first discovered the *Monitor.*

We hang the four-foot yellow torpedo-like device, the "fish," over the port side, attached via a long, waterproof electrical harness to a plotter in the radio room.

Figure 26 - The "fish" being lowered off the port side

I brought my own trusty 35mm Nikon camera and have also been provided a suitcase of cameras, including a Contax, Olympus, and Nikon. Also in the case is a selection of Zeiss lenses, a strobe, and a motor drive.

I am having some problems with the batteries of both the motor drive and the automatic aperture. I've disassembled and cleaned the cameras, which hasn't helped. Prior to departure I anticipated such a problem and did try to buy spare batteries. It was, however, impossible to find this type of battery, but I did place an order and they will be waiting for us at the next port. I'll re-clean the cameras and continue to use the motor drive for as long as possible.

The "fish" continues to bounce signals off the ocean floor while the plotter interprets the data into a crude display of hills, valleys, and boulders. John Newton thinks we're beginning to see the outline of the wreck.

We've anchored three bright orange temporary marker buoys to triangulate our position and narrow down the search. For security purposes, the buoys cannot be left unattended for more than a night or two.

The area is in a shipping lane, meaning a general area where there's merchant ship traffic, so to avoid the risk of *Calypso* being run over by a large freighter or tanker, we plan to relocate *Calypso* each night but leave the buoys in place. When we depart for good, we'll retrieve them.

The sea is calm with comfortable rolling swells. It's a beautiful day, other than the worrisome abundance of black smoke coming from the smoke stack. I'm told that we've been loaded with the wrong fuel.

The helicopter, located just aft of the stack, is normally bright yellow, but it is already covered in black soot.

The smoke complicates filming. There's been talk of returning to Norfolk to fix the problem, but it's decided we'll try to carry out the *Monitor* mission and then head to San Juan, Puerto Rico, for repairs. I was hoping they'd say Miami. Realistically I know we won't even make it that far.

By late afternoon we're still running a course, trying to find the wreck, crisscrossing back and forth, triangulating and mapping a grid. This is a slow, logical process, which would be impossible without the side-scan.

I finish another half-hour shift at the wheel. We continue to slowly troll the "fish" back and forth. I'm on every hour on the half hour until we find it.

Raymond, the cabin mate who was fired in port, left a half case of Heineken beer. Until now I thought I'd better not touch it, but since nobody's claimed it, I'm adopting it as my own.

It's the beginning of a new week, June 11 at 0400. We're at anchor. I'm on watch 0300–0500. The peace and quiet is nice, but I'm too sleepy to serve time.

At 0800 we resume the sonar sweeps. I stay at the helm all morning, continuing to sail and plot the grid. It's exciting as Captain Tranouil and Captain Cousteau rapidly fire new headings at me to steer. Papa Flash is in the adjacent radio room interpreting images on the plotter. The bridge is crowded as others surround us, helping with tedious navigational computations.

Captain Cousteau gives me ten bearings within three minutes. I stay dead on the mark, but the "fish" snags a marker buoy's line. Fortunately it isn't hurt, so we catch and release, recalculate the heading, and restart the pass. I'm embarrassed, but it wasn't my doing. I precisely followed orders.

Amazingly, after more than a full day's searching, on the next pass the new mark reveals the *Monitor.* But somehow we lose the wreck and scramble to re-drop the just-retrieved "fish." Luckily we find it again and re-drop more marker buoys.

As we prepare the diving saucer for a reconnaissance dive, the weather suddenly turns nasty. The wind is now near gale force and the rain is sideways. We abort and tie the submarine to the stern deck.

I'm shocked as, despite worsening conditions, Falco and Marc make the treacherous dive to secure a buoy line to the wreck. Note that the maximum depth on compressed air is said to be

66.2 meters (~217 feet). Upon return, they report she's sixty-seven meters deep with a manageable one half-knot current and fairly good fifty-foot water visibility.

The wind turns out of the north and worsens to a strong gale of forty-five knots. It occurs to me that a storm like this took down the *Monitor.*

The sea has got to be twenty-five feet, and there's torrential rain. We struggle to get the Zodiacs and chaland aboard before retreating. *Calypso* battles the dueling physics of gravity's downward force and buoyancy's upward force. We desperately yet unsuccessfully try to avoid putting the ship in the dangerous position of being parallel to the waves. *Calypso* rolls from side to side, to the point that the top of the radio tower nearly touches the sea. If the center of gravity shifts much farther we will capsize.

Figure 27 - Retrieving the buoys before we retreat

We never had a safety drill of any type. Nobody ever told me where the life rafts or life vests are, so I rush to find them, just in case.

Captain Tranouil is at the helm, his vision limited to a rapidly spinning, circular, dinner plate-size piece of hardened glass in the center of the bridge's windshield. First produced in 1938 by Speich of Italy, these screens are installed in all kinds of vessels for use in bad weather conditions like now: driving rain and heavy seas that throw spray and waves against the bridge. Other than through the plate, we can see nothing.

Again we're sideways, parallel to the large waves and rolling so severely that the captain is forced to turn the bow back into the wind, directly into the waves. *Calypso* pitches like a deadly seesaw. The bow rises twenty feet into the air while the stern submerges into the ocean. Then the reverse: the bow slams into the sea and plunges underwater while the stern ascends high above us on the bridge.

Calypso moans in pain. Amidships timbers shudder and creak. She's no match for the sea's strength and threatens to snap.

We limp the thirty miles to Hatteras Point. Eventually the storm passes. Reprieved, we anchor for the night.

This part of the ocean, off the southeast Atlantic coast with apexes of Bermuda, Miami, and San Juan, is known for its extraordinary number of lost ships, boats, and even aircraft. It's the Devil's Triangle, also known as the Bermuda Triangle.

There are said to be supernatural qualities inside the triangle. Many theories attempt to explain the disappearances, but perhaps the most believable is that this is one of only two places on earth where a compass actually points to true north instead of the usual magnetic north. If a navigator does not compensate for the variation, which can be as much as twenty degrees, he can unknowingly direct his ship or aircraft into harm's way, well off the intended course.

A magnetic variation does not, however, explain the phantom storm that didn't even appear on satellite imagery. We knew where we were and navigation wasn't a factor.

The triangle is likely caused by a combination of natural characteristics: the confluence of the Gulf Stream, weather patterns, and deep ocean trenches. The Gulf Stream is a powerful, warm, and swift ocean current that begins at the tip of Florida and flows up the eastern U.S. coastline.

Human error is probably also a factor in the triangle. All I know is that I now believe in the Bermuda Triangle.

Earlier this evening Paul took a large iron hook attached to a pole and gaffed a bale that was floating off the stern. He pulled it aboard and with his ever-present ten-inch knife slashed through the plastic exterior and burlap interior. It was about fifty pounds of marijuana. We assume a smuggler being approached by the Coast Guard dumped it, or maybe the smuggler's boat or plane was the triangle's latest victim. Who knows? Pink Floyd said the street value is about $50,000. To the visible disappointment of some, Floyd confiscated the pot and took it into custody.

I have a legal stash (candy and food) that I'm enjoying but conserving.

It's now after midnight and we're anchored in calm water off Hatteras.

I hope that today will be less eventful. At dawn we'll test the sub. Then we'll return to the *Monitor* site. Some of the divers are expressing fear about the depth of the planned dive.

By mid-morning I'm taking still shots of the sub test. Then Ken and Falco leave in the helicopter to scout conditions at the dive site. It's a crisp, cool day with brilliant sunshine. The clear aquamarine seas are choppy but diveable. However, the scouting report is that the *Monitor* site is too rough and we should remain anchored here.

We've all signed a NOAA flag for presentation to JYC at dinner tonight. I'm not sure what that's all about. It must be Pink Floyd's idea.

Papa Flash shows me his microscopic photography technique. It's actually very simple. A special film that's sensitive to blue light is placed in a tray. Dynamic water is placed on the film and a hue light flashes the exposure. The film is developed by rinsing it with water, developer, and hypo, and then rinsed again with water.

The chopper makes another inspection trip and returns with better news. I tie it down as we embark on the two-hour sail back to the dive site.

It's too bad we couldn't have left earlier, because by the time we get there JYC will have departed and our first real dive will be in the dark.

As we sail to the *Monitor,* I get a stunning view from my bunk's large window. Glistening placid water and seabirds are almost within reach. They say there's less rocking in the bunks below, but I've been there and don't think it's any worse up here.

It's later now and close to midnight. The first dive was just completed and now it's my turn. We descend into darkness, except for swaths of bioluminescence created by clouds of plankton releasing energy in the form of light.

The veterans fall like rocks with no regard for clearing their ears. So many deep dives have already taken their toll. They're all half deaf.

I am having trouble equalizing my ears and lag behind. I want to keep up, but I'm in pain, desperately pinching my nostrils, attempting to blow out of them, finally clearing and descending quick enough to catch up before the lights come on to reveal my delay.

Our descent continues. As we pass sixty meters, the powerful eight-kilowatt lights bring the wreck below into view. I hover above the stern and see a massive full-scale representation of the miniature model I'd seen days ago in Norfolk.

She's upside down and partially disintegrated. A nine-foot, two-ton, four-bladed propeller lies atop the exposed hull, with the broken rudder support lying nearby. The revolving gun turret is underneath, propping up the stern's topside. We work our way forward, along the armor belt, but unfortunately, due to the extreme depth, after only twenty-five minutes we must begin our ascent and lengthy decompression.

Such deep dives expose our bodies to extreme pressure. Not unexpectedly we're hit by a narcotic-like effect that's caused by the nitrogen in the compressed air we breathe being dissolved in our blood and body tissues. Our thinking and reactions impaired, we attempt to exercise caution and avoid confusion or panic.

A careful ascent is critical, stopping at prescribed depths for defined periods, allowing the body to purge the gas. Without proper decompression, the nitrogen won't satisfactorily escape the bloodstream and organs, resulting in a painful and dangerous condition called the bends.

We cling to the decompression line; it's cold, quiet, and with lights extinguished, the surrounding darkness is forbidding.

Finally with decompression complete, we follow the line to the stern ladder, climb aboard, and debrief on the aft deck.

It was a scouting dive to assess the condition and position of the wreck, useful for planning subsequent dives.

As the mental fog lifts, we slowly recall the rather large tiger shark. Sharks are all too common and usually harmless, but a few, like the tiger, warrant our attention.

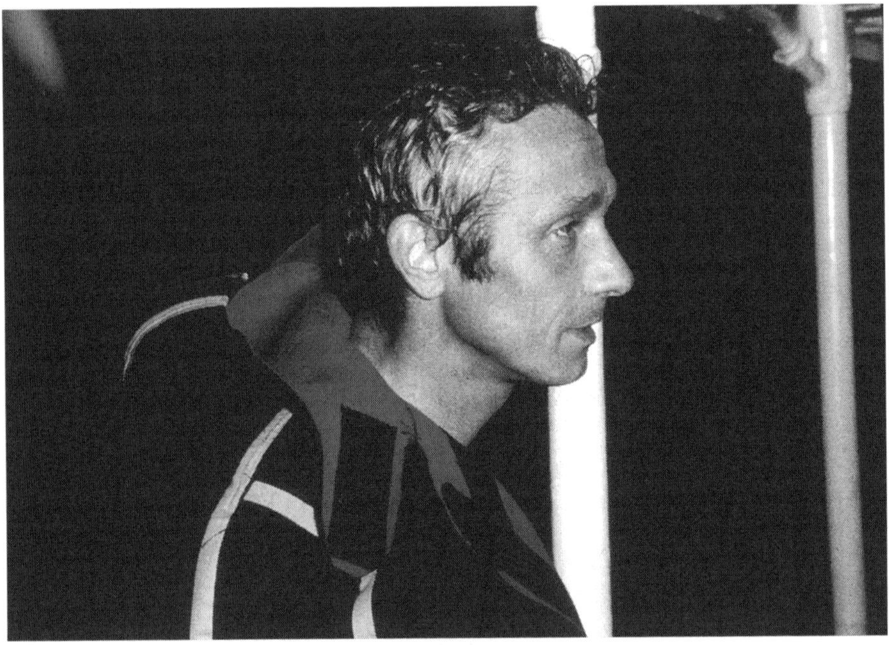

Figure 28 - Debriefing with Philippe

Between the increased three-knot Gulf Stream current and the depth, I'm wasted tired. But I go to the helm and steer for an hour, until 0200. We're underway, retreating to Hatteras, and shall return to the *Monitor* yet again tomorrow.

Pink Floyd, John Newton, and Papa Flash are all still aboard. That makes thirty-four, with only twenty-seven bunks. Patrick has been sleeping in the decompression chamber. Two people are sleeping on the cushioned benches at the dining table in the wardroom, while another is sleeping in the helicopter. I don't know where the other three are sleeping.

The next day, it's back to the wreck site. We wait for the increased current to subside, but it doesn't, so eventually we dive anyway.

This strong current should have cleared the water, improving visibility, but there's a chance that the visibility has actually deteriorated. It depends on what's upstream and the make-up of the ocean floor. We won't know until we dive.

We'll make two separate dives, with four divers each; same teams as before. I'm with Philippe on dive two.

We're the first teams to surface dive on the *Monitor.* Previous exploration was only via submarine. At sixty-seven meters, we've set a new record for depth on compressed air. Diving to this depth on compressed air is not advisable. If done at all, mixed gases are substituted for compressed air.

After completing the two dives, we're done for the day. It's too deep for anybody to safely make a second dive, so we return to anchorage off Hatteras.

It's just after midnight and I'm on watch. Even at this calmer, more sheltered spot this damn ship is really rolling and tonight's turbulent sea is irritating. The conditions at the wreck must be far worse. It's a difficult watch because with nomadic sandbars and wrecks all about I have to be vigilant about our location to ensure that we hold anchor and don't drift.

We return to the site by noon and learn of a tropical depression that's in the Bahamas and heading our way. With one of our two engines inoperable due to bad fuel, the decision is made to abort the *Monitor* mission. We can't risk riding out another storm in the Triangle, particularly as now we're on just one engine. There's no need for *Calypso* to set another diving record. We retrieve the marker buoys and retreat to Morehead City, North Carolina.

Captain Tranouil navigates as I steer. John, the American electrician, plays his guitar and sings. Gilbert and Jean-Paul, two mechanics, listen while I record the relaxed dialogue and music. First the Rolling Stones' "Angie," then the captain correctly guesses the next song is by Led Zeppelin and asks John if he knows The Beatles. John plays the Beatles' "Rocky Raccoon," which puzzles the French who ask if a raccoon is an animal.

The French sound so funny with their accents, trying to guess the names of artists and titles, loudly harmonizing and humming along. Then they make requests like "Cat Stevens, do you know Cat Stevens?" John plays "Morning Has Broken." Then the captain requests *Deliverance.* John plays "Dueling Banjos" and moves on to "Stormy Monday Blues" and "Hey Joe," while the captain asks for Chuck Berry's "Johnny B. Goode."

There's no such music aft and two decks below in the always hot and loud engine room. There the engineers keep vigil nursing the one remaining engine. Without it we're in trouble.

Considering that we're running on just one engine, we make very good time, arriving off shore of Morehead City the next morning at 1100. The seas were rough but fortunately the current, wind, and tide all worked in our favor.

In every American port, it's mandatory for visiting ships to have a pilot from the local port come aboard and escort the arrival. This is done for safety, to avoid collisions, and to provide local knowledge of tides, currents, and underwater obstructions, hopefully preventing ships from colliding or running aground. Some pilots like to take the helm and steer while others just watch the instruments and direct.

The fast-moving pilot boat pulls alongside *Calypso* and the pilot climbs aboard. He directs us to a dock at the North Carolina State

Port Authority's Port of Morehead City on the Newport River and Bogue Sound. It's a phosphate loading facility, where locally manufactured bulk fertilizer is exported to China and other countries.

Our first priority is to have *Calypso*'s fuel analyzed, and it's quickly confirmed that the fuel taken on in Norfolk is contaminated with sugar; either a sick prank or sabotage. So we'll unload and replace what fuel remains in the 847-cubic-foot tank. Then we'll wait an estimated four days for the engines to be repaired. It will take six hours to clean the carbon residue from each of the two General Motors engines' eight cylinders.

Ken and I head out to the store. I buy some cold, fresh milk. What a treat. He buys a case of cake mixes. I'm not sure why.

Due to the combined weather and engine problems, the *Monitor* expedition was essentially a failure. We didn't get nearly enough footage for even part of a television program. Some of the divers had flown from France to Norfolk specifically for the demanding *Monitor* dives. Now that we're done, they've already left for home. A few others are driving south to Florida. I'll stay on *Calypso.* I'm happy that I at least had the two dives on the *Monitor.*

Crap for lunch. Tongue! Pigs' feet for dinner last night, yuck, pork smorgasbord!

June 16 and this morning the entire crew is scrubbing the soot from the ship in the rain. It's actually great for morale as we joke around and work together. A local television camera crew arrives and they interview me for tonight's news. Unfortunately we don't have a television, so I won't be able to view it.

Captain Tranouil and I go ashore for lunch. We catch a taxi to Beaufort and visit the Maritime Museum of Beaufort[37] then eat at Clawson's on Front Street. Some of the crew shows up. We're all wearing our white crew shirts with the green *Calypso* logo, a naked sea nymph, which draws attention, particularly from the girls. The people are very nice, except for a few jealous rednecks. I'm not sure if it's prejudice against the French or because we're attracting the girls, probably both.

Beaufort is a very quiet, quaint, historic waterfront town. It strikes me as a wonderful place for a writer to live. To me the most magical aspect is the easily visible Carrot Island. Wild horses inhabit this as well as other surrounding islands. They're called the Shackleford Ponies, said to be descendants of Arabian horses that arrived here in 1739, when they swam to safety from a ship that wrecked on nearby Shackleford Banks.

The name "carrot" has nothing to do with the vegetable but rather evolved from the word "cart." The island used to be called Cart Island because fishermen used to net fish on the south side of the island and cart their catch across Taylor's Creek via a narrow man-made stone bridge constructed from the discarded ballast[p] of ships.

Perhaps my hunch about this being a great place to write is correct as in 1938, Rachel Carson, the famous environmentalist, came to Beaufort. Her visit to the U.S. Fisheries Station inspired her to write about shorebirds in *Under the Sea-Wind* (1941) and *The Edge of the Sea* (1955). She later wrote *Silent Spring* (1962), about the dangers pesticides pose to the environment.

The next morning, back at port, the doctor and I take a run, something you definitely cannot do at sea. We start out fine together, but soon he is too slow for me. I feel strong and leave him, pouring it on for seven miles. Afterward, since we're in port with access to a water supply, I even get to take a shower—hot, no less.

Lunch is eaten ashore with Captain Tranouil, Madame, Paul, and Michel Treboz, an electrician from the previous expedition, followed by shopping, not my thing and terribly boring. Madame always likes to have an entourage of men surrounding her.

Madame invites some of the crew and me to dinner at Man Chun House in Atlantic Beach. Her friends the Aquadros, who live in the area, have invited her. Dr. Aquadro is a diving physician whom I'm told was instrumental in the design of the decompression chamber. He worked with JYC on a number of other experiments

p A heavy substance placed in the draft of a ship to improve stability and control.

leading up to Conshelf III. Dr. Aquadro is also on the board of the *Monitor* Research and Recovery Foundation. Anyway, I decline the invitation, as one meal with the entourage is enough for me and I want to go back to Beaufort.

At night, back in Beaufort, I hang around Clawson's and make some new friends, Vicki and Keith Rittmaster. They're students at the Duke University Marine Laboratory that's located here. They're actually from Connecticut but live here. The lab, established in 1885 as the Johns Hopkins University Chesapeake Zoological Lab, originally operated out of the Gibbs House, located on the corner of Front Street and Live Oak Street. It was the first Atlantic Coast U.S. Marine Laboratory, later moved to Piver's Island and run cooperatively by both Duke and the U.S. Fisheries Department.

The next day I visit Vicki and Keith at their apartment on Front Street, where we change for a swim across Taylor's Creek to Carrot Island. This is an amazing adventure. We explore the shoreline's eelgrass beds, tidal mud, and sand flats, and then walk to a salt marsh where some wild horses graze among thickets aside a sand berm. We watch them for a while and then swim back to town, showering and changing at their place and spending the rest of the day together. It's my last day in Beaufort.

In the morning *Calypso* sails from Morehead, destined for Key Largo, Florida. The plan is to sail non-stop for two and a half days and arrive on Wednesday.

We have soft-shell crabs and spaghetti for dinner, a strange combination. The food this trip has been unusual. I think this chef is lazy. He makes his job as easy as possible and strangely, unlike the stereotypical French chef, he has no regard for presentation. Lunch was a crude pile of raw ground beef with raw egg yolks plopped on top. Steak tartar, they call it. I say it's a fancy dish that can make you pretty damn sick. I didn't touch it. I've been in the meat locker after heavy seas and seen the slabs of meat that have fallen off the shelves rolling around on the floor.

Ken didn't eat either and instead baked himself a cake and ate the whole thing. Something weird is going on. He's done that several nights in a row. He still has most of the case yet to go.

I stand watch early, 1700 to 1900, and am on again in the morning 0500 to 0800.

I'm in my bunk writing, my eyes heavy, struggling to stay awake. Sailing south, my starboard-side bunk looks east to the United States' Mid-Atlantic coast. The window is wide open. As the sun sets, darkness creeps in along with a comfortable enveloping breeze. Other thoughts will have to wait, *bonne nuit* (good night).

At 0830 a fire breaks out in the smokestack, just aft of our diver cabin. Smoke pours out from the door, vents, and the top and bottom. Fortunately Falco and I notice it quickly, and we empty two fire extinguishers. Then, since the helicopter pad is located just aft, we move the fifty-gallon drum of aviation fuel away onto the rear of the pad while others connect a fire hose and spray it into the stack's vents and door. As far as I can see, there's no major damage, just a big mess of yellow powder and water outside our cabin.

Captain Tranouil's comments: "Every day there has to be something. I wanted to have a quiet sunbath." I'm beginning to wonder about him.

It's almost noon now and we're some fifty miles off Charleston, South Carolina.

Next shift is 1900–2300. Since we're underway, two men stand watch together instead of one man when at anchor. With two men, one will check the radar, charts, and radios while the other steers the ship, switching duties every half hour. There's more work to do when sailing, and it's nice to have the company in the middle of the night. I enjoy working watch with Captain Tranouil, who tells me he takes only the best to stand watch with him.

For *Calypso* we're making very good time, flying at 9.5 knots, about fourteen miles per hour. Her top speed is said to be ten knots, so with both 580 horsepower engines humming at 900 RPM we can't expect any better.

Calypso's bow seemingly peacefully pierces the calm sea, but the flying fish think otherwise. Sensing she's a threat, startled, they retreat, scurrying along the glass-like surface of the ocean.

Occasional pastures of sargassum offer an astounding sweet fragrance. Then a pod of dolphins rides the bow wave.

I levitate from a balmy nap in time for the second service of *dejeuner* (lunch), wondering what delicacies we have in store today.

A week or so ago, John asked me if I would like to share my journal in exchange for his. At that time I was interested but told him I would think about it. He says he intends to write a book about this experience.

Marc, Bruno, and I finish lunch and clean our cabin. I'm glad that they're relatively clean and courteous guys.

For example, two days into the trip I found my new bottle of shampoo empty on the shower floor. I naively assumed it was an accident and didn't worry about it. Then, the other day when I went down for a shower, deckhands Christian and Nono were going through everyone's cabinets. When they grabbed the shaving cream out of my cabinet and emptied it onto the floor I got mad. They're morons.

Suddenly…one of the engines loses oil pressure and is quickly shut down. We're back to just one engine. *Calypso*'s speed has slowed to a painful four knots. The current and wind are against us, so we're literally fighting to avoid going backwards.

We're eighty miles from Savannah. Kathy lives in Atlanta, so I'd be happy to make port in Georgia. I'm sure we'll wait, though, and struggle all of the way to Florida.

Maurice, the steward, has something wrong with his foot and says that I should take over. Hell no! I hate being the catch all, having so many jobs. Everyone else has set jobs, but I do everything: photographer, diver, navigator, mate and steward.

The word is that we're almost out of water. That's not right, as we've only been underway for a day, with a reduced crew. We've discovered that two of the four aft water tanks are inoperable, somehow damaged by the same Norfolk fuel company that loaded us with sugar. This morning's fire used most of the fresh water from the other two working tanks, so we are in fact almost out of the recently loaded 1,850 gallons. There'll be no showers until we make port, now said to be Martinique, not Key Largo.

At one time *Calypso* had a distiller that produced 317 extra gallons daily, as well as two Allied Water Systems desalinization units capable of providing 900 more gallons of fresh water per day. They are not currently in operation, if even still installed. Since we're underway, we can't even cool off with a swim.

The worst thing is that some people are actually continuing to take showers, ignoring the usual rules about showering every other day for only a few minutes.

I wonder about our fuel supply. On one engine at four knots, that's at least eleven more days to Martinique. *Calypso*'s range on two engines, including her two days of reserve, is eleven days (2,640 nautical miles). In the past, for longer trips like Antarctica, Cousteau has carried additional fifty-gallon tanks on deck, but not this time. (A drum with a different type of fuel for the helicopter does exist.)

I'm standing next to Falco and John, and John throws a light bulb overboard. I tell them that it's bad to throw garbage over and that I've noticed the chef throwing bags of it over too. Falco denies it and then John throws a can over, saying we're far enough out that it's O.K. "The sea will eat it up." Perhaps this is true, but I don't like it, especially off *Calypso.* John says, "Look at all the other wrongs we do." I confront him and we go at it.

It's such a damn stupid thing to say. It's contrary to the mission and it disgusts me. I think the people serving on *Calypso* should be screened and have regard for the environment. They shouldn't be working here if they don't. The majority of the crew is guilty. It's global ignorance. You would think that of all the ships and crews, this one would be different.

It's midnight, now June 20, and I'm midway through a four-hour watch.

The mechanics have been working on the engine for ten hours and just concluded that the carbon residue from the bad fuel caused the oil pump to fail, which dropped the oil pressure and seized the engine. Since the same bad fuel shared by both engines caused the original problem, I don't understand why just one engine was cleaned in Morehead. Both engines should have been cleaned. This means another engine repair and several more days in port.

Captain Tranouil gets a fix on our location and begins figuring out the best port. The decision is between Charleston, South Carolina, and Savannah, Georgia. Savannah is of equal distance but farther south and particularly well equipped for repairs, so that's the decision.

We're limping along at 4.2 knots and with luck can be there in twelve hours. Imagine driving from Georgia to Florida at eight miles per hour. That's what we're doing.

Jean-Marie, the chief mechanic, says we can "probably" make it.

Now that all the engine chaos has died down and watch is ending, I ask Captain Tranouil for permission to take a short shower. All I want is enough to get the sweat off and slightly cool down. Normally I wouldn't ask for such a favor, but since we'll be in port today, able to take on water, I don't think it's unreasonable. Captain says yes but then Madame chimes in, saying she needs to think about it for a minute, so she thinks about it for a minute and then she says yes. (I would have taken a shower no matter what.)

Watch has ended and I'm ticked because, in the interim, Cousteau was contacted and has overruled Savannah, saying we must go to Jacksonville. He's in New York, so he doesn't even know what the hell he is deciding. As far as I know he doesn't know the condition of the engine, the weather, the information regarding the ports, or the time of travel. We're at risk of bad weather and the not so unlikely failure of the second engine.

I had a positive attitude, but it's hard to stay positive when you see all this shit. I have more to say, but since I got this much off my chest and onto paper, maybe now I can sleep…Aye, *Calypso*! Aye yi yi!

Watch 0800–1200 with Captain Tranouil. We've picked up Charleston's National Public Radio (NPR), which is playing great classical music. There is also an ongoing discussion about the Spoleto Festival and an interview with the owner of a Stradivarius violin. It's refreshing to hear the English language.

It's a gorgeous sunny morning as we creep along, hoping to get to Jacksonville tonight. Paul is taking advantage of our perfect trolling speed, using a drop line to catch two barracuda. As previously explained, we normally don't fish and instead barter with locals, but things are slow, literally.

JYC calls at noon and gives us permission to make port in Jacksonville. Even then we have to wait an hour for his call back, in case he changed his mind to direct us to another port, like Miami.

This expedition isn't going so well and I'm disillusioned. That's not a good thing because with this outfit ninety percent of the motivation is the ship, the crew, and Cousteau. When those areas weaken, motivation is vulnerable. Fortunately I'm motivated from within, going after what I believe in.

I stood watch this morning and then washed the decks. Now I'm on the foredeck with Ken. He's trying out the jump rope he bought in North Carolina, attempting to work off the weight he's gained from eating an entire cake every night!

Paul runs toward us, speaking French a million words a minute, saying we can't jump rope because it will bother the people sleeping below, and get this, we'll hurt the lights below. BS. If we had army boots on, maybe we'd wake someone, but we're in bare feet. He wasn't even below, so how does he know? If the slamming of twenty-five-foot waves didn't blow the lights, I don't think the pitter-patter of jumping rope will. Besides, we're even jumping forward of all the cabins, right above a hold and the shower. I was just down there a few minutes ago and there's no vibration from the jumping rope, just a slight tapping noise. Also, it's the middle of the afternoon and there's nobody asleep. If it were midnight I could understand, but if I pulled eight hours of watch in the last sixteen hours, I should be able to jump a little rope. Paul is very overtired. If he is always so unhappy, he should find another job.

It's too bad that we have to be inconvenienced by the ongoing repair delays but since we do, in a way I'm sort of glad to be making port again. Unfortunately this stop will likely mean the cancellation of Key Largo and/or Martinique. We need to make those films, but we must be in Venezuela by July 5 and ready to begin an oceanography study for the government.

I hate that we're missing so many days of diving in beautiful waters. I'm also somewhat familiar with the business side of all this and am sensitive about the cumulative cost of so many delays. Not only the cost of actual repairs and normal at-sea operating costs, but also the opportunity lost by not creating new films.

Land ho! As Jackie Gleason would say, "How sweet it is."

The chart indicates that we're north of Amelia Island, Florida.

I think that whenever *Calypso* makes port, whether scheduled or not, a press release should be sent. This would help promote The Cousteau Society. Instead we seem to quietly tie up to the most private dock and keep it all a big secret. As evidenced by our arrival in Norfolk, the public does enjoy the fanfare and the opportunity to see the ship. The few guests that I've brought aboard for a tour were fascinated. But even those modest tours seemed to be a bother to others aboard.

I don't think it's because of the superstition that a (visiting) woman on board a ship makes the sea angry. I think it is because Madame is shy and gets jealous of visitors, particularly females. It's her world, though. If she wants to keep it that way, I can appreciate that, particularly since I care so much for her.

The simple solution, and contradictory superstition, would be to have a naked woman on board, which is said to calm the sea. That must be the reason why ships used to have carved and painted wooden naked figureheads on their bow. Perhaps the sea nymph painted on *Calypso*'s smokestack and printed on our crew shirts is our modern-day figurehead.

We're close to land; cruising past Amelia and the ferry *Buccaneer*, which I once took going to the Tournament Players Championship professional golf tournament.

We call for a pilot, who meets us at the entrance to the Intracoastal Waterway. He pulls alongside, climbs aboard, and heads to the bridge. He wants to steer and does, nearly running us aground. There's real panic. Falco and Captain Tranouil go crazy yelling at the pilot in French. We eventually make it safely to the assigned pier, but not without considerable upset.

There's a lot of tension on board. The atmosphere is different than I remember. It's quite unpleasant with everyone on edge and bickering. Just like in the real world, all it takes are a few problem people to rock the boat.

June 22 – Bellinger's Shipyard, Jacksonville, Florida

I start the day by cleaning the shower area, sinks, adjoining hall floor, bridge, and radio room, then load the cameras for the divers who are going to drive to Key Largo. They will search for shipwrecks within the only other U.S. marine sanctuary, Key Largo National Marine Sanctuary, approved in 1975 by President Gerald Ford. I'll stay here on *Calypso* instead of going along.

Although I believe the *Monitor's* site is smaller than this, I'm told that a state park protects an area from the shore to three miles out, and the designation as a marine sanctuary extends the protection out to eight miles.

We film their departure. Then as I step back aboard, Paul has a cow because there's a plastic bag on the deck outside of my cabin door. I can't understand what he says to me either. It's impossible to understand him when he speaks so quickly. He doesn't try to slow down for me at all. I tell him that I didn't put it there and then I throw it away. What a pain in the ass.

Unfortunately this shipyard, at 13911 Atlantic Boulevard, is twelve miles from downtown Jacksonville. I call my college friends Carl and Cindy Powell, who lived in the apartment above me during school at Furman. They now live in Jacksonville, but I'm told they're away in Virginia. I was hoping to see them and am disappointed.

Captain Tranouil is very calm but unhappy. This being his first Cousteau mission, he tells me he already knows that he won't be back. He shows me photographs of his home on the historic island of Saint Moro, France, saying he wished he was there now for the summer.

As he waits for a ride downtown, he continues, telling me that whenever we're in port, everyone has him translate instructions for ordering things but that when they cruise the bars at night, they don't need his help and leave him behind.

Usually the captain of a ship is the ultimate authority and legally responsible. However, the official captain doesn't really run *Calypso*. JYC runs the ship when he's here, and when he's not, Falco is in charge. In the unlikely event that neither is aboard, Bernard takes over. Madame, of course, always has a very strong influence. Since neither Falco nor Bernard is licensed, we need a licensed captain to comply with port entry and departure requirements.

The hot day passes in this non-air-conditioned ship. For ventilation we insert long, metal, duct-like tubes into the cabin portholes to redirect any moving air into the cabin. Unfortunately after an earlier rain shower, someone pushed our cabin's single tube back through the porthole; the residual rainwater inside spilled onto my bunk and journal, which are now soaked...When it rains, it pours.

Like yesterday, Paul has me up early, so it's a good thing that I haven't been staying out late. When he wakes me, some of the guys aren't even back yet from their night out. How did I get to be in this catchall hellacious position of being Paul's helper? I guess it's because on the last expedition I was Paul's deckhand and he still thinks I am. I'm supposed to be a diver and photographer. It's much easier to be a specialist.

After lunch, the chef temporarily leaves a sack of potatoes on the portside walkway. Paul finally loses it. He literally reaches for his knife and attacks the chef. Several of us wrestle the knife-wielding Paul and restrain him. As quickly as it started, it's over, but now Paul will be going on an unscheduled vacation home to France.

Paul's an old-timer, so he'll be back. There's an unwritten rule on *Calypso* that after three months aboard you must take a break because you do go crazy. Paul snapped early this time. I saw it coming.

Things just don't seem to be getting any better. I've decided not to get uptight about it and instead try to study the incidents and laugh them off as best I can. Of course, that's easier said than done. This experience teaches me why and how mutinies occur.

News flash: we're into hurricane season and there's one heading toward Martinique, our next destination.

I'm listening to Jackson Browne, my favorite, glad another day is done and that it's close to dinner. Despite my complaining, I'm still happy to be here. I know it's a unique opportunity and I'm satisfying my appetite for adventure.

One lesson I've learned is what it feels like to be on the receiving end of prejudice. The French believe they're superior and always do their best to make me feel inferior, even in my own country.

The boatyard across the waterway is hosting us for an oyster roast tonight and it's time to head over.

What a great time at the roast. I meet a young guy who's building a wooden trimaran from scratch. He's two years into it with another year left. Once it's built, he and his girlfriend plan to sail it across the Atlantic.

Morning arrives, and although it's early, it's already uncomfortably hot and humid.

I use the nearby pay phone to make a morning call to Kathy. Afterward, walking back to the ship, I notice I'm walking on top of rusted metal filings several feet deep. The drainage runoff from this must be harmful.

I hear that there's more than just the fuel that's wrong with the engine. It's a mystery as to what other repairs might be required and how long we'll be here.

With the other divers away, I'm enjoying having the cabin to myself.

We're intentionally tied up to the dock backwards, with *Calypso*'s starboard side, including my cabin's window, alongside land, shielding Madame's portside cabin, which faces the river.

A gigantic twenty-foot propeller is outside my window, atop the field of filings. It's as big as two station wagons, for a ship many times the size of *Calypso.* I joke about it with Captain Tranouil, saying we should sneak over and put it on *Calypso* some night. He thinks it's a great idea, as this would likely sink the lower bunks into the soft mud, while our upper cabins would remain clean and dry above.

The things that these guys buy are hilarious. Tonight as we dine, there's an assortment of toys spread out on the wardroom table. A dozen little wind-up Star Wars and Disney characters are marching around. Imagine Mickey Mouse, Donald Duck, R2-D2, and Darth Vader with their sparks, sirens, whizzes, and other crazy noises weaving in between plates, baskets of French bread, and bottles of wine. It's bizarre yet amusing.

I'm feeling better about things. Maybe I was meant to read that book, *Darwin and the Beagle,* as making it on *Calypso* is akin to Darwin's survival of the fittest.

One hundred yards of telephone line slither across the shipyard's bed of filings, connecting our new telephone that rests precariously upon the portside's seven-inch-wide railing. It won't be of much use for personal conversations as it's in a high-traffic zone just outside the wardroom. Operator assistance is required for all calls too, which is expensive. So I'm still stuck having to pump silver into the distant pay phone.

It's hard to believe that it's almost July. Time flies when you're having fun.

Madame just informed me that the chef has quit because of yesterday's violent argument with Paul. Although I don't blame him, I won't miss fat Philippe and his raw meat.

Unfortunately Paul hasn't left for France yet. He's taking a few days of local leave and then flying home to Marseille. It's sad, as Paul doesn't want to go. Even now, he's still harping about how he's the only one aboard that works.

Paul does work very hard, but so do many other people. I'm amazed that after so many years of experience that he doesn't have more perspective. His behavior wouldn't be quite so bad if he wasn't enabled with so much authority and didn't subject us to his wrath. I think Paul actually had a nervous breakdown.

Pierre, a sailor, a position that reports to Paul and one rung above a deckhand, is also leaving. His departure is a surprise and I'm betting that he quit. We had previously had a long conversation and he was depressed, even before all of this happened with Paul. He just couldn't understand why I would want to come on board *Calypso*. "Why *Calypso*?" he asked. It's a good question. I suppose the "fame" is attractive, although there's little to no media exposure along the way. There is certainly adventure and an air of mystery to the entire experience.

Although most of my motivation is from within, I have to admit that some comes from wanting to please or impress others. I know that's wrong. I didn't need others to summon the courage or realize the value of the opportunity. It's obvious to me that very few people get this chance.

Pierre and the rest of us would of course be happier if we were doing what we had set out to do, traveling, exploring, diving, and filming. Being stuck in ports and shipyards beats us down. The less interesting maintenance work does play with our minds. I can handle it, as long as we get back to sea soon. I want to be back at the helm, navigating and diving.

Speaking of less interesting work, I again swab the decks and clean the shower area, sinks, and floors. I don't mind swabbing the decks, but a deckhand should clean the bathroom. I was a deckhand last expedition but have been promoted to diver. Cleaning the ship's one toilet, used by more than twenty men in rolling seas, is not a pleasant task, if you catch my drift. The term *head* is derived from its location in the 1400s at the head of the ship, so that splashing water could naturally clean the toilet area.

The ship seems very different from what I remember.

I'll wager that John the electrician is the next to go. He's raising hell in every port and neglecting his work, giving *Calypso* a bad image, always using foul language and smoking pot on board. Can you imagine if customs or the media found out about that?

Jacksonville is a real dump, at least where we are. I miss lying in bed, looking out my window at moonlit flying fish skipping on the water. Instead, now, around the clock, I see and hear fountains of welders' sparks.

It's Sunday morning so I hike to the pay phone and speak with Mom, Dad, and Janie, my little sister. It's a short but sweet call. I hate for it to end so quickly, but I'm out of change, so instead of having the operator cut me off, I end it.

Upon return to *Calypso*, en route to the galley for a cup of coffee, I pass Paul who looks like he's going to cry. Inside the galley, Madame is in heavy conversation with Pierre. Otherwise the ship is deserted and eerily silent.

We've been working non-stop maintenance the past four days, so when Captain Tranouil asks me if I'd like to windsurf with him, I tell him I'm ready for some fun and would like to give it a try. Despite the nasty shipyard water, it's great fun and I do well. He tells me he's a champion in France. He is also a good instructor.

I'm told that since there are crocodiles in the water, the way we'll work it is that while one man is on the sailboard, the others will circle him in the Zodiac. If he falls from the board, we'll swoop in, before the crocs do, and pluck him from the water.

After a while Captain Tranouil has to leave for a telephone call. Then several other guys leave and I'm left with the two deckhands; the guys who like to shower together. Christian is surfing while I drive the Zodiac. Nono is my passenger. Christian makes his second turn and mistakenly moves out of the inlet and into the current of the waterway. I ask him to come back, but he won't or can't. Now Nono wants to drive, so I let him. The punk doesn't know how to drive, though. He puts us into the current and then manages to break the outboard motor. I wrestle him to take control and then summon a passing boat for a tow. We retrieve Christian and return to *Calypso*. It was fun while it lasted.

Christian and Nono are nuts. For normal conversation they stand face to face and yell.

I'm sitting on the foredeck, totally drenched in sweat. Considering how late in the day it is, this heat and humidity is really something. The sun is getting low and now there are dozens of people windsurfing. I think the croc story was a crock.[q] It was a great motivator, though.

Many guys have gone into town, but I'm content staying aboard. Pierre asks me if I could write down the lyrics of John Denver's song, *Calypso*.

---

q Crocodiles are only found in the southern half of Florida and we are in the north. Also, crocs, like gators, are primarily freshwater animals. Although they'll occasionally venture into brackish water (water that has greater salinity than fresh water) the waterway is too close to the ocean to be considered brackish.

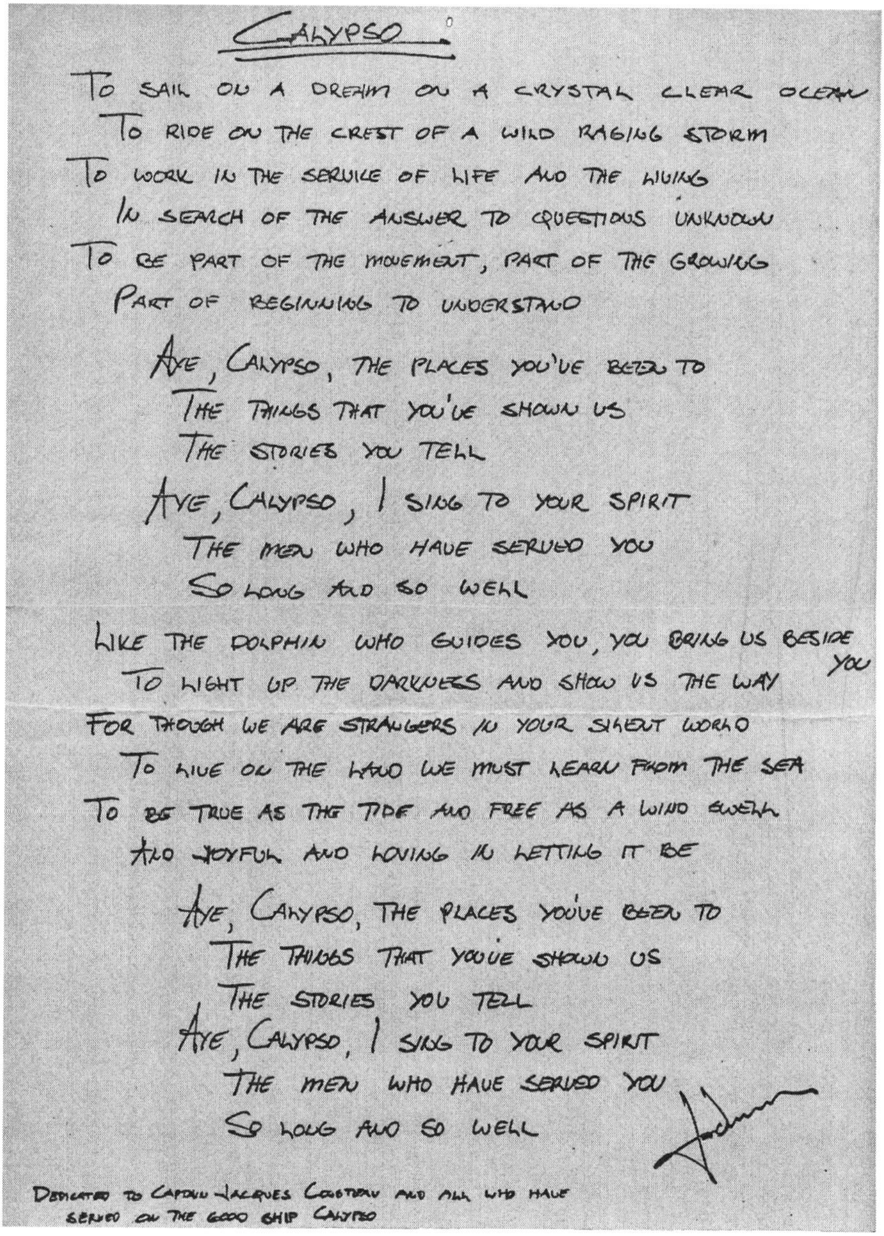

CALYPSO

TO SAIL ON A DREAM ON A CRYSTAL CLEAR OCEAN
TO RIDE ON THE CREST OF A WILD RAGING STORM
TO WORK IN THE SERVICE OF LIFE AND THE LIVING
IN SEARCH OF THE ANSWER TO QUESTIONS UNKNOWN
TO BE PART OF THE MOVEMENT, PART OF THE GROWING
PART OF BEGINNING TO UNDERSTAND

AYE, CALYPSO, THE PLACES YOU'VE BEEN TO
THE THINGS THAT YOU'VE SHOWN US
THE STORIES YOU TELL
AYE, CALYPSO, I SING TO YOUR SPIRIT
THE MEN WHO HAVE SERVED YOU
SO LONG AND SO WELL

LIKE THE DOLPHIN WHO GUIDES YOU, YOU BRING US BESIDE YOU
TO LIGHT UP THE DARKNESS AND SHOW US THE WAY
FOR THOUGH WE ARE STRANGERS IN YOUR SILENT WORLD
TO LIVE ON THE LAND WE MUST LEARN FROM THE SEA
TO BE TRUE AS THE TIDE AND FREE AS A WIND SWELL
AND JOYFUL AND LOVING IN LETTING IT BE

AYE, CALYPSO, THE PLACES YOU'VE BEEN TO
THE THINGS THAT YOU'VE SHOWN US
THE STORIES YOU TELL
AYE, CALYPSO, I SING TO YOUR SPIRIT
THE MEN WHO HAVE SERVED YOU
SO LONG AND SO WELL

DEDICATED TO CAPTAIN JACQUES COUSTEAU AND ALL WHO HAVE SERVED ON THE GOOD SHIP CALYPSO

Figure 29 - Calypso as written by John Denver

I like Pierre and I'm sorry to see him leave. In the middle of writing the lyrics for Pierre, I think about the line, "the men who have served you so long and so well." I can't help but think of Paul, so I go below to his cabin and ask him if there's anything he wants me to do or if he wants to talk. He doesn't quite understand and panics, thinking there is a problem with the ship. Then he figures out what I'm saying. At first he seems embarrassed but then appreciative, saying, "I am just quiet." I took a risk. I didn't want to offend Paul.

Like Madame, Paul is uncomfortable when he's away from the ship. So he's now foregoing the option of local leave, opting to return home to France as soon as possible.

Kathy calls the ship's phone. She's in San Diego. We have a nice talk and she sounds happy.

The divers who went to Key Largo should return tomorrow. We're looking forward to getting Falco back aboard to restore order. A good idea, but in reality he's too passive.

A local news crew approaches and interviews me while I'm painting the ship. It will air tonight.

I run a few miles just before dinner. It isn't a nice area to run. Although the heat is still stifling, it feels good to run.

Later, after dinner, Jean-Paul and I have a nice conversation. We walk to the nearby "Handy Store" where I buy a quart of milk and a few donuts. Upon return we listen to John Denver music and show each other pictures of our girlfriends, which in French they call *fiancées.*

It's a new week, June 25, and there's been little progress on the engine. The mystery continues. I wonder about this shipyard.

Paul wakes me early to paint…or am I having a nightmare. Why is he still here?

After painting I volunteer to wash the floor of the bridge and the radio room. Then I wash my cabin's floor, spray for bugs, and straighten up before Bruno and Marc return later today. Everything is spic and span.

The chef left this morning. Paul leaves in two days. I just put the call through for Paul so he could notify his wife in Marseille. *Mon pleasure!*

After lunch, I make the mistake of volunteering to help Maurice, the steward, clean up. He's temporarily taken over as chef, so I feel it's only fair to try and help him. Well, Paul comes over and says that I'll be the steward until the new chef gets here…No problem, but Paul, isn't it time for you to go to the airport?

The new chef is Maurice's brother. I figure he'll be here in two days. Well, I'm wrong; it's going to be more like ten days. That is too much for me. Thank God Madame steps in and says that everyone will take a turn. We'll see. Hard for me to take watch and do all the other chores while also being the steward. Regardless, Maurice is a real nice guy and these are special circumstances, so I want to help. Maurice is very proud of his job and appreciates the help. I know Madame appreciates it too. She tries to help me steward, but there's not enough room for both of us so I ask her to take a seat.

With so few people on the ship right now, we only have a single sitting per meal. That definitely makes it easier. Maurice bribes me, saying he will give me anything that I want to eat, tempting me with chocolate cookies and other goodies stored in a secret hold… Now we're talking, but no thank you on the steak tartar!

The usual mid-afternoon thunderstorms are passing through. Now I know to be aware of them. If the porthole in the cabin is left open, I'll have a waterbed.

The electric panel in the engine room caught fire so we have no power.

I'm beginning to think that we have a spy aboard. Sabotage, coincidentally derived from the French word *sabot,* for wooden shoe, seems to be a real possibility. I'm just kidding…sort of. It is amazing how every day there is a new problem.

A shipyard seems a totally unfit final resting place for *Calypso.* Here amid the torches, cranes, propellers, and rust.

In preparation for our survey of Venezuela's coast, we're taking this opportunity to have many new scientific instruments and apparatus installed, e.g. winches, shelves, etc. With all of this new equipment, the ship feels more crowded, even with just half of the crew currently aboard.

I work dinner without power, which isn't too bad. Except that after I have everything cleaned and put away, the four divers and Xerox return from Key Largo, and they want dinner. They didn't find any wrecks and no filming was done. Falco did find a nice field of rare black coral. It seems it was a boondoggle, but to be fair, I have learned that when dealing with nature and wrecks there are no sure things.

The power has just come back on, which is good. The entire electric panel had to be replaced.

I can't believe it. I just went to use the Xerox machine in the radio room and Michel, the radioman, locked the entire bridge. What a fool. He's so protective. He told me that JYC told him to lock it. I said JYC told me to use it whenever I want. There's politics even over a stupid copy machine. I'll be on watch later so I'll get into the radio room then and make my copies.

Not sure what's going on with Ulysses, Madame's Yorkshire terrier. He's way overdue for a bath, smells horrible, and is losing his hair. The worst is that during our meals she lets him beg for handouts and jump in our laps while we're eating.

I've served everybody dinner, so at 2100 I'm now finally sitting down to eat. Ulysses is bothering me and I feel like pushing him away, but Madame is here, thinking he's just the cutest thing. Several guys are sitting here watching, feeling the same way I do. We laugh about it behind her back. I love animals, but this thing practically makes you ill, particularly when you're trying to eat.

It's yet another day. I'm getting ready to help with lunch when I'm informed that JYC's given me a raise, up to $580 per month. I'll take it. I must be doing something right.

The problem with the engine has finally been determined: the crankshaft is off center. That has turned the inside of the engine into metal salad. Crunch! So it looks like we'll be here for a few more days. Why did it take so long to figure out?

I take a $26 personal advance from the ship's purser so while I'm out running errands for the crew I can buy myself some beer and tonic water. We're taking quinine pills for malaria and I figure the extra quinine in the tonic won't hurt.

En route back to the shipyard, the taxi's radio announces shocking news: Philippe Cousteau has been killed in a plane crash. I arrive at the ship and it's horribly strange as nobody seems to know. The news breaks, resulting in a flurry of telephone calls and an ocean of tears. It's confirmed; Philippe is dead. The PBY has crashed.

The next day, June 28, the *Florida Times-Union* newspaper reports "a seaplane piloted by Jacques Cousteau's son, Philippe, clipped a sandbank while landing Thursday, capsized and sank in the Tagus River, drowning the 37-year-old son of the noted French oceanographer ... Police in this Lisbon suburb (Alverca) said seven persons managed to escape from the 33-year-old plane, but despite rescue efforts by fishermen, Cousteau drowned at the controls."

Jean-Philippe, the co-pilot, was rescued but lost an arm and is in critical condition. Six other members of the team "were stunned by the collision" but rescued without injury.

JYC has arrived from New York and he's clearly in shock, coming aboard, saying, "We work as normal. We now go to Martinique, then Venezuela."

JYC asks me to go to the radio room and place a call to New York. I make the connection and go to his cabin to tell him. It's difficult to get anybody's attention without intruding, but Ulysses finally starts barking and that does it. Madame comes to the door in tears; this is the first time I've seen her cry. To my surprise, Jean-Michel, Philippe's older brother, is already here consoling his parents. He must have arrived last night.

It's uncomfortable to be here and I don't know how to act. I'm just following orders and carrying on.

I'm surprised when at sunset the flags are put back at the top of the mast. I ask if raising the flag so quickly, or at sunset, is a French custom, but it isn't. It's just that JYC is in denial, abbreviating our mourning, wanting everything ship-shape, including the flag. He says, "We'll go on despite the death."

The tradition of lowering the flag to half-mast likely originated on ships at sea. Technically the flag is to be flown at a distance of just one flag lower than the top of the masthead, allowing room above it for the "invisible flag of death." Nowadays the flag is usually flown lower, about halfway down the mast, symbolizing an untidy appearance due to neglect of normal duties during a time of mourning.

Now it's really as though this expedition was just not meant to be.

The PBY, known as *Calypso II* or the *Flying Calypso,* was purchased in 1979[r] by the Cousteau organization, then modified, equipped, and painted with the *Calypso* logo. It served as a self-contained mobile diving platform, enabling faster transportation and the capability of housing a nine-member amphibious team. Consolidated Vultee Aircraft Corporation manufactured the plane, a Patrol Bomber PBY-6A Catalina, originally used as a long-range bomber in World War II.

Known as flying boats, PBYs first flew in 1935 and have since served every branch of the U. S. military. Equipped with depth charges, bombs, and/or torpedoes, they could locate and attack enemy transport ships and submarines. They were also used for search and rescue and transport, as well as to escort convoys. Approximately four thousand PBYs were built. Today only a few dozen remain, one less than yesterday.

Cousteau's plane was unique as it still had its turret gun blisters and the interior had not been modified. Before Cousteau

---

r The PBY was purchased the same day that President Nixon defended his record in the Watergate case and declared "I am not a crook."

purchased it, the plane provided regular transportation between the U.S. and Costa Rica. Prior to that it served as a borate bomber,[s] and flew hundreds of forest fighting sorties.

It's now 1400 and JYC, Madame, and Jean-Michel are leaving for France. I'm supposed to drive them to the airport, but John is late returning with the rental car, so I arrange a taxi. John needs to be fired.

On July 1, a pleasant summer evening, finally, ten days after our arrival, the sleeping engines rumble back to life. We leave Bellinger's via the Intracoastal Waterway and the Saint John's River. The river is active with pleasure craft, commercial traffic, and military ships.

Captain Tranouil conducts the symphony, guiding me with headings while cranking the telegraph-like levers that transmit propulsion orders to the remote engine room below. The engineers reply by using their own levers, creating an exciting racket of bells. *Calypso*'s custom intercom system between the bridge and the engine room complements the madness. The radio chirps chatter from other ships, and the tug alongside lets out powerful groans from its awesome diesels.

The pilot and Falco supervise. We're all tense, hoping that this pilot, Bobby, won't scare us the way the other pilot did. As though he's used to such controlled chaos, Bobby suddenly interrupts, telling Captain Tranouil that he has a note written by his wife for "Mr. Cousteau." Then he says he wants to steer, so the captain replies *tres bien* (very well). Bobby says it's easier for him to steer than to give directions, to which the captain says, "But we have to be careful when we get in the big water because last time when we came we missed the turning."

Bobby asks Captain Tranouil where Captain Cousteau is now, to which he replies, Lisbon. A brief dialogue follows until Falco rudely gets it back to French, the way he likes it. Falco suggests

---

s Water was used as a fire suppressant, but because most of the water evaporated before reaching the fire, chemicals like borate were added to minimize evaporation.

a slight increase in speed, to six knots. Tranouil politely explains to Bobby that if we increase *Calypso*'s speed it allows for better steering.

Sam, on the tug, radios over, asking how far we want to be escorted. Captain Tranouil's first reaction is that the tug can leave now, but then he asks how many more minutes until we get all of the way through the channel. Bobby says twenty more minutes and the captain wisely says, "We can keep it (the tug)."

Bobby asks Captain Tranouil and Falco where they are from in France. Captain does the talking, responding Brittany and Marseille respectively. Bobby tells us he's been to Le Havre, Normandy, and La Police. Falco tries to keep Captain's attention with French dialogue, but Bobby continues in his southern American twang, "Y'all do great work, Captain. Everybody talks about this boat, everybody."

Bobby asks Captain if he liked Jacksonville and tells Captain that he has five sons and two shrimp boats. Captain thinks this is "nice, nice job because shrimps are very good." Bobby points to the little fishing village that we're passing, explaining that's where he lives. Falco is still struggling to regain control of the discussion and steer it back to French. Michel walks in and joins the melee, so now it's no contest. Michel's hyper French overwhelms the crowd and there's no longer interest in speaking English or talking to Bobby, who now suggests we can go even a little bit faster.

As we pass Naval Station Mayport, located on the south side of the river just inside the entrance jetties westward of Saint Johns Point, "Navy Mayport" and several of their vessels chime in on the radio. The tug pulls alongside; Bobby says good-bye and hops aboard.

I lower our flag, protocol for passing U.S. military ships, but the Navy ships don't reciprocate, apparently not recognizing that *Calypso* is a minesweeper nor acknowledging our American flag, which we raised since we were in an American port.

There are many such visual signs used at sea. An assortment of flags or other devices signify pilot aboard, taking on fuel, engine out, etc. In fact, after we pass the south jetty and finally re-enter the Atlantic, we need to use another sign. We've stopped with engine trouble—again. No, I am not kidding! We raise two vertically arranged black balls, signifying a vessel not under control. Black balls…no, I am not kidding!

The problem is supposedly remedied so we're finally back on our way, sailing south to Venezuela, with an intermediate stop at Martinique in the French West Indies. At least that's the plan.

The propeller shaft has started vibrating, so we've stopped—again. No, I am not kidding. Bruno, Falco, and Zonza dive underneath the ship to inspect. It's only a fouled propeller, so they clean it and we're back underway. I'm on watch, steering manually 1900 to 2300.

Although the ship isn't as orderly as when Paul was here, it's nice to not have him hassling me all of the time.

I want to shoot a portrait of Falco from a certain angle, but Nono refuses to move. He doesn't speak English, so I ask him in French to move. He says it's not necessary, so now Nono will have no-no portrait. The French men are very egotistical. Captain Tranouil told me that next time, just grab him and move him.

We finally have the autopilot working again. This Hardlandic Brown autopilot links a gyroscopic compass, hydraulic rudder mechanism, and an automatic steering wheel. We set a course for the autopilot to steer. It follows that heading, constantly responding to any deviations caused by wind, waves, or currents, automatically adjusting the wheel and thus the rudder. This makes watch much easier. However, in that our particular autopilot is unreliable, we must constantly supervise it and frequently override it with manual steering adjustments. At least it frees us from having to keep our hands on the wheel every minute of the long multi-hour watches.

I track our position, direction, and speed while monitoring the current and wind, keeping an eye out for ships heading our way. A variety of navigation instruments help, including an electric log that records the speed and course, an ultrasonic device that measures depth, and radar that surveys a forty-mile circle of the sea around us.

As predicted, John has been given notice. He'll be leaving us at the next port, Martinique. He cut his own throat when he didn't get the rental car back in time.

Only a few of us are being asked to take watches. Captain Tranouil told me he's only comfortable with having certain people handling the ship. I'm one of them. He and I generally take watch together for twelve hours per day, with five guys dividing the other twelve hours. It's very tiring working around-the-clock, but it is great experience and there's not much else to do while we're underway.

It's so nice to finally hear both engines working well. There's a comforting rumbling hum and no vibration sound. I hope the storm is over.

0500 on July 2 and we're twenty-seven miles east of Cape Canaveral. Captain and I are on watch until 0800. It's unbearably hot and humid. Neither of us could sleep ahead of watch, so now we're both struggling to keep our eyes open. We're in a shipping lane, with many larger vessels overtaking and passing us. It's bad enough to feel sleepy on watch when at anchor, but while underway we cannot afford to nod off...A massive oil tanker passes port side.

It's a long sail to Martinique, so again our fresh water is being rationed and showers prohibited. Since we're underway we can't swim, so to try and stay cool we've set up a hose that pumps water from the sea, enabling salt-water showers on the aft deck.

JYC calls to inform us that Philippe's body was found. Philippe's request was that if he should die he be buried at sea. Not cremation and sprinkling into the ocean but rather the casket off the ship. Captain Tranouil thinks that JYC will bring Philippe to *Calypso* for a ceremony at sea, but I doubt it.

Captain tells me that I've taken some of the last pictures of Philippe and that they're now famous.

I tell the captain about my grandfather, Richard L. Horne, a Commanding Officer of a U.S. Navy Warship on World War II's

Murmansk Run. They were arctic convoys that travelled a vital supply route from the United States, Canada (Halifax, Nova Scotia), the United Kingdom (Scotland), and Iceland, through the stormy Barents Sea and the White Sea, to the northern Soviet supply ports of Archangal and Murmansk. The allied ships were often within striking distance of strategically placed German air bases in Norway and German submarines, destroyers, and other threatening ships. Without the allied ships' delivery of critical munitions and food for the Russian front, the Russians may not have been able to resist the Nazi offensive.

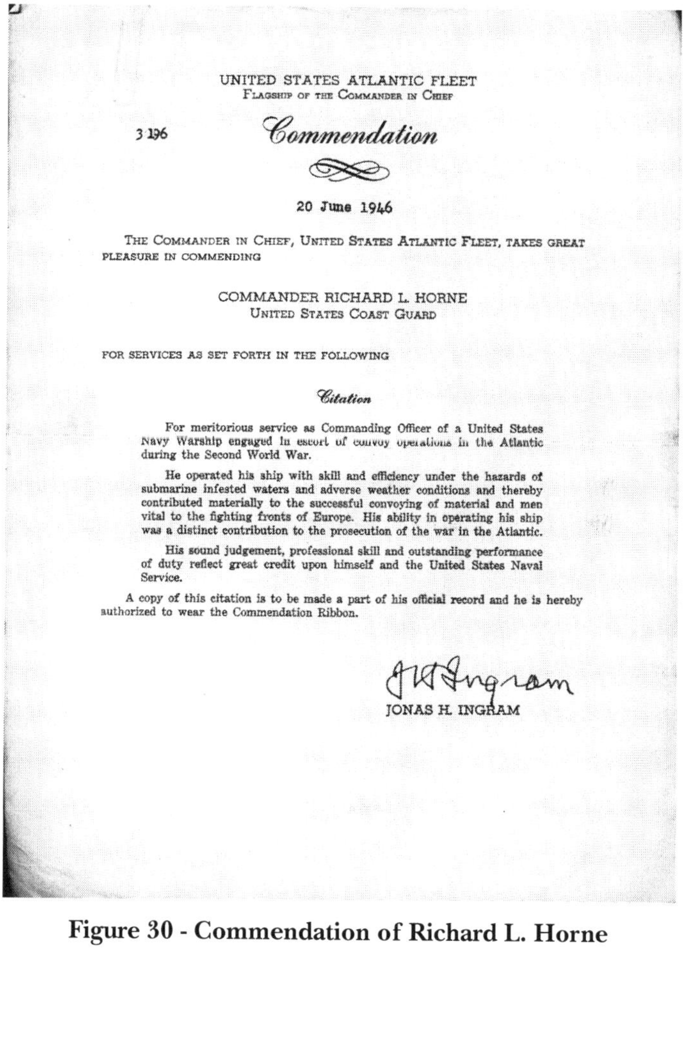

UNITED STATES ATLANTIC FLEET
FLAGSHIP OF THE COMMANDER IN CHIEF

3 196

Commendation

20 June 1946

THE COMMANDER IN CHIEF, UNITED STATES ATLANTIC FLEET, TAKES GREAT PLEASURE IN COMMENDING

COMMANDER RICHARD L. HORNE
UNITED STATES COAST GUARD

FOR SERVICES AS SET FORTH IN THE FOLLOWING

Citation

For meritorious service as Commanding Officer of a United States Navy Warship engaged in escort of convoy operations in the Atlantic during the Second World War.

He operated his ship with skill and efficiency under the hazards of submarine infested waters and adverse weather conditions and thereby contributed materially to the successful convoying of material and men vital to the fighting fronts of Europe. His ability in operating his ship was a distinct contribution to the prosecution of the war in the Atlantic.

His sound judgement, professional skill and outstanding performance of duty reflect great credit upon himself and the United States Naval Service.

A copy of this citation is to be made a part of his official record and he is hereby authorized to wear the Commendation Ribbon.

J H Ingram
JONAS H. INGRAM

Figure 30 - Commendation of Richard L. Horne

I mention that I have my grandfather's sextant, which Captain thinks "is very nice, as the sextant is the sailor's true tool." A sextant resembles a protractor but with mirrors and lenses. To use it in daylight you hold it to the eye and sight the horizon, or at night an identifiable star, usually Polaris. During the day it is always the sun. Navigation is achieved by using the inscribed scale to calculate the angle.

After a delicious lunch, I'm resting in my bunk, listening to Little Feat.

"Oh Atlanta, Oh Atlanta!
I said yeah! yeah! yeah! Atlanta, got to get back to you
Well, you can drop me off on Peachtree
I got to feel that Georgia sun
And the women there in Atlanta
They make you awfully glad you come
I said watchin' them planes
I wish I was on one
I'm sittin' here thinking 'bout my crazy dream
If I could only be there tonight

Oh Atlanta, Oh Atlanta!
I said yeah! yeah! yeah! Atlanta, got to get back to you"

Written by Bill Payne, Little Feat

Watch soon again from 1600–1900, to be followed by another in the early morning, 0200–0500.

Midday now and we're trying to not burn up in this sweltering heat. When not on watch, we sit on the foredeck listening to music and reading, making frequent trips aft to the saltwater hose. At one point we put the hose on the deck and all lie down, letting the water run over our heads. It's fantastic and reminds me of being a kid and running through a sprinkler.

Bruno and I take a detailed inventory of all the diving equipment. We want to be sure everything is in good working order for the larger dive teams planned for Martinique.

We stop again. An abandoned fishing net has fouled a prop. It is yet another sign of more and more garbage out at sea. We dive to clean the prop and move on, but now there's a clicking noise in the transmission, and it's progressively getting worse.

We're worried, and at 1700 we leave the shipping lane to move closer to shore. We're just a few miles off Palm Beach, Florida. We anchor and again dive underneath to check the condition of the drive shaft and prop. We don't find any problems, which is actually bad news, meaning that the noise must be coming from inside the engine.

It seems risky, but we're not going to stop in Florida. We're continuing on to Martinique.

We finish a pleasant dinner and have a special after-dinner drink, Martinique white rum. It's strong but delicious, enhancing the soft pastel sunset to our west over Florida.

I'd planned on being fast asleep by now, if you call seven knots fast, but the view from my bunk is captivating. There's a star-filled sky above the coastline's twinkling lights, reminding me of the comforts of home. To the east, scattered storms feature periodic lightning bolts piercing low-lying clouds. Dull rumbles of thunder follow, rolling across the sea. Above us it's clear, with jewel-laden constellations.

I would love to sail into the large Miami harbor at night and see my college friends Barb Crompton, Vicki Jackson, Peter Thompson, and Paul Wessell.

Falco and Captain Tranouil want to stop in Miami and figure out if the engine is all right, but they need permission from JYC, who's not aboard. It's crazy that there's not more delegation of authority. These guys are here and they know what's best. It doesn't make sense to head to the Caribbean on questionable engines.

I'm told that the autopilot is out again. That means when I go on watch I'll have to manually steer, 0200–0500. That's not good, as it's already difficult for me to keep my eyes open.

The ship turns even closer to shore. We're less than two miles out.

I'm back in the cabin. Bruno says Christian, the stupid deckhand, is down in the galley pitching a fit, saying he does all the work. What is it with this attitude? I hate to see the tensions rising again.

There's much more to say tonight, but I need to sleep.

I awake for the early 0200–0500 watch, then another from 1200–1600, and yet another 2300–0200.

The day has passed and as we finish the first service of dinner, only eighteen miles east of Cuba, once again the "*Calypso* Rectangle" strikes. A loud grinding noise sounds as though the putrid port engine's transmission has just eaten itself.

Maurice, the former steward who's now the interim chef, instantly realizes that our speed will halve—and that means good fishing. He finishes cooking and runs to the stern to cast a drop line and troll. He loves fishing, which has become an all too frequent recreation. The last time he fished, he caught three barracuda and three tuna. Christian, the angry one, tells us that Maurice has developed a Pavlovian[t] instinct for grinding motors. That's the first funny thing I've ever heard from Christian, and it's true.

We've made an about face and reversed course for a sixteen-hour return trip to Miami. That is, if we make it. We considered making port in Cuba but decided against it.

The bloodhounds are sniffing the bridge, looking for the source of a burning odor. They narrow it down to "just the radar," not too important when sailing past commie Cuba and ten thousand reefs

t Ivan Pavlov was a Russian physiologist and Nobel laureate. In the late 1890s he noticed that dogs salivated before food was delivered to them. He carried out experiments by manipulating stimuli before the presentation of food and established laws that he called "conditional reflexes." Today the phrase "Pavlov's dog" is used to describe someone who reacts to a situation rather than using critical thinking.

during hurricane season. The dogs say it's still operable, "just overheated." No worries.

Raymond gives me another interesting lesson on the maintenance, cleaning, loading, and unloading of the underwater motion picture cameras. He's leaving the ship in Miami, so I'll add camera maintenance to my list of chores.

I'm lying in my bunk with my head on the pillow by the window. Bruno walks up to my window from outside and tells me the ship is sinking. For some odd reason it's actually very funny. I guess nothing would surprise us now. Of course he was just joking, but we both have a great laugh.

Just starting 2300 watch and happy to have a friend in the captain. We're talking about how it's important to be able to understand situations and communicate. This came up because earlier Michel was mad about one of his gadgets. The incident reminded me of a story in the book I'm reading, *Zen and the Art of Motorcycle Maintenance.*

We're listening to Jim Hall's *Concierto* on my cassette player, discussing where the music would best be heard: near a fireplace, port wine in hand, dog at your feet, softly falling snow outside. Then Captain plays three classical tapes and quizzes me. Thanks to my Furman music class and cellist girlfriend, I'm able to name the pieces and composers.

Ken is down in the galley eating another cake. Every night he makes a cake and eats the entire thing by himself. It must be a nerves thing. As I suspected, his initial joy about being at sea was too much and short-lived. He's gained at least thirty pounds and there's still a half case of cake mixes remaining.

To sell or to sail, that is the question. Whether it is nobler in the mind of JYC to install sails or sell this tired slug of a "mind sleeper."

I feel guilty laughing, but you have to laugh. "If you're too busy to laugh, you're too busy." (I can't remember who said that, but it's true.) Besides, at this point almost everyone else is laughing too.

Ken and I have our own theory about the problems with the engine, transmission, radar, autopilot, stove, water, AC power, etc.

It's the COCKROACHES! Seriously, it's phase four, like when the lobsters invaded *Saturday Night Live.* These critters have organized themselves and are on the offensive. It is cockroach sabotage. (We haven't been able to figure out how they put all the sugar in the fuel, though.)

The roaches are about an inch and a half long. They're reddish brown with a yellowish margin behind their heads. I see them at night, before, during or after watch, when I like to get a snack. We don't have many sweets on board, so the best I can usually come up with is a peanut butter and jelly sandwich. At snack time, I enter the galley from the port side and open the Formica cabinet drawer on the left, where the French bread is stored. Inside, on the fold-down cutting board, are whole loaves as well as leftover slices of bread. Every time I open the cupboard, dozens of cockroaches that are crawling on top of and in between the bread rapidly scurry away.

Watch is over. It was good. The ship is quiet and the sea is calm.

We arrive at the head of Miami's harbor channel at 0930 on July 4. The sky is solid blue but for a few puffy abstract clouds. The pilot comes aboard and directs me through the harbor traffic and visible swirling currents, all of the way to the dock, which is particularly tricky on just one engine.

Our flags are again at half-mast as Philippe is to be buried today. A Portuguese Navy corvette with a hundred-man crew is sailing three hours with Philippe's corpse to his ocean burial site, some twenty miles southwest of Trafaria. A simple religious ceremony will precede a naval honor guard coming to attention while his lead casket, draped with French and Portuguese flags, will be coaxed off the ship to rest 6,500 feet below. I'm told that the sea there is calm and the sun is bright.

Jan is there, pregnant with Philippe's second child, along with JYC, Madame, and Jean-Michel.

It's night now and I'm going ashore to meet my friend and Furman swimming teammate, Peter Thompson. Pete drives me to

Barb Crompton's home, where her parents are having a family Fourth of July party. Barb was on Furman's women's swim team and she and Pete are dating.

It is fun to spend the American holiday with them. The traditional cookout is a welcome change. After dinner we all go see fireworks. Then Barb and Pete take me back to *Calypso* and I give them a tour.

After they leave I walk to the pier's front gate. As I approach the night watchman, I notice he's asleep. I help myself to his flashlight, borrowing it to see the dial pad on the pay phone, and call Kathy to let her know I'm in Miami. After the call, instead of waking him, I just set the light on the table next to him. He's an older guy. It seems sad that at his age he has to work a night shift. You can't sleep on *Calypso*'s watch. I wonder how he gets away with it. Well, at least it's nice to know we have tight security.

There's a kitten in the guard's booth. It's scared of me so at first I try to gain its trust, but then decide it's best to let it remain fearful of man.

Much of the crew is going to Disney World tomorrow. It's about a four-hour drive, so I'm going to skip it.

On this Fourth of July I'm grateful for our independence, although I wonder how independent we really are. The country's dependence on oil threatens our lifestyle and will continue to do so until we develop alternate sources of energy.

It's morning now. I'm deliberating about renting my own car, but I don't really have the time or the money. I drive a few of us in the ship's rental car to a doctor's office. We're required to have some additional medical forms completed and I need to determine my blood type.

Then I take Maurice to Miami International Airport to pick up his brother Jean-Pierre, the new chef. The airport television monitor says his plane arrived at Gate B-4. As we wait, I use the pay phone to call Mom and Kath. It's nice to hear friendly voices.

Meanwhile the plane comes to a different gate and we apparently miss Jean-Pierre. Maurice is very angry with me. I tell him that just because I'm an American, I can't make everything perfect.

We assume that Jean-Pierre took a taxi to the ship so we head back. Upon arrival back at the ship, there's no sign of him. I bet he wasn't even on the plane. So whose fault is that?

The next three hours are spent in the darkroom, working on cameras with Raymond. We practice loading and unloading film, which has to be done by feel in the dark. Then we work on the waterproof housings, which are custom designed and built by Davso.

Our laundry is back. That's good because the Jacksonville cleaner did a disgusting job. Although Miami's cleaner didn't do much better. I sent my only two pairs of long pants, and this cleaner burned them both. Fortunately they sent along two new pairs as replacement.

I'm off via taxi to my good friend Vicki Jackson's home for dinner. Afterward I try walking back to the ship but soon realize it's too far and that I'm suddenly in a bad neighborhood. I flag down a taxi. He gets lost but keeps the meter running. Soon the fare exceeds my funds so I try to barter the ride for a midnight tour of *Calypso.* The driver gladly accepts.

It's still very hot and humid. The few of us aboard can't sleep.

In the morning I make another trip to Miami International to pick up Jean-Pierre. He'd missed yesterday's flight but neglected to let us know, so Maurice was out of line getting upset with me.

The buzz is that Jean-Pierre specializes in sauces. Ask me if I care. The French do get wild about their food.

We're supposed to sail today, but I doubt we will.

I take the captain to the airport. He wants to go to the rental car office and have his name added to the contract so he can drive. Why is he doing this if we're to sail today?

Upon return to the ship, Bruno asks me to take him to the passport office and Ken wants to go to a camera store. Bruno tells me that some of the guys are angry because I'm driving around so much. They don't think I'm pulling my weight. That's bullshit. I drove all day. I don't mind the driving, but I'm not playing around. In fact, the only thing I wanted to do for myself was to get a haircut, and I didn't. I was asked to drive because I was the only one willing to sign the rental contract.

The captain tells me to ignore the others, saying, "They act like children and won't even finish the cruise." I'm wondering whether Bruno made this up, so I actually ask one of the other guys. He says there's no truth to it.

I now learn that the upset is because there's supposedly a packet of mail at the airport. The crew justifiably wants their mail. The captain never told me this or I could have picked it up when I was there with him. He says that now that he can drive the car, he'll get the mail later tonight, when he goes to the airport to meet Madame and Jean-Michel's flight. Of course the post office closes at 1700, so by the time the captain gets to the airport, it will be closed. If someone had told me about this earlier, I would have gladly picked up the mail.

The crew didn't pull off the trip to Disney, which is too bad, as that would have been good for morale.

I return Bruno and Ken to *Calypso* in time for the second sitting of dinner.

Since we're not leaving tonight, I call Pete and he is coming to pick me up for dinner.

The next morning I drop Jean-Michel at the airport and frantically rush back to *Calypso,* trying to get back before the ship leaves. After running around Miami doing errands for Madame, Falco, and the captain, I'm low on gas and can't find a gas station, so the car is on empty.

Of course after all that rushing, again, we're not leaving today. There is yet another engine problem. It seems that Bellinger's mistakenly connected an American drive shaft part to a European part. We're told this will be fixed quickly and that we'll leave tomorrow.

It's a melancholy evening abroad *Calypso.* I want to enter more in the journal, but Jean-Paul interrupts, asking me to take a walk. I like Jean-Paul. He's a very funny, upbeat guy, so I agree to join him.

We leave through our pier's guarded entrance, cross MacArthur Causeway, and take a short walk west toward downtown Miami before going right onto Fountain Street. This takes us to Palm Island, a beautiful, private man-made island in Biscayne Bay. The guard lets us on and we walk past beautifully landscaped mansions.

Upon return I trade Madame two of my warm beers for two of the cold ones in her fridge. She seems like such a lonely woman, but I guess she's had quite a nice life.

"The real cycle you're working on is a cycle called yourself."
Robert Pirsig, *Zen and the Art of Motorcycle Maintenance*

This morning, while taking another short walk, I realize that it is July 8, my twentieth birthday. I call home and give my brother Dean an order for sixteen belts for *Calypso* crew. At $15 each he should make a nice profit. It's fun to develop business for him.

Maurice and Jean-Pierre kiss each other on both cheeks every morning. It seems different, but I suppose nice for brothers.

I clean the bridge and then, since it is Sunday, our day of rest, we go windsurfing. It's wild in the harbor channel. We dodge and weave huge cruise ships full of waving tourists. It's quite different from the Jacksonville experience.

Barb's younger brother stops by. He's brought two friends, who will both be entering freshmen at Furman. I give them a good tour, which is always just as much fun for me.

Afterward I take a Zodiac and join the crew picnicking on a small island just across the channel. I'm really sad because as I tear into a piece of French bread, the post inside my top crown snaps. Years ago while playing ice hockey on Donavan's Pond, I took a wrist shot in the mouth and knocked this tooth out. Now it's out again and painful. It should be fun putting a regulator in my mouth, descending on deep dives. Of course it's Sunday, impossible to get to a dentist, and we're moments from sailing.

I'm disappointed that nobody acknowledged my birthday, but at least we are in port so I can call home. It is good to speak to Mom. I try calling Kathy but can't reach her.

We shove off at 1500. A small crowd wishes us bon voyage.

It's later now and hotter than hell tonight. My sheets feel like they're on fire. I'll be on watch 2300–0200 and again 0800–1200.

In Miami we had installed an Omega Magnavox Satellite Navigator with a video monitor. It indicates our real-time northern latitude (N), western longitude (W), Greenwich Mean Time (GMT, which is Greenwich, England; four hours later than our current eastern U.S. time zone), speed, drift, difference (the net of speed minus drift), heading, and setting.

Latitude N 23 47.26
Longitude W 79 21.24
GMT 12 37 36
Speed 11.0
Drift 0.4
Difference 10.6
Heading 144.1
Setting 336.9

For fun and practice I successfully shoot the sun with the sextant, determining the angle of the day's early sun above the horizon. My measurement closely matches the readout from the satellite.

Again, it's early morning but already extremely hot.

JYC will meet us in Martinique on July 14. We'll stay there until the twenty-fifth and then depart for Venezuela. He's bought two new engines for *Calypso,* which will be installed after the completion of the Venezuelan oceanographic research, assuming the current engines can last that long.

We sail south-southeast in the Santaren Channel of the West Indies. The chart indicates that we're south of Florida, between Clay Sal Bank to the west and Great Bahama Bank and Andros Island to the east. The Straits of Florida are to the north and Old Bahama Channel is to the southwest off northern Cuba. There's no land in sight, and we're making good time, with five more days to Martinique.

Just as my 1900 watch begins, a DC power failure again knocks out the autopilot.

I proceed to steer for two hours with yet another hour to go. The cockroaches are alive and kicking.

Bernard summons me to view the fantastic sunset, predicting we might see the coveted green spot. It's more commonly referred to as the green flash. A rare sight, lasting but a fraction of a second, occurring the moment the sun disappears over the horizon. Bernard's sixth sense is again right on. We see the green flash. If that isn't dramatic enough, at the moment the sun disappears over the horizon off the stern, the moon rises from the ocean directly off our bow.

Latitude 22 16.48 N
Longitude 77 35.35 W
GMT 01:54:41
Speed 11.0
Heading 119.1

I steer a course directly into the moon's luring reflection. It's a peaceful, beautiful evening. At least it would be if hyperactive Michel would stop running around.

Ken's left the bridge to bake another cake.

I'm up the rest of the night with a stomach bug, complete my morning watch, and then go straight to bed for the rest of the day. Raymond didn't leave *Calypso* in Miami as planned, so he takes my evening watch and the following morning's 0200–0500.

The useless doctor gives me an assortment of unlabeled medicine with no instructions. There's no way I'm taking all of it. I guess which ones to take, the dosage, and the frequency.

Bruno didn't leave in Miami either. He's now teaching me advanced diving skills and more about the scuba equipment. We've been rebuilding various types of regulators and servicing other items. Afterward he quizzes me to make sure I understand the mechanics.

Bruno's told me some wild stories about when he was a dive instructor at Martinique's Club Med. He says we'll meet some of his friends when we get there.

We enjoy a second comfortable day. The sea is like glass, but it's beginning to build. Slow-moving rollers rock us uncomfortably from side to side.

I'm still weak, shaky, and running a fever, but after sleeping the last twenty-four hours I feel considerably better. Captain Tranouil is now sick and in bed with the same thing. We've been designated "*le cart malade*" (the sick watch). Two of the mechanics are also sick. I guess in these close quarters, all it takes is one and then the whole ship becomes ill.

I join the first sitting of a rock and roll dinner. When the sea gets this rough we remove the tablecloth to expose the cribbage board-like wooden table, with hundreds of holes drilled in it. We insert four-inch wooden pegs into the holes around our plates, bowls, platters, glasses, and bottles. As the ship rolls and pitches, the pegs keep the tableware somewhat steady. The pegs can't stop the waves of wine from overflowing glasses or food from sliding off the plates. Most of us don't even feel like eating and don't dare to take a seat.

I don't know how he did it under these conditions, but Jean-Pierre made unbelievable apricot tarts. Dessert on *Calypso* is extremely rare and a real treat. To me it's more important than the rest of the meal. I'm surprised that dessert isn't prepared more often.

We're now into the trade winds and the waves are topping fifteen feet. We're pitching so much that the bow's entire false nose and underwater observation chamber lift out of the sea before slamming down with a thunderous bang. The timbers creak. She feels like she could snap.

The satellite shows two hurricanes to our north.

When the last laundry came in, I swiped an extra pair of sheets from the hold. There are plenty. With no showers and this heat, they get filthy, particularly in our cabin where, depending upon the wind, the smokestack exhaust blows in, literally turning the white sheets gray. We have to sleep on them until we're told we're allowed to make a sheet change. Today I quietly changed mine.

It's too rough to write. I'm on watch, feeling dizzy and sleepy and drifting off while underway, which is terrible. The captain is with me and I think he's also falling asleep. He won't admit it though and shouldn't.

Eventually the sea calms and we pass Haiti.

Captain Tranouil says *Calypso* is ridiculously uncomfortable. Her flat bottom lets you feel every ripple. He's captained ships one thousand feet long and two hundred feet wide where everyone gets a private bath and shower. The ships even have a swimming pool, ping-pong, and more. He says you don't even know that you are on a ship, with very little movement even when in rough seas. On the big ships you can even ride a bicycle, whereas on *Calypso* you can't jump rope. If I made this my career, I'd stick to large merchant ships, the hell with glory and fame.

Bruno rolls a cigarette. Tobacco flies all over the cabin. He says it's good because it kills the cockroaches. Actually he says it slows them down enough so that we can kill them. There's probably some truth to it, but he's still a slob.

I telex the New York office to ask if they're providing me with dental insurance. They answer no, but tell me to get the tooth fixed anyway and they'll pay for it. What a nightmare.

I don't know how deep the water is right here, but two days ago, when we were off of Cuba, it was three thousand meters deep

(1.86 miles). That's hard to believe and scary to think about. I just block it out of my mind.

Michel T, the radioman, just walked by and threw an empty paint can into the sea. That's becoming a typical scene that upsets me every time. He's a hyper guy who's great with electronics but lousy with people.

Just yesterday the sick watch was on the bridge and he was carrying on. He never talks at normal volume, he always yells. He was making a bunch of noise and smoking like crazy, which was obnoxious, considering the captain and I were sick to our stomachs and our heads were pounding.

We're traveling past Haiti and Santo Domingo. The distant mountains ascend into the clouds. Steep shoreline bluffs drop to the beach.

The electronics indicate that our ETA in Martinique is 2000 hour on *Samedi*, July14. Being that it's a French island, on the fourteenth they'll be celebrating Bastille Day, France's Independence Day. We'd hoped to arrive by noon to enjoy the festivities. The holiday honors the end of rule by kings and queens and the beginning of a new form of government. The name is derived from a French prison, the Bastille, where protestors were locked up. On this day in 1789, French citizens stormed the Bastille, freeing the prisoners and touching off the French Revolution.

We'd hoped that the trade winds would help us gain time, but instead they're hurting and setting us back. It's a daily cycle. The winds are caused by hot afternoon air rising from the islands. This creates turbulent seas. Then the islands cool overnight, allowing the wind and sea to subside. After this I will never again want to visit an amusement park or ride a roller coaster.

One of my written life goals is to dive in the wild with whales. I haven't seen any whales yet but still hope to. I've scratched from my list the dream of solo circumnavigation of the world. Realistically, sailing the globe alone is more than I want to bite off.

Latitude N 19 00.98
Longitude W 68 42.21
GMT 15:15:08
Speed 10.2
Drift 0.3
Difference 9.8
Heading 131.6
Setting 321

This voyage has proven to be quite different from the last, the length of the journey, the distance (more than a thousand nautical miles), the crew, the duties, and my age.

Listening to music on the bridge makes the time pass quickly and pleasantly. We try to shave some hours off our ETA by moving closer to shore, making for better views of the islands.

The white-speckled blue ocean leads to gold beaches laced by green palms. Pastures cover ascending foothills. Dense jungles appear in upper elevations. Cotton ball clouds hover in the light blue hue.

There's a certain peace that usually accompanies a night watch. We keep the lights off on the bridge to make it easier to see the navigation instruments and any lights of approaching vessels. The only illumination is the subtle orange of the radar screen and the vibrant green of the compass. It's too dark to read or write, so when we're not playing music or talking we meditate to the sounds of the blowing wind and the splash of *Calypso* cutting through the waves.

The daytime watches are different. The sea is usually more active and there are constant visits from the crew. Either way, night or day, spending so many hours on the bridge allows the ocean to cast its trance, causing periodic drifts into unconsciousness.

With watch completed, now it's time for the second sitting of lunch and then a nap.

I'm awakened and mad as hell. This guy Marc, who I thought was such a nice guy, is turning into a real bastard. Not only is he one of the guys who have been starting trouble, but he's got a habit of coming by and waking Bruno—and therefore me as well. I was just trying to catch up on some rest and Marc stormed into the cabin.

Marc starts playing with our fan and breaks it. That was inevitable because Bruno is always messing with it too. The fans can be distracting. Each cabin has one mounted on a wall. They're less than a foot in diameter and have soft rubber blades. When they're off, they're limp, but when turned on, the blades stand up and move the air quite effectively. The rubber blades are for safety as from time to time in close quarters, particularly in the dark of the night and in rough seas, we lose our balance and bump into them. Instead of injuring ourselves with metal blades, the rubber blades just jerk to a stop without causing any real harm.

The quotes below from Pirsig seem ironic and meaningful.

"We are not in the Dakotas yet, but the broad fields show we are getting nearer. Some of them are blue with flax blossoms moving in long waves like the surface of the ocean."

"I have a feeling none of us fully understands what four days on this prairie in July will be like."

"But to arrive after days of hard travel across the prairies would be to see them in another way, as a goal, a Promised Land."

Latitude N 17 18.77
Longitude W 66 11.89
GMT 10 49 24
Speed 8.1 Knots
Heading 113.1
R 328.0

I've discovered a couple of new data points in the satellite navigation program. Above, R 328.0 indicates the number of nautical miles remaining until arrival at our programmed next destination (Martinique).

Our ETA is now literally midnight at the conclusion of Bastille Day. I have another hour of watch and then it's back to the sack for me. I'm very tired and ready to make port.

After passing Santo Domingo last night, we entered a tropical depression and twenty-foot seas. *Calypso* has been pitching all night and although she feels like she's moving slowly, we're actually making eight knots, which is pretty good. It's amazing to think that you can fly from New York to Martinique in just a few hours but it will take us weeks.

I haven't had a shower since Tuesday. I keep postponing it until before going to bed, but by then the sea is so rough that the violent up and down pitching makes it impossible to go below in the bow for a shower. Last night I really wanted a shower, but it was just too dangerous.

For the bunks below it can be pretty hairy when she's pitching. Ken, whose bunk is down there, describes it as though he's inside the head of a prizefighter. That's a good analogy. Pow! Pow! Pow! In the divers' cabin way above, we feel her more when she's rocking and rolling side to side on her flat belly. When that happens, if we actually want to attempt to sleep, we have to use two seatbelt-like straps to secure ourselves in the bunk.

Here comes Michel, again strutting around with his loud voice. Not what I want to hear at 0700. There are some real weird crackers on this ship.

It's later now, 1600, on the bridge listening to cellist Leonard Rose. The sea is choppy and we're all getting anxious to arrive. The mood seems to be deteriorating. People are starting to get edgy and for some reason still always wondering why they are the only ones working. That gets to be a real pain in the A to listen to day after day.

I again practice my manual navigation skills, working the sextant and manually charting the course. Captain checks my measurements against the radar and satellite. I'm spot on. It's good to keep this skill up, just in case the technology fails, which obviously could happen on *Calypso.* The navigation skill is pretty easy, but it's cumulative, so if you let it lapse it's hard to get back, at least quickly when you may really need it.

At the beginning of watch Captain Tranouil tells me he's only concerned with fixing up his apartment. He tells me to keep an eye out, as he's not interested. He's sort of joking around, at least that's how I take it. He says, "Being at sea is a dog's life." I might agree, at least on *Calypso.* Speaking of dogs, Falco comes to the bridge and tells us that Ulysses almost fell overboard. Apparently a wave caught him and nearly pulled him over. Too bad! Hopefully it gave him a bit of a bath.

We can see the lights of Puerto Rico, just ten miles to the southeast.

Latitude N 16 43.19
Longitude W 64 53.64
GMT 22 33.06
R 245.3
Speed 8.9
Drift 1.1 Dif. 7.8
Heading 119.1
Setting 302.7

We plod along at a snail's pace, about fifty miles south-southeast of Saint Croix and eighty miles south of Saint Thomas. By tomorrow we'll be near Barbados, Antigua, and Guadeloupe. It is fun to be so close, but I wish we were stopping.

I can't believe that I'm navigating off a chart drawn in 1864. We have a more recent one from 1963, which is reassuring, but for some reason we're not using it. It's time to plot our position and then eat dinner. Watch later, after midnight, 0200–0500.

I promised myself that I'd get to bed by 2000 but here it is 2130. There was a birthday party for my pal Nono. I stuck around to be sociable and to have some cake. It was sort of hard to sit through a party with gifts, champagne, and photos, when they just passed up my birthday, but I'm happy for this kid.

On watch July 14 at 0255 and I see a meteorite that appears to be as big as a tennis ball. I wonder if it's a piece of Skylab but it seems too late for that.

It's Bastille Day, and I'm listening to Crosby, Stills, and Nash.

"*Wooden ships on the water, very free and easy, easy, you know the way it's supposed to be.*"

Written By David Crosby, Stephen Stills, Paul Kantner

We hear a sonic boom directly above the ship; three loud blasts. I think were being attacked (just kidding).

Just before finishing watch, the autopilot goes out once again. It's good to know the roaches are still with us. The real problem is a short circuit.

With more divers coming aboard tomorrow, the cabin will again be filled, so I've cleaned the cabin and compressed my belongings.

We're planning a ten-man dive; one of the largest Cousteau has ever made.

There are only about ninety miles to go, so we should arrive around midnight. We'll anchor offshore and pull into the dock in the morning. I have watch 2300 until 0200 and plan to be up by 0530 to shoot the helicopter's filming of our staged formal arrival at the pier.

John the electrician will be leaving in Martinique. He's the one who wanted to write a book about all this and for us to share journals. He told me today that he's only written twelve pages, but that he has it all in his head.

Latitude N 15 26.12
Longitude W 62 14.71
GMT 19 55 13
R 74.5
Speed 8.8
Drift 1.0
Difference 7.8
B 124.2
Heading 124.2
Setting 325.9

July 15, La Calypso à Saint Pierre, Martinique

We arrive at midnight and set anchor at 0100. There's an overwhelmingly beautiful fragrance of the jungle's soil. I finish watch at 0200, catch a few winks, and awake again at 0400.

As the sun rises, the church bell rings and we sail toward Saint Pierre's solitary pier. All goes well until a sudden early morning tropical storm rolls in and saturates the equipment and crew. The sun is in our faces, even while it's raining, making it challenging to film and keep the lenses dry. As we pull in to the dock, the bow hits, gouging the hull. Nothing serious, but it gives everybody a scare, including the people watching from the dock, who run in fear.

Once the warm crowd returns, the church bells resume and big bang fireworks are set off.

I'm glad I was filming and not at the wheel, but maybe I should have been. It's especially tough to maneuver *Calypso* at low speed, but I managed to smoothly put her into Miami in a current and traffic on just one engine. I'm told that eventually a bow thruster will be installed to enable better steering.

Christopher Columbus discovered Martinique in 1493, but he didn't go ashore until his return in 1502, when he named the island Martinica in honor of Saint Martin. In 1635, the French claimed the island but in 1762 the English occupied it, exchanging it for Canada a year later. In 1794, the English reinvaded and held the island until 1815, when they returned it to France.

The island is 1,100 square kilometers (425 square miles), fifty kilometers long and twenty-two kilometers wide, making it the second-largest island of the French West Indies. Its western shore is on the Caribbean while the eastern shore is on the Atlantic.[38] The closest neighboring islands are Dominica to the north and Saint Lucia to the south. The language is French and so are the cars, mostly Peugeots.

I've started recording the sounds of Saint Pierre, like this morning's Sunday church bell. It sounds beautiful ringing across the harbor. Although superstition has it that church bells heard at sea mean that someone on the ship will die. Maybe enough people have already died, both here in Saint Pierre and on *Calypso.*

Let me explain. Perhaps May 8, 1902 was an equally splendid day; at least until this hour, shortly after 0800, when nearby Montagne Pelée (Mount Pelée) erupted, causing the most devastating natural disaster in Caribbean history. Virtually the entire population of Saint Pierre, thirty thousand inhabitants, perished when burning volcanic ash moved at hurricane speed through the beautiful capital city.

Figure 31 - The eruption of Mount Pelée

It was the largest number of deaths from a volcanic eruption in the twentieth century, and strangely, it was not without warning. There was an election scheduled and the politicians had urged the citizens to stay and vote, assuring them that the previous few days of ash flurries were meaningless and that if there were an eruption, the lava would flow safely through the two ravines, sparing the town. Oddly, the lava wasn't the problem; it was the cloud of heat and ash that killed.

Those with the sense not to believe the politicians fled to nearby Dominica. From there they could see and hear the disaster. It was a while before they knew the scope, as a simultaneous earthquake had severed the undersea telegraph wire between the two islands. However, the Dominican fishermen at sea had a pretty good idea as they were closer to Martinique and could see the devastation.

It was said that everybody in Saint Pierre perished except for one, a prisoner, Ludger Sylbaris, but it came to be known there were at least two other survivors, a man named Léon Compère-Léandre—not much is known about him—and a little girl, Havivra Da Ifrile, who it is said rowed her boat into a cave when she saw the eruption begin and was found in her burned and broken boat two miles out to sea. It's likely that other residents and sailors initially survived but quickly died from burns. Thanks to the jail's thick rock walls, Sylbaris' involuntary feat allowed him to become an attraction with the Barnum & Bailey Circus and somewhat of a celebrity known as "The Man Who Lived Through Doomsday."

The volcano caused at least sixteen ships in the deep harbor to sink. Most have never been found and that's why we're here.

Saint Pierre was once known as the Paris of the Antilles. Today it is a small, primitive village of eight hundred people. They're good-looking black people, mostly descendents of slaves, who despite being rather poor are all very neat and clean, as are their homes and streets. I notice that they're particularly friendly to each other. For example when entering a shop, everyone says *bonjour* (hello) to one another.

I'm killing time before dinner. Afterward I look forward to taking a long walk by myself.

Unfortunately, despite the volcanic island's steep drop off, the depth of the water at the pier is too shallow. So we can't stay tied up to the dock. After we take on water and supplies we move *Calypso* two hundred meters off shore and anchor. It's a shame because that means we can't disembark the ship as easily and also that we must stand watch. At least since we're at anchor, we only need one person on watch, and as it doesn't always have to be a skilled sailor or diver, we can spread watch among the others.

The watch schedule is posted, and my time is set at 0400–0600 every other day. I was hoping for better hours, but at least it's only every other night, rather morning. I'll work tonight, which is fine because I'm too tired to go into port. I want to stay rested and strong for multiple daily dives. We're supposed to be here for twenty days, so I'll have plenty of time to see the town.

The captain tells me he's thinking of leaving right here. He again speaks of the merchant ships, where he could leave ship the entire time it was in port. On *Calypso* he's obliged to entertain Madame.

Ken tells me that Gilbert, the sub mechanic, said if he could find a job here, he'd also leave. Gilbert is one of the troublemakers, so I wouldn't mind seeing him go. He won't, though. I do admire the notion of staying here, as this seems like a wonderful place to get away from it all.

I'm in the photo lab for several hours, labeling, cataloguing, and storing a new case of film and also loading the cameras for our first dive this afternoon. Somebody's been snatching film, and I'm trying to do something about it. It's critical that we always have enough film on hand. I bought my own film for personal shots and the others should too.

As mentioned, we're only a couple hundred meters from shore, but as the island is the pinnacle of a mostly submerged volcanic mountain, the underwater vertical drop is steep. So even this close to shore, we'll be making dives of 65 meters (213 feet) deep.

Again, note that the maximum depth on compressed air is said to be 66.2 meters (~217 feet). The good news is that the water is tranquil, without a strong current.

I join a large team for our first dive, on the SS *Roraira:* JYC, Falco, Bernard, Bruno, Coll, Delcouterre, Sumian, and Zonza. It's great to be back in the water. We descend 182 feet and enter the 120-meter steel-hulled steamship, resting upright on a slope of volcanic ash. I quickly learn that diving on this ship will be gruesome, as among the colorful coral and fish are melted bottles and scattered human bones.

After the dive I take the cameras to the refrigerated lab to unload and clean them. It's funny that my instructor, Raymond Amadio, and I loaded two identical cameras and his camera jammed and wasn't operational, whereas mine worked fine. Raymond Coll used it to shoot sixty meters of film.

I jump in for another swim before dinner. This is the first time in a long time that we haven't been in either a dirty port, rough seas, or underway, so it's fun and refreshing to swim.

The climate is interesting if not bizarre. It seems to rain about every fifteen minutes, with the moments in between terribly hot and humid.

Dinner is delicious: steak, potatoes, salad, cheese, and fruit. It's a typical meal, but tonight it hits the spot. We so frequently have meat that we complain about not getting enough seafood, which seems odd given that we're at sea.

It's a new week, July 16, and I'm up for 0400 watch. I walk into the wardroom to get a snack and find Pierre and Jacques, who've been to the bar in port. Jacques joined us in Norfolk as the chief engineer. I think he's done a fantastic job, but he leaves this afternoon, as his "commitment has been satisfied." Jean-Marie France returns tonight, following coronary surgery. Obviously drunk, they're telling me they like me and they ask me many questions.

Pierre says something that's strange, that "Americans are all the same, and all look down the same tube." I contest, explaining that he's only met a few Americans and has a limited view. I don't even know how he can come to this conclusion because even the few Americans that he has met are actually quite diverse.

They continue with the usual arrogant stories of their region in France and how wonderful and historic it is. I don't understand why they so freely criticize Americans. Maybe they're trying to antagonize me, but I think its jealousy and ego. Anyway the talking helps pass the time of my watch in the wardroom instead of the bridge. Being on watch here, at anchor in a harbor, is nothing but a good way to keep people from sleeping. As the sun rises, I convince Pierre and Jacques to go to bed.

Then after watch, I join Ken for a sunrise flight over Saint Pierre, Mount Pelée, and then *Calypso* below in the harbor.

Figure 32 - *Calypso* with St. Pierre's church in the background

We return and Ken is in trouble. He didn't let Captain Tranouil know that I was going. I don't understand because anytime the helicopter takes off it's so noisy that everybody knows who is going. Also, I actually did let several people know I was going. Of course, now we learn of a never before heard policy. The line I got was that taking aerial pictures might interfere with other duties, and "whenever a passenger goes, the captain must be notified. He has to enter this in his log." Yeah, right, what log?

I can see the captain's point, but so many times we handle a situation satisfactorily and responsibly yet it isn't the correct procedure. Then we catch hell. The problem isn't me, or anyone else in particular, it's the fact that guidelines aren't laid out and clearly communicated. You always have to learn from a mistake. Anyway, now it is late afternoon and I've cooled off, in more ways than one.

We're again using the side-scan sonar, making slow progress trying to locate more deep wrecks in the harbor. The grid is sort of messed up, so we go back to the main marker buoy and restart plotting a matrix. We spend all afternoon sweeping the shore with the "fish" hung over the port side. Passing above what we believe to be hidden wrecks, we mark our discoveries with buoys. Four are definitely ships. Several others are good prospects, but might not actually be wrecks. We hope to find and dive upon the *Dalhia, Diamant, Gabrielle, Grappler, Tamaya, Teresa de Vigo,* and any others we can find.

I join Ken for another helo flight, this time letting the captain know ahead of time. I'd forgotten how much fun this two-man Huey is. It's so small that you feel like you're suspended in air. It's so cool to look straight down through the chopper's clear floor at the jungle below then rise above the banana plantations and rain forests to look right down into the volcano.

Later Raymond and I spend more time in the lab, cleaning all of the cameras and lenses and fitting the strobes for tomorrow.

It's too bad that Captain Tranouil has become so fatigued and irritable. He's like a different person and now we've drifted apart. Being at sea on a small ship takes an unpredictable toll. Now he's just going through the motions, getting us to the destinations and then hiding away in his cabin. When in reality, upon arrival is when the interesting things like diving and filming start to happen.

This morning the doctor, chef, and steward leave for the larger city, Fort de France. I'm supposed to join them, to go to the dentist, but the dirty laundry fills my seat in the car, which is absolutely fine with me. I'm in no hurry to see a French dentist on an island that practices voodoo. I'd rather stay here to walk around Saint Pierre and take pictures and make another dive.

I ask Captain if it's O.K. for me to take some time in Saint Pierre, and he says that I can after I wash Madame's Zodiac. We just inflated it this morning and it's still clean from when we previously stowed it. He's turned into a real bastard. I don't take it personally, as he's like this with everyone. He's become another man on the verge of a mental breakdown. This is worrisome considering he's the captain of the ship.

I do finally get to shore and explore Saint Pierre. I learn about the beautiful theatre that was destroyed and never rebuilt then visit the church and museum. There's a small, crude, open-air market in the town square, where every morning the wives of farmers sell wonderful produce. They come from local farms and plantations in the rich foothills and the mountainside above, offering tropical fruits and vegetables, including avocados, banana, cinnamon, coconut, coffee, guava, mango, papaya, pineapple, and sugarcane. The volcanic soil and the frequent tropical rains are ideal for growing. The variety of bananas is most interesting, ranging in size from extremely large to very small finger-like ones.

I discover the town's perimeter of lush vegetation, including wild hibiscus, frangipani, bougainvillea, anthuriums, poinsettias, orchids, and exotic hardwoods. Nearby tropical rainforests boast ferns as tall as trees. Many shades of green accent the cascading waterfalls, which are the village's water supply.

Ken buys an umbrella so he can walk around town without getting drenched every fifteen minutes. There's a maritime superstition that an umbrella on a ship is bad luck. Bruno says that if Captain Tranouil or Madame sees it, they'll quickly throw it overboard...Given our run of luck, I wonder if Ken bought the umbrella in Norfolk and never told us.

There are many maritime superstitions. They are universal and not French-specific. For example, saying the word "pig" or "hog" on or around a ship is bad luck. This fascinates me. I now realize that despite the abundance of meat we eat, there hasn't been a single pork product.

Bernard, Bruno, Jacques Delcouterre, and I leave in the Zodiac and slowly follow the chaland, which is looking for more wrecks by sweeping the "fish." Finally, after two hours and no success, as dusk approaches, we give up on the chaland and dive on a relatively shallow thirty-five-meter wreck we'd found yesterday, the *Gabrielle*. We explore the wreck with lights and find the anchor and again many melted bottles and human bones.

For a change we're using double hose regulators instead of the single hose type. At first it's tricky, but I like the lighter feel in my mouth. Also, the double hose releases exhaled air bubbles behind my head instead of in front, which makes it easier to film.

This water has lower salinity than the Atlantic and is therefore less buoyant. So now that I have too much weight on my belt, it's difficult for me to stay above the delicate volcanic silt that covers the wreck and the harbor floor. To be more buoyant on the next dive, I'll need to remove a kilo from my belt.

It's much later now, approaching midnight. We're anchored offshore and I'm watching the lights of the village sporadically flash on and off. It's weird how one street's lights will turn off for a second or two and then come back on, to be followed by the next street and so on.

We're close enough to shore that tropical bats visit us at night. They're particularly prevalent off the stern, where we have high-intensity work lights illuminating the deck and the surrounding water. Bats usually don't like light, but these are taking advantage of the fish being attracted to the light. Bats are important to the island's ecosystem and agriculture, helping pollinate the flowers as well as disperse the seeds of trees, shrubs, and plants.

It is lights out for me; solo watch in five hours at 0400.

During watch, the night sky gradually lightens. Then the sun rises on the sea's eastern horizon and the village brightens.

After watch I photograph the early sub launch and then head to the lab to prep more cameras.

Later in the morning it's off to Fort de France for the dreaded dentist appointment with *Docteur* Michel Bourrouët. First he takes x-rays, and then he yanks out the post, telling me afterward that it was necessary.

This is more serious than I expected.

He inserts a new post in my gum and a temporary tooth, saying the previous work was good but "not strategic," and that he's surprised, having expected better from the American dentist...I should have figured on a comment like that.

I make an appointment to return for more and then join the other guys that came along. We spend the rest of the day walking around the city, not returning to *Calypso* until dusk.

After dinner, Bruno and I take a Zodiac to shore, to the solitary bar of Saint Pierre. It's a nice clean bar and restaurant with bright white walls, floor, ceiling fans, and pastel paintings. We're the only ones in the place. Bruno and I get along real well, which has sort of taken the pain away from what has become a terribly cold Captain Tranouil. I sense that the captain is plain unhappy but wonder if it's because now that we've left the U.S. he doesn't need my help anymore with the American ways.

Bruno tells me that the plan for one of tomorrow's dives is for me to take still shots of the dive team. Normally I'm one of the working divers who are off camera, wearing a plain black wet suit or, given this warm water, no wet suit at all. On this dive, however, I'll be on camera, wearing one of the fancier one-piece suits with the familiar Cousteau logo and yellow stripe running down the side. These suits look great on camera and are a Cousteau trademark. Bruno says I'll wear Philippe's wet suit because it's the only one piece that will fit me. That will be a strange feeling, wearing Philippe's suit.

Marc, our cabin mate, joins us at the bar. He's normally rather quiet, but he isn't tonight. He's had too much rum, which the locals call punch.

Then I notice a couple of men dancing with each other. Bruno warns me not to stare as the men will think I'm putting a voodoo spell on them.

When Africans first came to the island of Martinique as slaves, they found in their faith a common thread: religious beliefs that included forms of witchcraft. They called it voodoo, originating from the West African word *vodun* meaning "spirit."

The next morning Bernard, Falco, and I dive on the rather shallow, twenty-seven-meter deep *Teresa de Vigo*. Wow! I feel that if I died right now, I'd be satisfied with my life. It's not even the best wreck, but these experiences are just so unbelievable. She's an upside down fifty-meter wooden ship, still needlessly secured by two chains extending from her bow to dual anchors embedded in the white sand. Her hull, encrusted in pink, orange, and white coral, hosts thousands of fish strolling alongside and darting in and out.

This was a preparatory dive. Unfortunately we have to clean garbage from around the wreck so it won't appear in the film. This is one reason we prefer the deeper, untouched wrecks that are too deep for others to have spoiled.

Since we're recovering an unexpected quantity of garbage, some other divers decide to suit up and film our repeated ascents. This footage might be used in this film or as stock for the future.

The sacks get so heavy that we have to drag them, disrupting the ash, destroying visibility. Somehow there are even several tires, which we also drag away.

In order to carry the weight of the garbage to the surface, I remove and drop all the weight from my belt. I make two dozen ascents, which despite the modest depth is still tricky and a bit dangerous. It would have been much safer and less exhausting if we'd stayed on the bottom and had someone above hoisting the bags, then lowering them after they were emptied.

I appreciate Bernard continuing to include me on all of his dive teams. He's a gifted teacher who quietly and patiently explains improved diving technique. Bernard's mannerisms and the way he speaks are all so calculated. It's said that he turns his tongue around seven times before he speaks. I believe it's true. He tells me I have a lot of heart.

I want to do everything perfectly, but to do so is unrealistic. I need to log more hours of practice. There's no substitute for experience. The Cousteau team has been diving for decades. Their form is perfect and seemingly effortless.

After lunch I'm so tired that I practically pass out. I grab a quick nap. Upon awakening I'm soaked from the heat and humidity.

Then Bernard and I make another dive, this time deeper on a wreck sixty meters deep.

Things are really shaping up. Everybody's spirits seem to have lifted. Maybe the variety of problems and tragedies are behind us. We're busier now, doing exciting work. This is the way it's supposed to be.

At 1700 JYC arrives from New York, with mail. For me two letters from Kathy and another from home. He also brought me a new journal and reading material. It's Christmas in July.

JYC suddenly looks old to me. No doubt due to recently burying his beloved Philippe.

The first thing he does is put on his wet suit. I join him. His energy, enthusiasm, and sincerity are unmatched.

JYC works hard, burning both ends of the candle. When I'm on watch I often see him in his stateroom writing. He works out daily, doing simple stretching and strengthening exercises. He's now stoop-shouldered but lean and strong, believing that a clean body supports a clear mind, and that fatness is inexcusable. He previously told me that he likes to leave the dinner table a little hungry.

After the dive I stand and write in the beautiful new journal that JYC brought me, set upon my top bunk. A pleasantly cool breeze passes through the cabin.

It's been without question the busiest, most productive day of the expedition. I made three of the day's six total dives.

The sub also dove today, for four hours at 150 meters. It is less restricted on time and depth, primarily only limited by fuel and oxygen supply.

Suddenly there's commotion. There is a problem. Bernard is in pain. His joints hurt and they're stiff. These are common symptoms of the bends, so when this happens, no matter how mild, we treat it promptly and seriously. He enters the decompression chamber, just five feet outside my cabin, and he'll be there for several hours.

The chamber is being pressurized, slowly, artificially returning him to depth. This will recompress the expanded gas in his body to a manageable volume and relieve his pain. Once his blood flow is restored to normal, the chamber's pressure will then be gradually reduced, eliminating residual gas from his body, just like he'd normally do during underwater decompression. Although Bernard's case is believed to be mild, if we don't properly decompress him, he runs the risk of a gas bubble passing to his brain or heart and killing him.

I was with Bernard on his most recent dive, but I have no symptoms and have not joined him in the chamber.

This is a two-man Galeazzi-type decompression chamber, so the doctor could have chosen up-front to be in the chamber with Bernard and make the simulated descent, but once the pressurization of the chamber begins it's no longer possible to enter. Another type of chamber, a twin lock chamber, has a second lock, which does allow another person to enter the chamber during pressurization.

We're amused that Bernard takes a half-gallon jug of wine into the chamber, which is of course not the protocol. We watch him through the small portholes while the doctor, who's outside with us, remotely monitors Bernard's vital signs.

We easily communicate with Bernard via an intercom, and there is a small portal to pass objects in and out, such as food and medical supplies. It's not, however, large enough for another jug or even a slender bottle.

Bernard's shoulders still hurt. Now I hear that they actually hurt prior to our dive. Apparently he'd banged into something a few days ago, so this may be a false alarm, but not necessarily so, as bruising can actually make it easier to get bent.

The decompression schedule has been extended and now Bernard won't be out until at least 0200. I'm going to try and sleep before my 0400 watch, but with the chamber and crowd just outside my cabin door it is pretty loud.

It's later now. I'm on watch and Bernard is out of the chamber. He seems to be O.K.

The next morning it's back to Bourrouët, the dentist. His office is in the same modern building as the American consulate, which puts me at ease. He makes a mold of my mouth and plays around with the giant hole in my mouth before telling me to return yet again on Wednesday.

Luis and the ship's doctor rode with me to Fort de France, so we eat lunch together and have an enjoyable conversation. Luis is related to the political leadership of Venezuela. I'm told he is second in command of the Venezuelan Navy. He's been with us since Norfolk, apparently a favor to his family. I've lost my cool with him a few times, but we're still on good terms. He's very wealthy and lazy, aboard for fun, doing absolutely no work. Every day he oils up and lays in the sun to work on his tan. Then he does his push-ups and sit-ups. He's a dapper dude who impresses the chicks in every port by strutting into town in his pressed white military uniform.

I think that Luis has been treated poorly. He says it doesn't matter to him because he knows who he is. We haven't even arrived in Venezuela or started the contracted research, and he already says the Venezuelans don't need Cousteau's ship for the oceanographic study. He'd prefer that the university receive the funds because they're actually better equipped, which is probably true.

We leave Fort de France, making the scenic drive back to Saint Pierre. After returning to *Calypso* we wind surf for hours and swim. Then there's the second sitting's dinner bell.

Since it's Saturday night, I want to call Kathy, but I can't get to shore. Calling from Saint Pierre is a real production anyway. I have to walk three kilometers to a phone at the hotel. It's difficult to get change for the pay phone, so I stand at the front desk using the main phone.

Tonight will be a spectacular midnight dive that will even include the *soucoupe,* the submarine. The sub has a set of underwater cameras, so I prepare and load them, along with our hand-held still and motion cameras.

It's time. Leading the descent are five on-camera divers carrying underwater torches. Bruno and I trail, lighting the scene for three cameramen. Two more divers hover behind us, tending the electric light cables. I hustle and successfully equalize to keep up with the team's rapid fifty-two-meter descent.

Normally there are only one or two stars on a dive, but on this one we have five. It's extremely dramatic to have a night dive with underwater torches and to see five divers wearing the black and yellow one-piece wet suits.

The dive plan even calls for Bruno and I to be filmed on camera, so I'm again wearing Philippe's wet suit, along with JYC's bright yellow one-piece air tank case. I was hoping JYC would be with us, but he had an earlier deep dive and it wouldn't be safe for him to dive again so soon. He plans to dive at 0600 with a smaller team.

The usual sequence is that the cameramen follow the actors, lighting is behind the cameramen, and the underwater cable tenders trail the lights. The cameramen only have to worry about the actors' bubbles, but the lighting men have bubbles in their faces from the actors and possibly another nearby lighting man. The cable tenders get it all, sometimes creating a whiteout in which they work mostly on feel. With so many on this dive, it's an unusually dense flood of ascending air bubbles. So visibility is tricky, and keeping everybody in the right spot at the right distance is challenging.

It's even more fun when someone kicks up volcanic sediment. The bubble-filled dark clouds of silt are disorienting. We all try to keep up with the actors without getting in the way of a camera or light or tangled in the web of cable.

I carefully follow Bernard, lighting him aside the wreck's starboard exterior. I stay with him as he moves inside the wreck. At least for as far as the length of the cable allows. Then the cameraman and I back out, continuing to shoot and light the scene as Bernard swims toward us.

Bernard then turns and glides toward Falco at the bow. We stay with him, following, thankfully with a perfect amount of cable slack. Any poor feeding of cable right now will jeopardize this otherwise perfect scene. A shortage of cable will cause a jerk or a shadow. Too much cable will get caught on the wreck, a rock, coral, or even a diver. The cable tender hovering behind me is a critical helper, keeping a few extra loops in his hand, feeding it out and reeling it in, depending upon my movement. At the same time he's also in contact with the person feeding or retrieving cable from the attached generator in the chaland above.

Eventually we've shot all of the film in the cameras. The cable tenders jerk a signal to the chaland for them to retrieve the lights. It goes dark.

This huge dive couldn't have gone any smoother. We want to continue exploring the wreck, but the lights are gone, we're low on air, and although exhilarated, we're exhausted, as we didn't touch the sea floor once during this long sixty-five-minute dive. It's time to begin our ascent and extended decompression.

A dozen of us hang on the line. Extra air tanks are lowered. It's dark and quiet. The only sound I hear is my own inhaling and exhaling and the bubbles of surrounding divers.

We finally complete the final decompression stop and swim to the surface.

It is 0200. I've got watch in two hours (0400). I'll enjoy the beer that Bruno just offered and then I'll sack out.

I'm awakened for watch. Startled, I can't believe it's already 0400.

JYC's up at 0500, so while the others are asleep we have a nice visit alone on the bridge. He says, "My friend, I will be here until the eighth and we shall have several long talks. If you ever wish to write a book or if you have any other uses, you are free to use any of the photographs."

As watch ends at 0600 I take still shots of JYC leaving on his dive.

While they're gone, I work in the lab, unloading and reloading all of the cameras.

Later, following lunch, it's pouring rain and I'm holed up in my cabin. There are four in the cabin. Marc has moved back and another diver arrived last night. It's crowded, the ship is full, and there are even a few more divers staying at a nearby hotel. It's very interesting here in Martinique with so much diving going on. We're all dreading the switch to Venezuela, where all we'll do is collect water samples day and night, with no diving.

This afternoon we dive again on the *Roraima*, the ship with the skeletons. This time with *Calypso* directly atop the wreck, we descend right off *Calypso*'s stern dive ladder. It's another pretty big dive team, with JYC, Bernard, Falco, Coll, Sumian, Delcoutere, Zonza, and Cappello.

The water is very clear, but the dive is deep enough that lights are still needed to film. The wreck is covered with wavy green seaweed. Inside are colorful coral and gorgonians. My unenviable job is to dig through the ashes, melted bottles, and other unidentifiable objects and collect several bags of human bones.

It doesn't seem right to disrupt the bones that have been resting in peace for seventy-seven years, and I don't like doing it. It's one of JYC's corny ideas, to give these victims a proper burial at sea. It's actually bizarre considering that he just buried Philippe at sea. Maybe there's a psychological explanation. I guess I don't really care what I have to do as long as I can keep diving.

Bernard offers me more praise, telling me I'm diving very well and that "you know how to dive when the fish accept you." I can't say that the fish accept me, but they do accept him, *Calypso*'s Dr. Dolittle.[u]

This afternoon there's some confusion. It's high tide, so the water is deep enough for us to have brought *Calypso* back to Saint Pierre's dock. We need fresh water and also want to film another take of a staged arrival, hopefully this time not hitting the pier.

Falco gives me permission to go ashore with some others, but then JYC says that anyone who works on the decks has to stay aboard. Since I have so many jobs, I'm not sure whether that means me or not. I should just leave, but I feel obliged to stay. Later, as the tide turns, we move *Calypso* back offshore and re-anchor.

It's night now. I get a ride ashore to call Kathy. I haven't spoken with her in more than two weeks. I walk to the hotel and discover that the phone is out of order. Disappointed, I head back to the pier, where the chaland picks me up. Later I join the 2300 night dive, which includes the submarine.

Another new week begins, the morning of the twenty-third, and Ken tips me off that at 1000 he's going to fly JYC to Saint Pierre. I poke around and quickly discover that a film crew has already disembarked. I grab my camera and film and try to get a

---

u Dr. Dolittle is storybook character who can speak to animals in their own languages.

ride ashore. Since Paul is gone, Christian is now the acting first mate. He is his usual bastard self.

I have to wait a half-hour for the electrician to prepare the generator. Then we leave, in the pouring rain, in an overloaded Zodiac with too many people and the generator. Upon arrival a few guys unload the generator. I try to keep the camera equipment dry, and Christian loses his cool, cussing me out for not helping. I don't understand why he's so upset; reminds me of Paul.

I leave these guys and catch up to the camera crew atop the mountain at the ruins of the local theatre. JYC joins us, landing in the helicopter and then strolling through the ruins with the curator of the small local museum. We film JYC's tour and stage conversations inside the adjoining museum, where the curator tells the story of Mount Pelée's eruption. This excellent museum portrays the disaster with before-and-after photos of the city below.

Then we drive to the observatory on the top of a neighboring mountain. We pass a farm of magnificent palms that line both sides of the road, boasting huge hanging bunches of bananas. We stage another conversation between JYC and the operator of the observatory, who explains that here they constantly measure the seismic activity of Mount Pelée, the adjoining mountains, and other volcanoes throughout the Antilles.

Here in the higher elevations, the farmers seem to be more industrious. The people below in Saint Pierre seem less interested in working; they just want to eat, sleep, and drive a big car.

We descend to town and board Zodiacs. On the way back to *Calypso*, Jacques Delcoutere and I spot a pair of breaching whales.

Tomorrow we leave Saint Pierre and sail south to Fort de France, where we'll take on fuel, get cholera vaccinations, and possibly leave for Venezuela. It's been a wonderful day and a special stay here in Saint Pierre.

We took some great footage here but could use even more, so some divers will remain behind in the hotel and use local fishing boats to continue diving and filming. I'd like to stay. We leave tomorrow and nobody knows which divers are staying.

It's hard to believe that it's July 25. This time has passed so quickly. It seems like we just got here and now we're leaving.

Around 0930 I call the ship from shore and request a ride back. Raymond is on watch and therefore supposed to drive an hourly shuttle. But he's in the lab, away from the radio, which isn't good. He doesn't retrieve me until 1130. By that time several of us have gathered and fallen asleep on the dock.

Later we again bring *Calypso* to the pier, disembarking some supplies and divers to stay at Hotel Latitude. Then we leave for Fort de France.

In Fort de France, Falco, Maurice, Nono, Alain, and others leave for the airport, returning to France. We take on fuel and water and I make one last trip to the dentist. We spend the night and the next afternoon. Sadly we're now leaving Martinique.

A couple miles offshore we pass the imposing Diamond Rock. In the early nineteenth century the British fortified it by hauling guns to the top, securing this passage and port from the French, who were battling the British to dominate the Caribbean.

It will be a thirty-six-hour sail to the Venezuelan port city of Cumaná.

JYC, Dad, and Jacques Constans, The Cousteau Society's vice president for Science and Technology, previously went to Caracas, to meet with Dr. Luis Herrera Campins, the president of Venezuela; Dr. Neri, the minister for the Eastern Provinces; and Mayor Oswaldo Graziani, and signed a contract for a seventy-five-day study of the Caribbean along the coast of Venezuela. *Calypso* shall be used as a platform from which to collect water samples and data at 110 locations along the county's coastline. The project is planned to take four months. Venezuelan students will come aboard to study the hydrology, geology, and biology of the coast's water, reefs, and marine life, with the objective of quantifying the environmental impact, if any, of the offshore oil drilling operations.

Venezuela's eastern border is the Atlantic Ocean and the Caribbean Sea but the country has fallen behind in the science of oceanography. There is no national agency similar to those established by members of the United Nations Educational, Scientific and Cultural Organization's (UNESCO) program on Intergovernmental Commission on Oceanography (ICO), that coordinates on a national scale all activities that pertain to the education, training and research in maritime and underwater activities.

I go below and work in the photo lab until midnight. Since most of the cameras will no longer be needed, I clean them and put them into safe storage.

It's a restless night. After being at anchor in Saint Pierre's calm harbor for two weeks, it takes time to readjust to the movement of the ship and the sea.

Another day passes. We're twenty-nine hours into the journey and I'm on watch 2000–2400.

Latitude N 1027.08
Longitude W 64 12.53
GMT 9:58:55
27 07 70
Heading 119.3
Setting 256.9

At 0300 we arrive at Cumaná, the capital of Venezuela's Sucre State, one of twenty-three Venezuelan states. We anchor offshore. At sunrise we'll proceed into the harbor.

Cumaná is said to be the first South American city founded by Europeans, initially by Franciscan monks in 1515. It was subsequently repeatedly attacked by local Indians and reestablished several times, including in 1521 by Spaniard Gonzalo de Ocampo, and again in 1569 by Diego Fernandez de Serpa.

The city is situated in northeastern Venezuela at the mouth of the Manzanares River on the Gulf of Cariaco, an inlet of the

Caribbean. The natural harbor enables busy maritime trade, including exports of coffee, tobacco, cacao, sugar, fruit, and beans.

I was anticipating several days in port and a nice reception with festivities similar to those in Norfolk, but I am disappointed to learn that we should not expect anything and that we'll be sailing again tomorrow.

We dock at 0615. Indeed, there is not a big welcome. It's just JYC, Graziani, and a handful of other VIPs greeting us. JYC holds a brief press conference from atop the helo pad and leaves for a lunch reception. That's it. The rest of us just hang around.

So it's back to work, loading three dozen crates of fresh fruit and vegetables, slabs of meat, and boxes of other food staples. Ken and I take a walk into town, which is poor and uninteresting. We want to exchange some money, but by the time we find a bank I've decided I no longer need money because there's nothing to buy. Ken, however, changes a ten, and the cakeman buys me a piece of cake…No, I am not kidding. We sit and talk for an hour or so. It's really nice to get off the ship and just sit and talk.

Things are looking up for him career-wise. He's thinking of staying on with Cousteau.

I'd like to stay on and would if I could be sure JYC would be at this long enough. My sense is that JYC is getting on in years. If I want a business career, I might as well get on with it. I don't want to go ten years on the ship, have something happen to JYC, and then be stuck making a living diving on oil rigs in the Gulf of Mexico. Not that there would be anything wrong with that, but it's just not what I want to do…Dinner bell. Have to go.

I can't wait to leave Cumaná and get back to sea. Sitting still tied to the dock here in this heat and humidity is unbearable. There are people all over the dock, constantly harassing me, wanting to come aboard. We've again put the starboard side against the dock, so my bunk is only a few meters from the pier. People just walk aboard, day and night. There's no port security so we're careful of our personal belongings and the ship's equipment, particularly expensive lightweight items like cameras.

At dinner this young Venezuelan guy just comes aboard, uninvited, and walks into the wardroom while we're eating. He gives us bananas, mangoes, and other fruit and then starts serving us. When JYC walks in, the guy asks for a job. He says he'll pay JYC just to work on the ship. We finally have to ask him to leave. It's interesting. He might have actually had a chance if he hadn't overdone it.

After the first sitting I have a nice visit with a young American couple that walked to the pier from their hotel. They work in Caracas and are having a disappointing vacation here in Cumaná.

Then, although I've already eaten, I join the second sitting of dinner, already in progress. I want to make myself known to Graziani, who's dining with JYC. It's incredible as everybody at the table can speak English but they're all speaking French, which Graziani can't understand. Graziani probably doesn't realize this or notice it as much as I do, but I think it's very rude. Graziani is very complimentary of Dad, saying, "Freddie Hyman is a very good friend of mine."

Later Bruno and I take a long walk through town. Small packs of dogs and loner cats roam the streets, scrounging for food. An occasional attempt at a nice house and yard is plugged in between shacks and old cracked plaster buildings. Repeated earthquakes in 1684, 1765, and 1929 have destroyed much of the city. They've tried to rebuild each time.

Worn and tattered political posters are everywhere. I see why revolutions occur but sense that those who may start with legitimate complaints and ideas become just as corrupt as their predecessors.

Bruno is by profession a diver, but with our diving finished he's back in a sailor role. He tells me that Christian and Marc can't understand why I'm on the ship. That only French should be aboard. I'm so bored with this and don't really give a damn what they think. I know that photography is the backbone of this operation and that's my job. These guys are more focused on the physical labor and don't understand that we're here to make a product.

Bruno asks me if I've noticed that JYC may be getting a little senile. I tell him I hadn't noticed—until tonight, when JYC repeatedly interrupted Graziani and then got up to get a spoon and rummaged through the drawers, banging loudly, while Graziani was speaking. I suspect this was more than just an ego thing and perhaps JYC is slightly failing. I find something mysterious about the French habits. They're always arguing and interrupting each other. Is it big egos, rudeness, both, or what?

While here I've learned a little bit about the Venezuelan culture. If an unmarried girl is asked out on a date, she must always have an escort, a chaperone. It seems to be a very laid back culture. Typically everybody takes an afternoon siesta. I doubt too many people are stressed out and die from heart attacks.

I stop in the photo store to buy special negatives for projecting images of plankton. Papa Flash showed me how when he was aboard. JYC wants me to give it a try, but my photo lab has been taken over by the scientists and transformed into a chemistry lab, so it's going to be difficult to develop the film. This is a sign of things to come...sailing the coast collecting water samples.

There's talk of detouring to Trinidad, to film a new oil spill. It's not in the Venezuelan contract, but JYC is tempted to try and sneak over to it.

It's almost like we're bored with the water sampling, even before we get started.

This morning I photograph another press conference and notice that Jacques Constans and JYC are pushing a side project, a United Nations experiment. The Venezuelans are visibly unhappy about this, wanting the media focused on their country.

We leave Cumaná at 1500. On the first leg, we'll sail to the mouth of the Orinoco River, through the Gulf of Paria, into the Atlantic near Barbados, and back to Puerto La Cruz. Then we'll head northwest to the Gulf of Venezuela and Maracaibo, stopping at the ports of Puerto Cabello and Punto Fijo.

Falco had planned to leave us in Fort de France but didn't. He and Constans will co-direct this mission.

It's 1930 and I'm just out of the shower, lying on my bunk, with new life after leaving port and being back out at sea. That always seems to happen.

With most of the divers gone, my cabin mates have left, and now I have three Venezuelan scientists in the cabin. This could be interesting—or a real drag. None of them speak English. They all seem like egg heads, but we'll see. One guy's shirt is a baby blue top of a pajama suit; the short-sleeve type that buttons up the front middle. Another is also wearing a pajama shirt, with a pattern of hundreds of little Budweiser logos.

I have a new job recording all of the water data. This may be an interesting way to be involved with the research.

It's funny to watch the French. Already they don't like having the Venezuelans on board. They seem to feel threatened. I think having the Venezuelans aboard could help the overall atmosphere. Maybe the added diversity will make it start to feel more like my previous expeditions, with multiple nationalities. However, nothing is ever the same.

This is strange, though. The French are now like a bunch of fish out of water. This isn't their bag, limping along the coastline collecting water. They're meant to push the envelope, exploring and filming; adventurous explorers stuck doing boring research. This isn't a good idea.

We call the designated measurement locations "stations." Our first sampling station begins at 2345 (almost midnight) and concludes around 0330. Then I try to grab some sleep before 0600 watch. I go to my bunk and there's a Venezuelan in it. I wake the idiot up and tell him to move.

Latitude N 11 00.16 – 10 34.78
Longitude W 63 30.14 – 61 45.00

The next day we clear the large stern hold to make room for storage of the submarine, but we can't stow it yet as we're into heavy seas with a forty-five-knot strong gale.

It's 1330 and the three Venezuelans are still asleep in the cabin. One of them is seasick. Joy. Welcome aboard, Bud Man.

So far I'm not impressed with the quality of the science. My university chemistry training taught me to be more careful and precise. I enjoy collecting data, but only if it is done using standardized procedures and exact measurements.

2100 now and we still haven't started tonight's seven stations. The procedures are running slowly and this will be an all-nighter. I've decided that I'll leave at the next port that has an airport.

We pull the all-nighter and complete the scheduled stations. The day passes as we sail to the next station. The weather eases, but we still need calmer water before we can safely stow the sub.

By evening we approach a gorgeous island, Trinidad. We find a harbor and drop anchor. There's a small, inviting village, surrounded by beautiful lush vegetation. I want to go ashore and explore, but there's work to be done and unfortunately we're not stopping here for long.

Finally we store the sub below, which opens up some badly needed deck space. Now it's time for dinner. But the chef has been seasick all day, so we're having lousy meals prepared by the new steward, JoJo, whom we picked up in Martinique. Now we have a Nono and a JoJo. Well, as mentioned, Nono already left.

I'm admiring a magnificent sunset when an overcrowded Trinidad Coast Guard vessel suddenly pulls alongside. They seem suspicious and aggressively come aboard, wanting to see what we are up to. We calm their concerns and they are off.

Another week has passed and it's now July 30. We're heading to Güiria to load fuel and unload the three seasick Venezuelan scientists. They certainly didn't last long. Their replacements come aboard.

It's too bad we won't be stopping to dive in a famous nearby fishing area. It's said to be abundant with snapper, grouper, swordfish, and tuna, but onward, we've got water to sample.

At dusk Ken and I start on a walk but quickly sense danger. A small boy follows, poking us with his finger, begging. We see a young girl, maybe barely a teenager, carrying a lifeless baby by the elbow out into a field. I think it is dead.

Later JYC asks me to stay on with him for the future. I thank him and explain that with this expedition's diving and photography completed, I've fulfilled my role and plan to take my leave. He says he understands and agrees it's time to take leave, but that I should come back on the next expedition to Clipperton Island, a small, two-square-mile volcanic island located six hundred miles off the west coast of Mexico. The film will be on sharks and the island's hydrography, microbiology, physical characteristics, as well as other creatures such as crabs and birds. He hopes to have visiting scientists from Paris, Scripps Institute, the University of Southern California, and Canada's Université Laval and McGill University.

The next morning we head from the Caribbean toward the Atlantic. There, where the two seas clash, the water promises to be rough.

We arrive at the day's fourth station and rock and roll at latitude N 10 35.35 – 09 22.95, longitude W 62 00.55 – 60 31.50. This is relatively shallow water at 23.5 meters deep, which makes for faster sampling. Today's earlier stations were also shallow at twelve, twenty-four, and twenty-five meters respectively, contrasted to one of yesterday's stations of 1,763 meters.

At greater depths it takes several hours just to lower and then raise the water collection bottles, called Niskin bottles. They are twenty-five-centimeter-long metal or PVC tubes that serve as water collection canisters. At each station the first bottle is clamped to the end of a cable. The entire cable is measured and marked and lowered to a specific depth, which is usually the bottom of the ocean. As a winch lowers it, additional bottles are attached at prescribed intervals, e.g. every 250 feet; in other words, a bottle is sent to the bottom and other bottles are positioned every 250 feet above it. As the bottles descend, their top and bottom remain open. When the bottom canister reaches the ocean floor and the other bottles are therefore at their corresponding depths, from the surface we drop a weight, which slides down the cable. We call it the messenger and encourage it to sink by yelling "go, devil."

There are actually a series of messengers. Each descends at a rate of about one meter per second. The first messenger that's released from the surface descends until it reaches and strikes the shallowest bottle, which then triggers the top and bottom of that canister to close, thereby collecting water at that prescribed depth. A second messenger that's fastened to the bottom of that bottle is then jolted free and released, descending to the next lower bottle on the cable, and the process repeats itself all of the way down the line. When the last weight finally reaches the bottom canister, it also hopefully closes. The cable is then raised and all of the canisters and their contents are retrieved.

It is all extremely time consuming. For example, at yesterday's mentioned depth of 1,763 meters, it took the messengers more than twenty-nine minutes to reach the bottom Niskin (1,763 divided by 60 seconds). Add to this the preceding time to lower the actual bottles attached to the cable that the messengers ride on and the subsequent retrieval of the bottles, and you're looking at hours per station.

This type of sampling is called surface and hydrocast sampling. After the samples are collected, the water is transferred to individually labeled plastic sample bottles. A portion of each sample is filtered. Each filter with its residue is carefully catalogued and, along with the sample bottles, stored in the converted photo lab. Eventually the materials will be transported to the Venezuela university for more detailed analyses including salinity, nutrient, and plankton content.

We have been lent an expensive computerized probe, which is proving to be a lifesaver, helping us obtain better real-time data. Although the Cousteau team is still very amateur at this, with practice we're all getting better at handling the myriad apparatus and associated winches and hoists.

Other instruments we're using include a Sechi disc, bucket thermometer, precision radiation thermometer, and a fluorometer. The Sechi is a thirty-centimeter-diameter white plastic disc that's attached to a line marked in meters. The disk is lowered in the water. The depth at which its reflection disappears is measured on the line and recorded, providing crude data on water clarity and turbidity. An above-water observer on *Calypso* also makes a *dry look* measurement. When practical, an in-water observer wearing a facemask with head submerged takes a *wet look* measurement.

The bucket thermometer is a thermometer that's contained in a plastic cylinder, or bucket. The bucket is open on one side so water can easily flow in and out while surrounding the thermometer, permitting an accurate reading of the surface water temperature.

The precision radiation thermometer measures the sea surface temperature. Readouts are viewed and printed in the radio room.

The fluorometer measures the organic content of the seawater. It's located below deck. Water is pumped to it from an external intake beneath the stern. Life forms in the seawater are shredded by the fluorometer and fluoresced in ultraviolet light.

Right now we're laboring through the murky brown plume of the river delta. Tropical plants, leaves, and branches float by. Suddenly we violently collide with a huge floating tree and suspect that it has dented the bow's observation chamber.

A gigantic waterspout passes by. Probably a fair weather spout, the type that develops at sea. We do, however, see onshore cumulus nimbus clouds and scattered thunderstorms, suggesting that the spout could have developed on land and may therefore be tornadic. It's a towering spinning column with a dark curtain of rain below. Eventually it diffuses into softer, wispier clouds. When we converge, we're pelted with golf ball-sized hail.

Ron and I have a nice chat. He's a visiting American scientist who previously served in the U.S. Navy and then studied biochemistry and worked as an oceanographer. He recently joined us as a volunteer to help us for a couple of weeks before he returns home to change careers, going to work for a Norfolk port newspaper.

It's afternoon and as I set a surface bottle, a slick of *Calypso* sewage floats by...This should make for a nice water sample.

We still haven't reached the Atlantic, but as we get closer the sea steadily intensifies.

The next station stop is in forty minutes at latitude N 0922.95, longitude W 6031.50. We'll anchor there and spend the night. The captain doesn't want to hit any more trees, particularly in the middle of a dark night...Can you see the headlines, *Calypso* totaled after hitting tree?

Our master schedule needs to be corrected. The Venezuelan student who mapped the 110 stations made a huge mistake, plotting our navigation with straight lines, point-to-point, disregarding reefs, shallows, and even islands in between. For example, one leg is scheduled to be five days total, but now it will actually require nine days—seven days of travel plus two days for data gathering.

Dinner is great: roast beef, potatoes, salad, and fresh pineapple for dessert. After dinner Ron and I have another talk while watching lightning off in the distance.

I prepare the special Photo-Sonics camera for JYC's flight over the delta tomorrow and then bring it up from the lab to show him. He says it looks great. Photo-Sonics is a California-based company and one of the pioneers of high-speed photography.

I'm lying in bed as *Calypso* meanders over waves. Lightning continues to flash in the distance. A half moon illuminates the clouds and a slim white ribbon of sea.

Not bad, I've made it to August 1. It's so strange contemplating departure. I desire everything I miss, yet for some reason I hesitate to leave. I'm one of just a few who have been aboard since Norfolk. I am, however, approaching the three-month craziness milestone.

0200 and there's no way to sleep in this heat. JYC is rationing water. For two days we haven't been able to shower, wash, or even brush our teeth. The sink faucets are even disconnected, so we drop buckets over the side to get salt water.

0500 watch and I notice that we're not at the correct location, not where we dropped anchor. We're at latitude N 08 52.87 – 09 40.25, longitude W 59 59.90 – 60 08.75. The previous watch didn't realize the anchor wasn't holding and we've unknowingly drifted several miles.

The sky is particularly dark, highlighting the slow-moving satellite overhead. Slowly the sky brightens. It's an inspiring sunrise.

JYC's planned helicopter flight over the delta has been cancelled due to bad weather. Well, at least I got the practice of assembling and loading that special camera and showed it to JYC.

I'm in my cabin listening to the real Pink Floyd. I just sneaked a new bottom sheet because soot made the other a dark, grungy gray.

At dinner, Madame argues with JYC because she doesn't want the scientists using the food freezer to store water samples. I love Madame but feel that some of her complaint is only because the scientists aren't French.

It's after dinner and I just had my first shower in three days. The next shower will be in three more days. It's tough with physical labor, tropical heat, and no time to stop to cool off with a swim.

Although the scientists are recording their samples and some associated data, Constans wants us to also keep our own records. I started helping him do this several days ago, but he keeps changing the format, which is irritating. Everything is done by hand with paper and pencil, so every time he changes the format, I have to rewrite the entire thing. He's super-hyper and disorganized.

JYC changed my watch from day to night. I'm on with him now 2300–0200. Madame joins us.

We can see flames near Trinidad sixty miles away. We think it's from the two oil tankers that collided last week, but we're not sure.

The autopilot is working well, so I don't have to manually steer, but it's of course still temperamental and the cockroaches are looming, so I have to stay close, inside the hot bridge. Otherwise I could step out the starboard side into the breeze on the flying bridge. JYC is too distracted by Madame to help me at all, so I'd best continue to pay close attention.

Today we complete another four stations. Since it's deeper here, in order to get a bottom sample and set bottles at the same intervals that we have used at the other locations, we must now double the usual three or four bottles to six or eight. The deeper the location, the more bottles we use.

The replacement scientists are better at sharing the lab with me. It's a pretty tight squeeze, though. They seem to congregate and lounge in the lab for hours to take advantage of the refrigerated air. The scientists also disrupt the cabin all night long. As we arrive at each collection station, they storm in, turning on the light and yelling.

Everybody is starting to drag. This is a different kind of work than we're used to and it's twenty-four hours a day, every day. The Cousteau team misses the diving and adventure.

I'm so tired of banging my head. The doorways are low and I'm tall, so I bang my head daily. After months, my sore scalp feels like soft pulp. I'm also tired of having my beer stolen from the fridge in the lounge—I mean the lab.

Today we finally enter the Atlantic and complete four stations of 773, 1,170, 1,278, and 2,500 meters. Six, eight, ten, and twelve bottles sampled per station, respectively, taking hours per station.

We haven't seen flying fish since we were last in the Atlantic. Now that we're back, a huge school surrounds us. I enjoy them; they're entertaining and fun to watch.

These are larger than the ones we saw off the Carolinas. They're up to a foot long with pectoral and pelvic fins the sizes of a bird's wing. They don't actually fly but rather swim at up to thirty miles per hour and then launch into the air as they approach the water's surface, vibrating their outstretched fins, gliding for hundreds of meters.

Flying helps the fish avoid predators such as tuna, mackerel, and dolphins. This larger species uses a lobe on the bottom of the tail to steer, changing course to fool predators. They seem fooled by us, thinking that *Calypso* is a large predator. I guess we are, unintentionally, as in the rough sea we're finding them all over the deck. We toss back the live ones, but for those that it is too late, we give them to the chef, who prepares a tasty appetizer.

Pouring rain wakes me from a nap. It's pouring through the porthole's air scoop and onto my bed. I'm lying here sweating, knowing there's not another shower for two more days when it dawns on me that when, not if, it rains again, I'll shower in the rain.

I had three dreams, all related to losing something, my tooth, two camera lenses, and a brand new baseball under the bleachers, whatever that means.

Lunch features unbelievably good homemade chocolate pudding for dessert.

I'm blown away by a conversation I just had with JYC. He said I could fly home from the next port and he again encouraged me to rejoin the team in Los Angeles in October for the expedition to Clipperton Island.

We've now traveled well into the Atlantic and have arrived at a station located at latitude N 11 19.86 – 12 11.54, longitude W 60 30.01 – 61 00.04. Thirty-foot swells roll the ship like crazy. Everything is falling all over the place. The pegs are back in the table, but nobody is eating. We've been here all day long taking samples. At 2,300 meters it's too deep to anchor, so we drift and use satellite positioning to constantly maneuver back to the vicinity of the specified station. Being battered like this is not fun.

Late in the day we have another heavy rain, so I lather up and take a rain shower. I was the only one. It felt great.

The word got around pretty quickly that I'm leaving. I would have preferred to go quietly. The few that never wanted to get along will be glad to see me leave. The friends I've made want me to stay.

I think about telexing New York to see if they can make plane reservations, but JYC tells me not to. He says to have my bags ready and he will do the rest. It seems like he expects me to be able to just walk on the plane with no reservations. That's crazy, but if that's what he wants, he's the boss. He says if it takes a few days to get on a plane they'll put me up in a hotel. He also informs me that I get fourteen days of paid vacation for every month I worked. That's a nice surprise.

The first sitting of dinner is in ten minutes and then I have watch from 1900–2300. It's bound to be a rough watch as we're still in heavy seas, fighting to keep the same position and complete this station. It's impossible to sleep so it is just as well to be busy on watch. Tonight I'll have plenty of company.

I'm torn; sad to leave yet excited to do so. I suppose that's a good way to leave. It's a crazy ship, but emotionally it grabs you. Joe and I talk and he says that working for JYC aboard *Calypso* is as though "you have to leave yet you have to return." My plan is to go with JYC and Graziani to Caracas on the eighth. If I have to leave, it will be very nice to be able to leave with JYC.

Raymond Coll asks me to familiarize Bruno with the underwater cameras, just in case they do any filming. Bruno taught me about the dive equipment, so now I can return the favor. We have a good session. He's smart and learns fast.

I ask JYC if they plan to film and if I'm making a mistake by leaving? He thinks it's a good decision for me to take some leave and then continue with the organization, meeting them in California. He says I'm too serious and that I need to relax.

The Cousteau Society has asked me to take some photographs of JYC, which they need for a new book, *The Cousteau Almanac,* so I take some photographs of him working in his cabin.

During my watch in an hour with JYC, 2300–0200, we'll finally move to a new station, so that will break up the time.

I'm convinced that we have a kleptomaniac aboard. Ron hid several Cokes in the cool lab but now they're gone. I gave up storing beer there.

At lunch Christian makes an ass out of himself. We need four seats to feed people who are assigned to work on the upcoming station. Many people have already sat down, including Ken and me. There are still four open seats. Christian orders me to give up my seat. I just look at him. Then he tells Ken to get up, but since Ken doesn't understand French, he stays. I tell Christian that there are four seats available and nobody needs to move.

I retrieve my duffel bag from a hold below in the bow. It is in bad shape, damaged by seawater that leaked through the hull into the hold. That's comforting, a leak in the hull. My bag is entirely covered in mold, inside and out. I wash it with Ajax and seawater and now it's drying in the moonlight. Apparently other people already had their bags ruined too but didn't bother to pass along the warning.

The stations are proceeding well but continue to be a slow process. We've spent the past fifteen hours at an even deeper station of more than a mile and a half (2,600 meters).

The schedule is starting to take a toll on the equipment too. The only winch that we have has been overheating. Also, the pressure from the depths has caused a leak in the computerized probe. I take some close-up photographs of the probe to possibly help with diagnosis and repair. It appears that the pressure caused the batteries to implode and that other components exploded. The inside is entirely ruined.

After the station is completed, we anchor near Isla Norteste of Islas Los Testigos. I join a group heading to the island in a Zodiac to explore this most remote Venezuelan island. It's inhabited by only a few related families who protect the abundant fishing ground resulting from the combined flow of the Orinoco River and enriched ocean currents.

Later, upon return to *Calypso,* I'm soaking wet with sweat and bug spray, but since we're hoisting anchor, there's no time for a swim. No showers are allowed, even though we'll be in Porta La Cruz for water tomorrow.

We're at anchor and I'm on solo watch. It's August 8, my last day aboard *Calypso.* At dawn a mother humpback whale and calf wander close by. Everyone's asleep. The mother seems to be waiting, so I wake Patrick. We don our fins, mask, and single tanks and jump in. As we approach, she's naturally protective of her young, yet accepts, if not welcomes, our gentle touch.

She's maybe twelve meters long, mostly black with some spots. Her flukes and underside are white. The baby is less than four meters in length. They're in no hurry, and we enjoy each other's company, until eventually she moves away, the baby by her side. Patrick and I climb the stern dive ladder and sit aboard the silent *Calypso.* Shortly thereafter a male whale passes by.

As mentioned, it was one of my life's goals to dive in the wild with a whale. I could not be happier.

Eventually the crew stirs to life. We keep the dive quiet, only telling Bernard, Patrick's older brother.

Constans asks me to photocopy all of the science data. The Xerox machine won't pick up the pencil, so I have to hand copy fifty pages of numbers, which takes four hours. I don't understand why he needs a duplicate because I'm leaving him the original.

Today, instead of working stations, we anchor outside Porta la Cruz and have some fun with recreational diving and investigation of surrounding islands. On one island I go inside a cave and discover a dead goat and other animal skeletons.

In the evening we pull in to the dock in Porta la Cruz and load fuel.

There's room on tomorrow's Viasa flight #826 to Miami, so JYC and I will leave, together.

EPILOGUE

My journeys with Captain Cousteau and his crew were positive, life-altering experiences.

Even today, more than thirty-five years later, wonderful memories still come to mind each and every day.

It's a bit of a curse, though, particularly at a young age, as I wonder if I'll ever experience such exciting work or adventure again. I am, however, now beginning to sense that in my older years, with responsibilities partially fulfilled, new, different opportunities are on the horizon.

I desperately try to preserve my favorite feelings, such as the freedom of going shoeless for days and weeks at a time. Also the peace of the night watch; standing on the flying bridge in the warm midnight air listening to the wind as the ship cuts the sea's moonlit path.

Also, strangely, still, whenever I smell diesel, I'm quickly and fondly taken back to *Calypso.*

I do not miss the sleep deprivation or banging my head on the ship's doorways.

I did not return with the Cousteau team for the Clipperton expedition. At times I wish I had, but instead I took advantage of a business opportunity and began my career, in pursuit of a "normal" life.

Thanks to Dr. George Low, NASA's alliance with JYC and The Cousteau Society grew. Astronaut Russell Schweickart, the former Apollo 9 pilot and backup commander of Skylab, successfully managed the Cousteau relationship.[39]

I interned for Rusty in Washington, D.C., during the exciting bicentennial summer of 1976. On that July 1, I saw Gerald Ford, Chief Justice Warren Burger, and Vice President Nelson Rockefeller cut the ribbon to open the popular National Air and Space Museum on the National Mall. I spent much lunchtime there viewing the new IMAX film *To Fly.*

I worked on technology transfer for the Landsat program, formerly known as Earth Resources Technology Satellite. The twin satellites, Landsat 1 and 2, proved that unmanned spacecraft could be used to help geologists, hydrologists, and agriculturalists map, plan, monitor, and manage land use, forests and ranges, and water and marine resources.

Viking 1 landed on Mars that summer, which we witnessed with Carl Sagan, who spoke at NASA the day of the landing.

Dr. Low, who'd been with NASA twenty-six years, since its inception, retired that summer and became president of Rensselaer Polytechnic Institute in New York.

John Denver also became a dear friend of JYC and The Society. He joined The Society's council of advisors and was an active participant. John completed his song, "*Calypso,*"[v] and in June 1975 I heard him sing it live in concert in Atlanta, taking my friends back stage after the show.

John generously gave his copyright and royalties from the song to The Society. The song, an ASCAP hit, went gold worldwide. It was first released on his *Windsong* album and now appears on seventeen albums. In the U.S. alone, fans bought more than ten million copies of his *Greatest Hits* album, containing "*Calypso,*" the most in RCA history.

Also in 1975, *Beavers of the North Country* aired on television, followed in 1976 by *Mysteries of the Hidden Reefs, The Fish That Swallowed Jonah,* and *The Incredible March of the Spiny Lobster.*

On January 20, 1980, Jan Cousteau, Philippe's widow, gave birth to Philippe Jr.

That spring, when I moved to Seattle, Kathy and I parted ways.

---

v John performing *Calypso* http://www.youtube.com/watch?v=Q8SPqTlgmfE&feature=related

The Society also relocated headquarters then, to Chesapeake, Virginia, near Norfolk.

On September 3, 1980, following a dive on a sunken schooner in eastern Lake Ontario, Rémy Galliano did not surface. Rémy was my replacement. He was handling the light cables in just ninety feet of water. They said it was an embolism, but they weren't sure. At the time I was living in Seattle, and JYC called me to discuss my previous electrical accident.

Danger and death were a reality. I was young and naive, unmarried with no responsibilities, so I rarely contemplated the dangers.

In 1983, after 120 years on the ocean floor, the *Monitor*'s 1,300-pound anchor was recovered.

John Newton died of a heart attack in 1984, before the 1986 naming of the *Monitor* as a National Historic Landmark. The propeller was recovered in 1998, as was the steam engine in 2001.

In 2002, almost twenty-three years after we dove on the ship, the gun turret was raised, and the remains of two *Monitor* crewmen were recovered. Their remains were sent to the U.S. Army's Central Identification Lab in Hawaii for identification. The turret is currently undergoing a long-term preservation process at The Mariners Museum,[40] selected as principle museum for curator of USS *Monitor* artifacts and papers.

In 1985, Carrot Island, near Beaufort, was renamed the Rachel Carson Estuarine Reserve.

I kept in touch with Madame and last saw her in 1986 at JYC's seventy-fifth birthday party. Madame, JYC, Mom, Dad, and I, and others, made the short sail aboard *Calypso* just down the Potomac River from D.C. to Mount Vernon, Virginia. It was quite a gala with John singing *Calypso* and many celebrities attending including Hoyt Axton, Jimmy Buffett, Jose Ferrer, Jack Lemmon, Stephanie Powers, Loretta Switt, Ted Turner, and Ben Vereen.[w]

---

w John sings Calypso at JYC's 100th birthday party http://www.youtube.com/watch?v=RyivrvEwU6Q

In 2004, coincidentally also on the banks of the Potomac River, in Alexandria, Virginia, I met Philippe Jr. I met his older sister, Alexandra, in 2008.

My Furman friends, Barb and Peter, wed and attended my wedding to Margaret in 1987.

Vicki worked several years on *Saturday Night Live* while living in Connecticut and then happily returned to Miami to marry Paul Wessell, a fellow Furman graduate.

In 1996, a barge in a Singapore harbor accidentally struck *Calypso*. She sunk but was later raised and moved to La Rochelle, France, where she sat and rotted for years. In 2004, Carnival Corporation announced they bought *Calypso* from Loel Guinness and committed one million euros to her restoration. This was to occur in the Bahamas. I was skeptical. It didn't materialize. In 2007 she was towed from La Rochelle to the Piriou Shipyard in Concarneau, Brittany, France.[41] [42] [43] She was well on her way to being refurbished but work subsequently stopped. In Jacksonville, I'd said "a shipyard seems a totally unfit final resting place for *Calypso*...amid the torches, cranes, propellers, and rust." Hopefully she will not meet this dim fate.

Earlier my dad and I had wanted to organize an effort to save *Calypso*. Move her to the U.S., restore the ship, and build an adjoining scientific conference center and museum.

Death has met too many of my *Calypso* friends, most prematurely.

Patrick died in a car crash in Rwanda on the 1978 Nile Expedition.

Doc Edgerton died in 1990 from a heart attack.

Joe passed in 2002. I'd visited his home in San Diego several times and met his lovely wife. Every time we met, Joe would share his passion to search for Spanish galleons and the gold within. I always told him I would join him when he was ready. We ran out of time.

Madame and Dr. Low both died of cancer, George in 1984 and Simone in 1990. George passed just two days after the White

House announced he'd been awarded the President's Medal of Freedom.[44]

It deeply saddened me when both John Denver and JYC died in the same year, 1997. John crashed a Rutan experimental plane off the coast of Monterey, California. JYC's health failed and he passed in a French hospital.

JYC would have been one hundred years old in June 2010.

His legacy endures. The generation that listened to his accented narration and watched his pioneering television programs today view breathtaking nature photography from wonderful new documentary filmmakers.

Some brave individuals struggle to preserve precious parcels of land and water from overpopulation and greed.

The devastation of earth's irreplaceable habitats accelerates, taking on even grander scale with the destruction of rain forests, construction of gargantuan dams and massive oil spills.

Remember Jacques-Yves Cousteau—what he accomplished and that he warned us to protect our fragile water planet. He said, "Protect what we love."

There will never be another Captain Jacques-Yves Cousteau nor a ship and crew like *Calypso*'s.

ACKNOWLEDGEMENTS

The information contained in this personal account is derived from personal journals, memorabilia, photographs, and audiotapes. Other supplemental information and material has been obtained from public sources, e.g. in the in the public domain, or reproduced with the permission of the respective owner. Every effort has been made to contact copyright holders. In the case of an inadvertent omission, please contact the author. No association is claimed between this account and/or its author and any other accounts or organizations.

Thanks go to Fred Hyman and Renee my editor. I am also grateful to Ken Bowden, Ed. L Bucher of Collection Jeannette for the use of Cliché de Mai 1902, Jean Cahill, Jan Cousteau, David Fine, Harry Follas of the Catalina Group of New Zealand, Fran Gaar, Cheryl Gilmore of PADI, Dive.com, Bill Herrnkind, Janett Hyman, Olivier Laguette and Dominique Sumian of Aqua Lung International, Bob McKeegan, Brian Meehl, Randy Olson of Beaver Lodge, Lev Poliakov, Louis Prezelin, Gary Roush of the Vietnam Helicopter Pilots Association, Ryan Spence of Flashback Scuba, Estela Valdez, Belinda Williford and Helen Nearing of Duke's Marine Lab, and the many supportive people who expressed their interest and encouragement along the way, including Joe Eannotti, Eve Stockton, Katie Thomson, and Gail Zembsch. Thanks too to my uncle, Mark Sheldon, who allowed me to borrow his boat, *Sliver*, which helped further stimulate my writing.

Finally I thank my wife, Margaret, for transcribing my original journals and insisting that I write, and our children, Brent and Sarah; all three sacrificing countless hours that we may have spent together so that I could write this book.

ENDNOTES

More info is available from the following sources and links.

For those who wish to read more about marine biology, an excellent cumulative bibliography can be found at: http://scilib.ucsd.edu/sio/hist_oceanogr/Day_Bibliogr_Biogr_Ocean_Scientists.pdf

[1] Professor Andrew Benson http://scripps.ucsd.edu/Profile/abenson
[2] Mr. Ray Bradbury http://www.raybradbury.com/
[3] Mr. John Denver http://www.johndenver.com/biography/biography.html
[4] Dr. Harold Edgerton http://web.mit.edu/invent/iow/edgerton.html
[5] Mr. Dick Gregory http://www.dickgregory.com/
[6] Dr. Henry Kendall http://www.whoi.edu/page.do?pid=10934&tid=282&cid=815&ct=163
[7] Dr. K.O. Emery http://www.whoi.edu/page.do?pid=10934&tid=282&cid=821&ct=163
[8] Dr. Gabriel Nahas http://en.wikipedia.org/wiki/Gabriel_G._Nahas
[9] *Washington Post,* June 10, 1985
[10] Actual footage of Cousteau testing an early aqualung http://www.youtube.com/watch?v=jgXGeZzzHD8&feature=channel
[11] Captain Cousteau and Monsieur Gagnan *http://web.mit.edu/invent/iow/cousteau_gagnan.html*
[12] Mr. Orson Welles http://www.wellesnet.com/
[13] Mr. David Wolper http://www.davidlwolper.com/
[14] Photos of *Calypso* both early and late in life http://www.flashbackscuba.com/museum/Calypso_Restoration/Calypso_Restoration.html
[15] Information about the Blackfeet Nation http://www.blackfeetnation.com/
[16] Map showing Yellowstone to Glacier and into Canada http://www.ngmapcollection.com/product.aspx?cid=1540&pid=15991
[17] Information regarding dust off http://www.vietnamdustoff.com/fatherofdustoff.html
[18] Information about the Cree Nation http://www.creeindian.com/
[19] Dr. William Herrnkind http://www.bio.fsu.edu/faculty-herrnkind.php

[20] Map showing the Yucatan Peninsula, including Mujeres and Contoy http://www.ngmapcollection.com/product.aspx?cid=1540&pid=15899
[21] Isla Contoy http://www.islacontoy.org/
[22] NOAA http://www.noaa.gov/
[23] *The CoEvolution Quarterly*, Summer 1976, Jacques Cousteau at NASA Headquarters, interview by Stewart Brand
[24] Beaufort Wind Scale http://www.spc.noaa.gov/faq/tornado/beaufort.html
[25] Map of the Belize coast and reefs http://www.lib.utexas.edu/maps/cia10/belize_sm_2010.gif
[26] Turneffe http://ambergriscaye.com/pages/town/parkturneffe.html
[27] Lighthouse Reef and Blue Hole http://ambergriscaye.com/pages/town/parkgreatbluehole.html
[28] Glover's Reef http://ambergriscaye.com/pages/town/parkgloversreef.html
[29] Medusa http://en.wikipedia.org/wiki/File:Medusa_by_Carvaggio.jpg
[30] USS *Nimitz* http://www.nimitz.navy.mil/
[31] NOAA National Marine Sanctuaries http://sanctuaries.noaa.gov/about/welcome.html
[32] Pernod http://www.absinthebook.com/of_pontarlier19.html
[33] Harold "Doc" Edgerton's photos http://edgerton-digital-collections.org/galleries/iconic
[34] USS *Monitor* http://www.graveyardoftheatlantic.com/USS_Monitor_Today.htm
[35] NOAA chart showing location of the USS *Monitor* http://sanctuaries.noaa.gov/pgallery/atlasmaps/monitor.html
[36] Mariners' Museum and USS *Monitor* Center http://www.marinersmuseum.org/uss-monitor-center/uss-monitor-center
[37] North Carolina Maritime Museum http://www.ncmaritimemuseum.org/
[38] Map of Martinique http://www.infoplease.com/atlas/country/martinique.html
[39] Mr. Rusty Schweickart http://www.well.com/user/rs/index.html
[40] Mariners' Museum and USS *Monitor* Center http://www.marinersmuseum.org/uss-monitor-center/uss-monitor-center
[41] Restoration of *Calypso* Part 1 (towing from La Rochelle to Concarneau) http://www.youtube.com/watch?v=hnv-ZmArDxA&feature=player_embedded
[42] Restoration of *Calypso* Part 2 http://www.youtube.com/watch?v=icF4JRvqc7U
[43] Historical photos of *Calypso* and other interesting imageshttp://www.flashbackscuba.com/museum/Calypso_Restoration/Calypso_Restoration.html
[44] Dr. Low http://www.lib.rpi.edu/Archives/history/presidents/low,gm.html

8290856R0

Made in the USA
Charleston, SC
25 May 2011